75

20

Marks of the Beast

Marks of the Beast

The Left Behind Novels and the Struggle for Evangelical Identity

Glenn W. Shuck

NEW YORK UNIVERSITY PRESS

New York and London

NEW YORK UNIVERSITY PRESS
New York and London
www.nyupress.org

© 2005 by New York University

Library of Congress Cataloging-in-Publication Data
Shuck, Glenn W.
Marks of the beast : the left behind novels and the
struggle for evangelical identity / Glenn W. Shuck.
p. cm.
Includes bibliographical references and index.
ISBN 0–8147–4004–9 (cloth : alk. paper) —
ISBN 0–8147–4005–7 (pbk. : alk. paper)
1. Evangelicalism—United States.   2. Eschatology.
3. LaHaye, Tim F. Left behind series.   I. Title.
BR1642.U5S38   2004
813'.54—dc22   2004014840

New York University Press books are printed on acid-free paper, and
their binding materials are chosen for strength and durability.

Manufactured in the United States of America
c 10 9 8 7 6 5 4 3 2 1
p 10 9 8 7 6 5 4 3 2 1

Contents

Acknowledgments

I have benefited from the insight, patience, and kindness of many people during the production of this manuscript. Indeed, I would never have had the opportunity to undertake this project without the support and encouragement of many more. I would like to begin by thanking the Department of Religious Studies at Rice University for their support, financial and otherwise. Specifically, this includes Sylvia Louie, the department coordinator with all the answers; and the chair, William Parsons, who introduced my work to Jennifer Hammer of NYU Press. Likewise, I thank Jennifer for recognizing the project's potential and urging her editorial board at NYU Press to publish it.

This manuscript emerged from my dissertation project at Rice University, and I benefited much from the wisdom of my dissertation committee. Edith Wyschogrod, the committee chair, encouraged me to develop my ideas and produce a project at once both rigorous and readable. Always oracular in her comments, Dr. Wyschogrod gently implied her suggestions, not wanting to unduly influence the final product. Nevertheless, as anyone who knows Edith Wyschogrod recognizes, her mildest suggestions often contain "hidden imperatives" one would be wise to heed. John M. Stroup constantly barraged me with bizarre Internet links and helpful e-mails, patiently read large portions of the incomplete manuscript, and provided abundant and welcome insight into issues both of us believe require greater scholarly attention. Mark C. Taylor, ostensibly operating out of Williamstown, Massachusetts, proved a constant source of insight via his avatar on the World Wide Web. Mark has also recognized the importance of the work, and I am grateful for his support and encouragement. Finally, Michael O. Emerson, although a latecomer to the committee, did as much work as anyone to counsel me through the various stages, patiently reading drafts and providing an excellent example of professionalism for me to emulate.

A number of other scholars also read portions of the manuscript and/or discussed the project with me at length. The list begins with Robert C. Fuller, whom I met during a conference at the Esalen Institute in April 2003. Bob, rather plain-spoken himself, urged me to clarify portions of the text and make my claims more explicit. Bob also made several incisive and helpful comments in subsequent communications. Jeffrey J. Kripal, whom I assisted with a number of research projects at Rice along with the Esalen conference, also read the manuscript and made many helpful suggestions. Jeff pushed me during the publication phase of this project more than anyone, actually, and his advice—as always—was sound. I hope this book draws at least a measure of the attention garnered by his first monograph, *Kali's Child,* although I could do without the parliamentary debates on the merits of burning it. I would also like to thank Cathy Wessinger, who heard a summarized version of the manuscript's main arguments at the 2002 National Meeting of the American Academy of Religion in Toronto, Canada. Dr. Wessinger asked many incisive questions about the project and encouraged me to publish it.

A number of friends and colleagues also assisted me during this process. David A. Adcock consulted, challenged, and debated many portions of the manuscript; and, no matter how much I may have agreed or disagreed with some of his readings, I never left our meetings lacking fresh insight into the *Left Behind* phenomenon. I also owe a debt of gratitude to my friends and colleagues, notably Alejandro Chaoul, Randi Clary, Robert Erlewine, Stephen L. Hood, Julie Kutac, Molly Robey, Anna Solberg, Matthew Schunke, and Carter Wagner. Some of you read portions of the draft, while others provided an indulgent audience for my descriptions of *Left Behind* and its cultural significance. Still others reminded me that life goes on outside academia, difficult as that is to believe sometimes. I wish also to thank two of my teachers who became good friends, Richard Milk of Texas Lutheran University, and Rosanne Barker of Sam Houston State University—who believed in me when I needed it most.

My family has always provided me with plenty of understanding and encouragement. Dorothy Fitt, David and Sherry Teller, Rosemary Treichel, and Johnny (who always knew) and Mary Lou Ulrich have all played important roles in my ability to produce this manuscript. I would also like to thank Hermann and Waltraud von Laer—my German host "family." Hermann and I have spent many a late night discussing and debating American evangelicals, the state of the global economy, *Der Stop-*

pelmarkt, and anything else we have thought of while enjoying his favorite local brew, Haake-Beck Pils. Finally, I owe thanks to three very special people. My late grandmother, Dorothy Ida Ulrich, made sure I followed my academic dreams and would have been quite proud to see them coming to fruition. And last but certainly not least, I thank my parents, Colleen and Charles Shuck, who provided support, read drafts, sent love, sent money, and basically anything else I needed during those lean years known as graduate school. My academic work would simply not have been possible without you, mom and dad. It is to you that I dedicate this book.

Preface

About American Evangelicals

Before moving into the substance of the book, I want to provide readers with a sense of how I deploy the term "evangelical."[1] "Evangelical" is a much-misunderstood descriptor, owing in large measure to the many different ways it has been used. Throughout American history it has indicated related but politically and culturally dissimilar groups. Even evangelicals occasionally disagree about which groups belong in the fold and which count as heretical. In this text I am describing what evangelical media theorist Quentin J. Schultze calls the phenomenon of "popular evangelicalism," emphasizing "people in the pews" who mix and match beliefs, rather than denominational leaders who hold to more precise definitions.[2] I understand a popular evangelical first as a conservative Protestant who holds the Bible as a guiding authority. Second, a popular evangelical will also cite the necessity of a saving experience of Christ (sometimes called a "born-again" experience). Third, an evangelical understands "witnessing," or the need to share one's experience of Christ with others, as an important responsibility for the believer. Fourth, popular evangelicals believe that each individual must freely choose to either accept or deny Christ. Finally, and perhaps most important for the purposes of this study, popular evangelicals believe that Christ will return soon to establish his literal, millennial kingdom on Earth.

Put differently, despite using various forms of the term "evangelical," I am actually talking about prophecy believers, most of whom *are* evangelicals—at least in the *popular* sense. Prophecy belief represents what historian George M. Marsden calls a kind of folk piety.[3] It overflows theological and denominational boundaries and proves most influential at the popular level. Prophecy believers cluster within denominations associated with evangelicalism, to be sure, but they can also be found outside its bounds even among progressive denominations or among traditionally nonmillennial groups such as Lutherans. Denominational leaders of most groups, in fact, typically deride prophecy belief. Yet it keeps springing up via its own networks in Christian media, especially television networks and bookstores. Prophecy belief is indeed what historian Paul S. Boyer calls "a theology of the people."[4]

So if I am discussing prophecy believers, why do I not just use the term "prophecy believers"? This is the strategy Boyer uses quite effectively in his study. I try as often as possible to follow Boyer's usage because it suggests that prophecy believers can be found throughout the American population, and not simply isolated in a few denominations. But the same is true of popular evangelicals, and again, I believe that prophecy believers are much more often than not popular evangelicals—or potentially so—hence, I think I ought to be explicit about the fact that this is a study of a major subset of evangelicals, not simply "prophecy believers." Moreover, my overriding concern in this study is with evangelical identity and the potential consequences the acceptance of prophecy belief may carry for evangelical identity. Thus, I am concerned on one level with prophecy believers, but their beliefs may have repercussions for evangelicalism, too.

While recognizing that some may find my usage either too restrictive or too broad, my goal here is to avoid what philosopher Anthony Flew called the "death of a thousand qualifications," or the excessive use of qualifiers that breaks the narrative flow. For example, the correct descriptor might read "conservative dispensational premillennial pretribulational American evangelicals"—quite a mouthful. Let me be clear: I am not saying who is or is not an evangelical in any definitive sense. Indeed, that is not my task. Those evangelicals who are not prophecy believers, for example, members of the Christian Reformed tradition, may take comfort that I am not denying their status as evangelicals. Nevertheless, most evangelicals are conservative—at least theologically—and many if not most conservative evangelicals are prophecy believers, even if they fail to accept everything that books like *Left Behind* preach to them. Hence, one will always find important exceptions, but the term—as unwieldy and riddled with qualifications as it necessarily appears—remains meaningful.

Finally, I have also chosen not to use the term "fundamentalist," although a number of scholars I greatly respect do. This is not necessarily because the term has no explanatory value. Like "evangelical," it has been used to cover a number of Protestant groups in many different ways. Sometimes writers label as fundamentalists conservative Protestants who reject the world and cleave to their own communities. Often scholars add the necessity of prophecy belief. Still other writers, typically in the popular presses, label as fundamentalist any religious community whose beliefs exceed the bounds of what the writer considers legitimate. Nevertheless, it remains a useful term, but one I do not use here except when referring to the work of scholars who do use the term.

My avoidance of the term "fundamentalist" has more to do with my belief that the evangelicalism depicted by the authors is a transitional one. I think it fair to suggest that most of their beliefs could be considered fundamentalist. But I am attempting to track a sense of dynamic movement within the evangelical subculture, the tension one finds in the novels that asks which direction evangelicalism ought to go. Granted, the dominant voice within the novels points toward fundamentalism. The protagonists, especially late in the series, turn away from the wicked world and sharply—even militantly—define the boundary between "us" and "them," surrendering their moral responsibility in deference to allegedly inerrant prophecies. But I also find another fainter, yet nevertheless significant voice that warns against the dangers of too narrowly defining the line between friends and foes, especially in a world of increasing ambiguity and uncertainty. In sum, the *Left Behind* protagonists explore a continuum of possibilities within the evangelical subculture, albeit the conservative side. Thus, I opt for the term "evangelical," but with qualifications.

Introduction

First Words on Last Things

> Hardly anyone doubts that ours is a day when people are running "to and fro" and knowledge has increased. Both secular knowledge and the knowledge of prophetic truth have increased tremendously in this century alone.[1]   —Tim LaHaye and Jerry B. Jenkins, *Are We Living in the End Times?*

> We are living in a moment of unprecedented complexity, when things are changing faster than our ability to comprehend them. This is a time of transition betwixt and between a period that seemed more stable and secure and a time when, many people hope, equilibrium will be restored.[2]
> —Mark C. Taylor, *The Moment of Complexity*

This book explores contemporary evangelical prophecy fiction, especially the best-selling *Left Behind* novels by Tim LaHaye and Jerry B. Jenkins.[3] *Left Behind* represents the most prominent example of this increasingly popular literary genre, culminating a nearly three-decade trend of novels that have combined edge-of-your-seat suspense with critical aspects of the evangelical End-Times message. Although the reasons for the *Left Behind* novels' popularity are by no means simple, many of them center on the anxieties the novels articulate, especially their thoroughgoing suspicion of modernity. More specifically, the tensions the novels expose correspond to the emergence of what social scientists and media theorists have dubbed the "network society"—sometimes also known as the "network culture."[4] The network culture represents a pervasive matrix of rapid technological, social, and cultural changes that have emerged across the world since the end of the Second World War, and especially since the late

1960's. It has featured the explosive growth of new technologies, a global economy, and an increasingly free-flow of information that has toppled walls, erased borders, and menaced cultures holding exclusionary beliefs. Prophecy writers claim that these unwelcome developments mark the rise of the "Beast system."

The network culture has provoked sharp responses from those menaced by the drastic changes associated with it, drawing, in particular, the attention of LaHaye and Jenkins, whose novels attest to an impassioned attempt to maintain the integrity of evangelical identity while also adapting, however reluctantly, to the inevitability of change so characteristic of modernity. As the authors sense their traditional worldviews threatened by pervasive yet elusive economic, political, and cultural forces, they articulate their anxieties in the familiar language of apocalypse, creating protagonists who give voice to their deepest concerns. The texts feature, on one level, a desperate attempt to find the face of Antichrist under every suspect cultural development.[5] When one takes a closer look, however, the *Left Behind* novels indicate that LaHaye and Jenkins play more than an unwieldy and uninformed game of "pin the tail on the Antichrist." They ultimately take issue with the network culture and its perceived allies: New Age spiritualities and secular humanist philosophies that allegedly make humans and the natural world, rather than a wholly transcendent God, the measure of all things.

The network culture may give prophecy writers pause for alarm, but their response is by no means one of panic. Irony marks *Left Behind*. LaHaye and Jenkins, like many of their forebears in American evangelicalism, exhibit both an attraction and a repulsion toward modernity. A number of historians, in fact, consider evangelicalism almost "coterminous with modernity," existing in a kind of "symbiotic relationship," as Paul S. Boyer and Joel A. Carpenter put it, respectively.[6] Contemporary evangelicalism is, as Carpenter argues, a highly adaptive religious impulse that feeds upon modernity, even while railing against it, using, ironically, its own tools to transmit the evangelical message.[7] Technology, for example, saturates the pages of the *Left Behind* novels. Believers wield the latest gadgets against the forces of evil, who also outfit themselves with a full array of high-tech devices. Technology appears to carry for LaHaye and Jenkins both the promise of successful cultural adaptation, as well as the peril of overaccommodation. Indeed, their protagonists are torn between a desire to reject the sinfulness of the modern world, and a drive to enjoy the middle-class creature comforts afforded by contemporary American culture. Believers want it both ways. LaHaye and Jenkins, however, do not appear entirely comfortable with this liminal arrangement.

A second, related irony characterizes the *Left Behind* novels. *Left Behind,* after all, describes the End, yet the End takes its time in arriving. It is tempting to dismiss the authors' reluctance to bring forth the End in their novels as nothing more than an attempt to wring as much revenue as possible from a lucrative literary franchise. This does have a ring of truth about it. The enterprise began with a single novel, then became a trilogy and kept stretching to meet market demand. But one must not overlook the fact that readers continue to purchase the books in record quantities. A cynical attempt to cash-in or not, the novels obviously meet at least some of the psychic needs of their readership.[8] In a nutshell, LaHaye and Jenkins succeed because they offer meaning, however stark and gloomy, to believers struggling to make sense of the rapid cultural changes they perceive swirling all around them.

Moreover, it is easy to read the *Left Behind* novels and come away with the impression that American evangelicals are a defeated, forlorn, and desperate group, but this seldom verifies in the world outside the novels. Prophecy believers may dream of their heavenly "pie in the sky, by and by," but for the time being, they are not going anywhere. The recent upsurge in evangelical political involvement—even by traditionally reluctant figures such as Jerry Falwell—bears witness to the notion that although their fictional musings often address questions of escape, prophecy-believing evangelicals remain hesitant to leave the world behind.[9] Despite the undeniably escapist orientation of the series, the *Left Behind* novels reflect both the ambivalence of their readership vis-à-vis the world, as well as an implicit knowledge that as long they remain earthbound, they must make the best of it.

If prophecy believers are not going anywhere soon, they must take adequate measures to adapt to American culture without surrendering critical aspects of their evangelical identities. Prophecy writers specialize in articulating and defending evangelical identity by ferreting out hidden sources of evil in their midst, encouraging readers to construct their identities by determining what they are not. This process includes the setting of firm symbolic boundaries between those within the evangelical community who strive to uphold God's commandments and outsiders who do not. Just as the Antichrist emerges as the evil inverse of Christ, prophecy believers come to view themselves as the inverse of what they perceive as evil. This need to identify the evil *other* is so strong that, as sociologist

Christian Smith suggests, prophecy writers may even manufacture their images of evil, because an identified adversary provides prophecy believers with a tension and sense of purpose that energizes, rather than enervates their identity as evangelicals.[10] As Smith argues in *American Evangelicalism: Embattled and Thriving*, conservative evangelicals require an adequate level of tension between themselves and the cultural mainstream. Without this tension, they may lack the ability to differentiate their existential offerings from those of their competitors in the American spiritual economy. This is not to suggest that prophecy writers spin paranoid delusions with a pragmatic purposefulness. Indeed, as I argue later in the text, the network culture does indeed pose a serious threat to the particularity of prophecy believers. Nonetheless, such rigorous identification of evil can have serious consequences if the tension becomes excessive, and the symbolic boundaries between insiders and outsiders become too rigid.[11] Prophecy believers must, after all, still find their place in *this* world.

Thus, I suggest in the following pages that prophecy belief may serve to safeguard evangelical identity by acting as a kind of "cultural thermostat" that attempts to provide prophecy believers with just the right amount of tension vis-à-vis the contemporary world.[12] With inadequate tension they will have little to distinguish themselves from ordinary Americans, and their religious particularity may erode just as it arguably has already begun to slip away among a number of mainline churches in the United States.[13] With excessive tension, however, prophecy believers face the risk of turning too far inward, of separating themselves from the cultural mainstream and losing dynamism as a movement. Indeed, during times of crisis the rhetorical attempts of prophecy writers to distance their communities from the mainstream may backfire, and the thermostat may become unable to adjust to the massive infusion of cultural anxieties. A certain amount of critical distancing may be necessary for prophecy believers while too much may result in the loss of their particular identities as evangelicals, just as surely as too little.

Onward Christian Publishing: Left Behind and Its Precursors

Tim LaHaye and Jerry Jenkins have succeeded in a publishing market in which many prophecy novelists have failed, building upon the efforts of their predecessors to create a franchise with substantial appeal. Since

1970, a number of prophecy writers have opted to include fictional texts along with their more expository prophecy manuals.[14] One can attribute part of this success to Hal Lindsey's *The Late Great Planet Earth*.[15] Lindsey took a complicated eschatology and simplified it into a checklist of current events which signaled the last days. Lindsey, with the assistance of writer Carole C. Carlson, added a light touch to an otherwise ponderous topic and helped make dispensationalism trendy at a time when many Americans were searching for answers after the social uncertainty of the 1960's.[16] Christian novelists, encouraged in part by *The Late Great Planet Earth* and its astonishing sales figures—which made it the best-selling nonfiction title of the 1970's according to the *New York Times*—created narratives strikingly similar to Lindsey's formula, albeit with an overtly fictional turn. To demonstrate the depth of Lindsey's influence, Tampa Bay nurse turned novelist Carol Balizet, author of *The Seven Last Years,* even formally acknowledged Lindsey's influence, claiming that his "book started it all."[17]

One could classify the first efforts at novelization as hybrids between Lindsey-style pop-prophecy and serious attempts at fiction. Evangelist and popular prophecy speaker Salem Kirban tried such a formula in 1970, actually publishing his prophecy manual/novel *666* several months before Hal Lindsey's opus appeared.[18] Unlike Lindsey, however, Kirban failed to generate massive public excitement and sales. Part of this could be pinned on his prose. *666* did not demonstrate a mastery of the genre, perhaps since Kirban lacked experience as a novelist—his self-emphasized background was actually in journalism. The result exhibited a directness of style not conducive to narrative flow or character development.

Still, one cannot fault him for any lack of creativity or imagination, especially in his choice of illustrations. Although Kirban often relied on "stock photos" that he relabeled and recontextualized for the reader, he also included a number of original illustrations. In one frame, a guillotine stands before a church symbolizing Antichrist's eagerness to decapitate those unwilling to accept the Mark of the Beast.[19] In another, a woman is branded with "666" on a communion altar by two men who look more like bored security guards than agents of the Antichrist, Brother Bartholomew.[20] Even with such colorful innovations, however, *666* lacked the populist "common touch" so remarkable in *The Late Great Planet Earth*. Nevertheless, Kirban helped to pioneer contemporary prophecy fiction. His efforts, along with Lindsey's, encouraged a flood of novels that entered the market—with only slightly greater success—in the 1970's.[21]

Kirban's successors also wove into their apocalyptic narratives a number of equally colorful if not always credible themes. Still, many of the plot devices pioneered during the early years of the genre would later resurface in the *Left Behind* novels. Kirban's *666*, along with Donald Thompson's film, *A Thief in the Night*, both prominently featured decapitation for those refusing to accept the Mark of the Beast. Carol Balizet focused on the supernatural aspects of the Tribulation in *The Seven Last Years*, depicting locust plagues and other maladies with gruesome precision, reflecting her background as a nurse. Ken Wade, author of *The Orion Conspiracy*, highlighted the deceptive possibilities of virtual reality, with his main character confronting a seductive but ultimately demonic figure bearing an unusually close resemblance to the late pop music superstar Karen Carpenter.[22] Finally in *Abaddon*, evangelical radio personality and part-time exorcist Bob Larson suggested multiple personality disorder as a symptom of demonic possession, resulting from repressed memories of ritual abuse and compounded by death metal music.[23] More significantly, "Abaddon" denotes the chief of the demonic hordes, a notion LaHaye and Jenkins would later pick up—albeit in Greek—in their novel, *Apollyon*.

None of these themes, however, compares—at least on a visceral level—to one found in Gary M. Cohen's 1974 effort, *The Horsemen Are Coming*. Cohen combined the notion of *Soylent Green* with Exodus-style food drop programs, creating an Antichrist who—with an obviously wicked sense of humor—processes Christians and other political dissidents into edible wafers called "Manna." Cohen's narrative explains the concept, "The letters that spell Manna, M-A-N-N-A, represent something. They stand for Mammalian Animal Nutriments, Neutralizers Added. . . . According to World Network TV, the flesh of dead human corpses is being included."[24] Although LaHaye and Jenkins have yet to add their own version of refined cannibalism, the desperate food shortages they have already depicted may ultimately necessitate another serving of this familiar theme.

Prophecy novels of the 1970's may have failed to generate much interest, but one cannot say the same for evangelical prophecy films, especially those of Donald W. Thompson. Thompson, using Panaflex cameras and a directorial acumen that would later attract Hollywood offers, managed to stretch extremely low budgets and questionable if enthusiastic acting to create an End-Times phenomenon among evangelical churches in the 1970's.[25] His four-part series included *A Thief in the Night, A Distant Thunder, Image of the Beast,* and *The Prodigal Planet.* The four films, especially *A Thief in the Night,* dramatized the End-Times scenario familiar to evangelical audiences and transformed it into a powerful conversion tool.[26] Typically screened at churches or Bible camps for youthful audiences, the films raised an apocalyptic awareness among their viewers, encouraging them to accept the Gospel message before they were "left behind."

Most of the aforementioned novels and films differ from the *Left Behind* franchise in one important characteristic, however. For the earlier projects, the End is fixed and Antichrist is all-powerful—at least during the seven years of the Tribulation. Believers can do little more than hide out and attempt to escape the wrath of Antichrist and his repressive forces. The authors depict believers as remarkably powerless with only limited hopes for resistance or redemption. After all, they have been left behind, so all bets for salvation are off. *Beast,* written by journalist Dan Betzer, best exemplifies the early passivity of the genre.[27] Betzer's Antichrist, Jacques Catroux, literally bears the eyes, heart, and mind of his predecessor, Adolf Hitler, and fashions himself as the "Ubermensch" [sic] revealed in the German philosopher Friedrich Nietzsche's *Thus Spake Zaranthustra* [sic].[28] Catroux, moreover, can place his victims in a catatonic or paralytic state by a mere glance. Resistance against him is obviously out of the question. Protagonists can do nothing more than shake their fists against God and wonder what they will suffer next. Although an attempt to explain the passivity of the early novels is beyond the scope of the present study, I suspect it reflects the novelists' total emphasis on evangelism at the expense of what they viewed as pointless, overt political activism.

Oregon pastor turned novelist Frank Peretti changed much of this in the late 1980's. Peretti's first two best-selling novels, *This Present Darkness* in 1986 and *Piercing the Darkness* in 1989, proved groundbreaking in many ways.[29] Peretti's plots effectively dramatized evangelical anxieties in a shadowy, dualistic, but surprisingly realistic world, except perhaps for Peretti's fascination with demons and angels who fight for the souls of humans. Peretti's novels, while still burdened by an overwhelming need to find evil lurking behind every cultural entity with which he disagreed, nevertheless advanced the genre not only with his sales—which topped several million by the early 1990's—but also through his innovative prose. Peretti took an introspective turn, narrating the lives of protagonists who had lost their identities due to demonic influences, and who subsequently found themselves the objects of a cosmic struggle between demon hordes and angelic hosts. Peretti also eschewed the typical seven-year apocalyptic formula and experimented with new styles, while retaining the critical edge and sense of imminent danger characteristic of the genre. More important, Peretti's characters were more than passive victims; they fought back, struggling with mundane manifestations of evil, while their angelic counterparts fought demons in the ether surrounding them. Peretti's dynamic plots and realistic protagonists also proved appealing to consumers, who helped make Peretti's novels highly successful both within and outside the world of Christian booksellers.

Spurred on by celebrity endorsements, including one by Christian pop-singer Amy Grant, Peretti's novels topped mainstream best-seller lists, a first for an evangelical prophecy novelist. Peretti continued to churn out hits in the 1990's with *Prophet,* a bracing critique of modern technology and the mass media, before moving on to *The Oath* in 1995 and *The Visitation* in 1999—with both novels achieving best-seller status.[30] Other prominent evangelicals, doubtless influenced by Peretti's unprecedented success, also tried their hand at prophecy fiction. The list includes such notables as long-time "700 Club" host Pat Robertson (*The End of the Age*) and Christian financial advisor Larry Burkett (*The Illuminati*), although neither matched Peretti's commercial appeal.[31] Even Hal Lindsey tried his hand at fiction in the 1990's, although his novel, *Blood Moon,* met with disappointing results.[32]

Larry Burkett's *The Illuminati,* despite lacking significant commercial success, added additional wrinkles to the genre of prophecy fiction. Although Burkett clung tenaciously to a sharp, dualistic polarization of friends and adversaries, he introduced a number of themes LaHaye and Jenkins would also deploy several years later. *The Illuminati,* published in 1991, like Peretti's novels, reflected the changing cultural climate of the emerging post–Cold War period.[33] Whereas Peretti began with external concerns and moved inward, Burkett's paranoid prose detailed a laundry list of evangelical enemies and advocated a plan of cultural intervention that closely matched the goals of the New Christian Right. Even as Burkett promoted the causes of the New Christian Right, however, he also depicted evangelical Christians as a disempowered minority, displaying a less than credible measure of self-marginalization. *The Illuminati,* for example, features blood-thirsty liberal groups hunting down persecuted Christians and transporting them to detainment camps.

Consistent with the novel's familiarity with the New Christian Right, Burkett's characters do not idly accept their fate but fight against the forces of evil. Specifically, the protagonists oppose several figures, including Thomas Galt—a thinly veiled reference to CNN founder and media mogul Ted Turner. Galt oppresses believers with the power of his media empire. Believers fight back with an opposition newspaper titled *Truth* (a theme LaHaye and Jenkins also deploy in the *Left Behind* series). Galt, however, turns out to be not so unreasonable after all and eventually converts to evangelical Christianity, using the power of his media empire to spread the Gospel of Jesus Christ. Galt even hosts his own Sunday morning public affairs program called "Face the Truth," leading forty million Americans to accept Christ, according to an "Insta-pol."[34]

Burkett also observed the increasing power of networks. Data-Net, an advanced computer network designed to track citizens and bring forth a one-world government, becomes a major adversary in *The Illuminati*. Burkett's protagonists, while initially resigned, do take action, albeit with reservations. Led by a Georgia pastor, John Elder, and a computer expert, Jeff Wells, believers interrupt the prospective Antichrist's network, crippling his ability to carry forth his planned persecution of believers. In fact, Wells and his allies thwart their adversaries. But it is all just a false alarm. The real Antichrist has not yet arrived. Burkett makes it evident that if this were the real Tribulation, believers would have less success resisting Antichrist.

Frank Peretti touched upon the existential concerns of evangelicals, while authors such as Burkett focused their critiques on domestic issues more broadly construed and offered a glimpse at themes that LaHaye and Jenkins would more fruitfully articulate in the *Left Behind* series. Thus, the originality of LaHaye and Jenkins lies not in their novel discovery of such ideas but in their successful combination of them. Peretti's success demonstrated the potentially broad appeal of the genre, and LaHaye and Jenkins captured the market by writing blockbusters that addressed evangelical concerns with issues of cultural and personal identity, deploying a sophistication and resolution not often found in previous novels. Of course, savvy marketing helped, too. Literary agent Rick Christian of Alive Communications noted the genre's potential. Unlike other agents and authors, however, Christian knew which levers to pull and brought together two of the most prolific writers in contemporary evangelicalism, Tim LaHaye and Jerry Jenkins, to produce a fictional rendering of the Tribulation.[35] Together they formed a literary "dream team" that further popularized prophecy fiction, taking it out of the Christian bookstores and into the malls, megamarts, and even the more respectable mainstream booksellers.

LaHaye, already an evangelical superstar who had written and spoken widely on topics as diverse as secular humanism, conservative family advice, pop psychology, politics, Christian sexology, and, of course, prophecy, lent his considerable experience as an evangelical trendsetter and activist to the project.[36] Jerry Jenkins also brought significant commercial success, having authored, most notably, numerous best-selling biographies of American sports legends. LaHaye and Jenkins demonstrated an extensive knowledge of the evangelical subculture, and together they understood their readership and its needs. LaHaye conceived the ideas behind the *Left Behind* novels, while Jenkins used his solid, workmanlike prose to bring narrative life to LaHaye's vision. The combination proved explosive.

Their expectations were modest. After all, several publishers had already rejected the initial manuscript; and, just as importantly, previous attempts by major evangelical luminaries had failed to muster much interest.[37] *Left Behind,* released in 1995, while neither immediately nor extraordinary successful in the mainstream, did quite well among Christian bookstores. Its massive success came soon after, however, as the novel and its successors gained momentum and the publisher, Tyndale House—goaded by Rick Christian—successfully marketed the novels to prominent mass retailers, including Barnes & Noble, Costco, K-Mart, and Wal-Mart.[38] As *Christianity Today* contributor Steve Rabey notes, the *Left Behind* series may not have single-handedly initiated the surge of Christian publications onto the shelves of mass retailers, but it certainly benefited from the trend, as did retailers.[39] Although Rabey, writing in April 2002, estimated the total sales of the series at thirty-five million, recent estimates have exceeded fifty million.[40]

On the surface *Left Behind* differs little from its predecessors. It follows the basic dispensational script with Christ removing true believers during the Rapture, with everyone else left to suffer seven years of Tribulation under Satan's proxy, Antichrist.[41] What sets *Left Behind* apart, however, has been the ability of LaHaye and Jenkins to perceive acutely the cultural changes around them, sense the anxieties of a significant number of Americans, and build novels around such fears, explaining—much as Lindsey did—that these are signs that Christ will return soon. The worse conditions become, the more believers know that God is in control. Moreover, LaHaye and Jenkins offer their readers much more than a depressing list of painful plagues and unmitigated torments—they offer them the hope that even those "left behind" can effectively struggle against Antichrist, taking at least a portion of their fate into their own hands.

LaHaye and Jenkins have kept busy with other projects, however, with LaHaye updating his prophecy manuals and both authors producing a new guide to that most enigmatic of Biblical books, Revelation, suggestively titled, *Are We Living in the End Times?*[42] Moreover, the authors and the marketing staff at Tyndale House Publishers have recognized that a niche exists for children's novels, selling over ten million copies of a series entitled *Left Behind: The Kids*, geared toward existentially anxious youngsters aged ten to fourteen, who might lack the maturity required by the adult novels, but who can nevertheless benefit from the authors' gloomy interpretation of current events. Such texts largely repeat the themes of the adult series, with four juvenile books corresponding to each adult version. In addition, *Left Behind: The TV Series* is scheduled to debut soon, along with a radio version to be broadcast on Christian radio stations.

The existence of so many spin-off products, along with a mind-boggling proliferation of assorted *Left Behind* merchandise, further indicates the extent of the *Left Behind* phenomenon. The authors have also parlayed their joint success into lucrative, separate ventures. Tim LaHaye recently signed a book deal with Random House, the publishing wing of media giant AOL Time-Warner, that includes an estimated advance of $45 million. The publishers hope LaHaye can transfer his success with the *Left Behind* novels to a new action series centered on the exploits of a Christian "Indiana Jones."[43] Jerry Jenkins has also remained active, raising his already strong profile within evangelical circles. Besides his work with Billy Graham on the latter's autobiography, *Just As I Am*, Jenkins cofounded the Christian Writer's Guild, an organization that offers training and marketing opportunities to prospective evangelical novelists.[44] Jenkins also released his own prophecy novel in September 2003, aptly titled, *Soon: The Beginning of the End*.[45]

Finally, a film version of *Left Behind* appeared in February 2001, although without the authors' permission, which has resulted in extended legal wrangling. The film also lacked the luster that the novels brought to bookstores, never cracking the Top Ten, despite weak competition. One can blame part of this on the marketing strategy of coproducer Peter Lalonde. Lalonde's decision to "pre-release" the film in October 2000 directly to video was particularly inexplicable, as it effectively undercut any box office bounce the film might have enjoyed.[46] Thus, despite the success that the Trinity Broadcasting Network (TBN) achieved in 1999 with their own low-budget, End-Times thriller *The Omega Code*, *Left Behind*, even with triple the number of screens and a much higher production and promotional budget, could not equal the box office success of *Omega Code*.[47] None of this reflects upon the cultural impact of the novels, of course, which continue to dominate their own genre. The film's failure, however—on the big screen at least since it did perform quite well in the secondary DVD market—sufficiently inspired Tim LaHaye to sue the filmmakers for "failing to make the film into a blockbuster."[48] After the success of the novels, one cannot blame him for his disappointment.

Left Behind: A Brief Summary of Key Characters and Themes

Evangelical prophecy novels typically begin with a catastrophic event of unprecedented scale. Christ comes to "rapture" or "beam out" his faithful followers, leaving those who remain in a state of panic and despair, doomed to suffer seven horrible years under Satan's minion, Antichrist, in a period known as the "Tribulation." In *Left Behind*, the Rapture—at least from the perspective of three of its protagonists—occurs just after midnight aboard a transatlantic flight halfway over the North Atlantic. The authors skillfully capture the liminality of the panic-stricken passengers, who suddenly realize—at least metaphorically—that they are nowhere in particular, caught between night and day, and lacking any particular direction. Symbolically, the captain, faced with the chaos aboard his plane, feels compelled to turn the jumbo jet around and return to the perceived safety of home, where he hopes he can find some meaning in the disappearances.

Sleepy passengers awaken to find numerous empty seats. Clothing, glasses, and jewelry remain in the seats, but their owners have vanished. An elderly woman seated in first class cannot find her husband. A fellow passenger claims he must be in the lavatories, but the reader instantly recognizes the hopelessness of her situation; her husband, it seems, was a more devout Christian than his grieving wife and just received the ultimate upgrade. The captain, Rayford Steele, assisted by his chief flight attendant Hattie Durham and another first-class passenger, the young, Ivy League–educated journalist Cameron "Buck" Williams, move to subdue the remainder of the frightened passengers. The situation on the ground mirrors the anxiety on the plane, forcing them to reroute to Chicago O'Hare.

As fate would have it, Captain Steele lives in Chicago along with his family, among whom only his rebellious, free-thinking collegiate daughter Chloe remains. His wife and son have both disappeared. To make matters worse, he knows where they have gone. He should have listened. When his wife, Irene, implored him to attend New Hope Village Church, he turned away, alarmed by the total commitment demanded by the evangelical congregation. Now, he has nowhere else to turn for answers. Upon his arrival at the church, he is stunned to find the associate pastor, Bruce Barnes. Pastor Barnes preached the message but did not hear the *word*. All is not lost, however. Pastor Barnes, Captain Steele, Chloe, and Buck Williams each come to realize their errors, accept Jesus as their personal savior, and band together to form a core group within the church called the "Tribulation Force." Initially led by Pastor Barnes, the Tribulation Force sets out to oppose the Antichrist and save as many souls as they can before it is too late. The plots of the first two novels, *Left Behind* and *Tribulation Force,* besides portraying a post-apocalyptic world, introduce readers to the basic problems and personalities that prove crucial to the remainder of the series.

The Tribulation Force does not encompass all of the important characters, of course. The global unrest causes widespread panic, and grief-stricken citizens search for answers amid their rapidly fading hopes for the recovery of lost loved ones and a return to a normal life. This sense of bereavement and shock enables the rise of a charismatic leader with a comprehensive plan to rebuild damaged cities and chaos-stricken nations. Nicolae Jetty Carpathia, a hard-charging European businessman who becomes the president of Romania and the leader of Europe in rapid succession, also assumes control of the United Nations. Proficient in many languages, devilishly charming, handsome, and a mesmerizing speaker with a prodigious memory, Carpathia seems like the right person for such a perilous time. He not only gives comfort and answers for the disappearances, but he also offers the hope of building an even better world than the one currently lying in rubble. The crisis, it seems, brings to the world a spirit of cooperation and unity. Carpathia's commanding presence and his appreciation of the need for hope and order make him beloved among the people, who eagerly grant him additional authority. He uses his emergency powers to implement the widespread calls for unity, amalgamating the world's nations, religions, and currencies under his authority, which he acquires from the United Nations but soon expands well beyond its diplomatic capacities.

His blueprint for peace includes ten regional kingdoms placed under his control, a move to a single currency, and a unified world religion called "The Enigma Babylon One World Faith" led by Pontifex Maximus Peter II, formerly Archbishop Peter Mathews of Cincinnati, Ohio. Carpathia also requests and elicits the cooperation of the world's great powers in the destruction of 90 percent of the planet's weaponry with the remainder donated to the United Nations, renamed the Global Community. Although Carpathia ostensibly believes in the principles of free speech and an independent media, he buys all the major media outlets (including the Trinity and Christian Broadcasting Networks!),[49] using money gleaned from international bankers, and consolidates his power in a rebuilt Babylon, dubbed, "New Babylon."

His trustworthy aides assist him in his global takeover, especially including his ultimate False Prophet, Leon Fortunato, and his mysterious "aunt," Viv Ivins.[50] Both prove vital to Antichrist's success, despite occasional lapses into incompetence.[51] Finally, Carpathia signals the beginning of the Tribulation by signing a seven-year peace treaty with Israel, promising Israel protection in exchange for botanist Chaim Rosenzweig's formula that turns deserts into arable cropland. Briefly stated, Carpathia offers the world total peace and unprecedented prosperity, just after it seemed all had been lost.

The remaining novels, beginning with book three, *Nicolae,* chart the unraveling of Carpathia's unimpeachable image, even as his power continues to expand. The Tribulation Force, although suffering the loss of Pastor Barnes due to an apparently diabolical poisoning, sets up "cell churches" across the world and uses its connections—technological and otherwise—to infiltrate the Global Community and undermine Carpathia's plans. Although they know they cannot defeat him, they hope their efforts can convince many that he is a deceiver and a false messiah. Both Captain Steele and Buck Williams find themselves in serendipitous positions to gather information for the burgeoning underground resistance movement that grows out of the Tribulation Force. Carpathia hires

Buck to publish his flagship magazine, *The Global Community Weekly,* while Rayford becomes captain of Carpathia's newly built and exquisitely furnished Boeing 757 jet.

Moreover, the Tribulation Force never lacks technological expertise. Rayford's boss, Earl Halliday, plants undetectable listening devices in Carpathia's cabin, allowing Rayford to monitor the activities of Carpathia and his top lieutenants. Meanwhile in Chicago, a young computer expert named Donny Moore assists Buck in developing top-of-the-line always-connected laptops for each member of the tiny underground movement. This forms a pattern within the series. Although Donny dies in the great earthquake, which concludes *Nicolae*, a replacement arrives in the person of Dr. Floyd Charles, just as Tsion Ben-Judah, an orthodox rabbi who declares Jesus the Messiah on international television, replaces Bruce Barnes as the spiritual leader of the group, and the informal leader, via the Internet, of the nascent cell churches scattered across the world. Ben-Judah's teachings, which are coterminous with dispensational theology, allow the authors to insert extensive dispensational content without interrupting the narrative flow. Certain roles, in other words, replicate, albeit with different personalities. The Tribulation Force never lacks pilots, spiritual authorities, medical staff, technological consultants, or even economists.

Despite their apparent dependence on technological specialists, however, the Tribulation Force retains a healthy suspicion of Carpathia's technological infrastructure. After all, the same networks that allow them to spread their message also permit Carpathia to consolidate his global empire and polish his image, as well as potentially infiltrate the Tribulation Force. Although it seems at times that the Tribulation Force has an expert for every problem, the authors ostensibly recognize that Antichrist controls the bigger picture, at least until Christ's triumphant return.

Textually, the novels rely on fast-paced action sequences often at the expense of sustained character development. The protagonists also lack credibility. The novels turn on the assumption that members of a suburban Chicago Bible church will rise to a prominence of cosmic significance. Banality often results when the authors give an implausible level of sophistication to otherwise ordinary people. Coupled with the gross incompetence of Antichrist's support staff, the result just does not appear credible. The authors often depict evil characters like Leon Fortunato as humorous fools, as when Fortunato develops an extremely painful hemorrhoid during the first few chapters of the ninth novel, *Desecration*. The lack of credible adversaries may have even damaged the series' appeal, at least temporarily, as one can gather reading chatroom and bulletin board complaints about *Desecration*.[52]

The authors have nonetheless overcome such difficulties and maintained a large readership. Perhaps the idea of ordinary people challenging the Antichrist even works to the novels' benefit. The characters LaHaye and Jenkins create resemble ordinary churchgoers one might expect to meet at a bake sale or potluck dinner—except they fly transport aircraft and have knowledge of advanced weapons systems and complicated electronics that many governments would envy.[53] They modify their fatalism and demonstrate extraordinary capabilities when God calls them. Such hopefulness in the face of perceived cultural marginalization may prove appealing to those who cannot otherwise imagine how they can adapt to bewildering cultural conditions. Nevertheless, an extended discussion of the authors and their writing ability lies outside the scope of this book. I do suspect, however, that what secular critics find banal, the authors and their readers view as a winning formula—so long as it is not overdone.

The Rhetorical Appeal of Left Behind

A sampling of evangelical prophecy fiction indicates that authors believe recent economic and technological changes threaten their very identity as evangelicals, pushing aside a world undergirded by God and replacing it with one generated by complex technological forces prophecy writers collectively name the "Beast system." In the face of such pressures, prophecy novels such as *Left Behind* exercise a rhetorical appeal that showcases for believers the alleged comforts and simplicity of a premodern world, while gradually easing them into the multiplicity of postmodern worlds, in which their identities as Christians are miraculously safeguarded, and the complex economic and technological forces that threaten them are nothing more than the latest of Satan's deceptive machinations. In effect, the novels appeal to a mythical past in order to shape believers' understandings of a troubled present and an even more troubling future. Joel A. Carpenter in his study of twentieth-century Protestant fundamentalists, *Revive Us Again,* notes a similar tendency at work, calling it a Christian "Primitivism" that overlooks historical nuances and hearkens back to an allegedly pristine time when everyone followed Biblical precepts.[54]

The promise of a mythical golden age provides one incentive for believers to accept the evangelical message of the texts. But the strategy is not exclusively a positive one. Punishments await those who fail to make their decisions for Christ in a timely manner. LaHaye and Jenkins seek to foster an intense and uncanny sense of existential crisis among their readership and carefully heighten such tensions throughout the series, gradually revealing a world in which no believer would wish to be left behind. A kind of ironic escape becomes the only option. The authors, besides depicting foolish characters who suffer for their willful unbelief, also inform readers how they can avoid similar fates. LaHaye and Jenkins design their novels to bring their readers to a moment of personal crisis in which a faith commitment seems the only logical course. By intensifying, or exaggerating, current trends and making them much more palpable to their readers, the authors suggest that the undecided have little time remaining to make a rational decision.[55] One must merely observe the "signs of the times"—read current events as apocalyptic portents—to recognize the work of Antichrist.

Visions of finality tend to concentrate meaning in the present moment, sparking significant interest among those seeking to understand changes which might otherwise appear meaningless. Such a concentration of meaning no doubt proves tempting to many Americans. Potential believers are more likely to make a commitment if they understand the importance of the times. LaHaye and Jenkins attempt to convince their readers that *this* historical moment is a unique one in God's plan of salvation and requires an immediate and affirmative decision. Those who fail to accept the message of Christ will face eternal damnation, while those who do will receive a handsome payoff for their investment of faith.

The authors also deploy another, related technique: the use of *Schadenfreude*. Not only do evangelical readers get a foretaste of the delights that await them, but they also get the pleasure of imagining the suffering of those who sneer at their religious ideas. Readers, for example, can discover in graphic detail just what will happen to those obstinate neighbors who refuse to attend Sunday School with them. Those accused of marginalizing evangelicals receive satisfying comeuppances in the *Left Behind* novels. Those who come close to conversion but stop short of making a commitment receive perhaps the greatest punishment, however. They know the hell that awaits them during the Tribulation, along with the Rapture they could have enjoyed had they simply accepted Jesus.

One can also posit a fourth, less obvious but arguably more significant reason why the authors devote so many pages to exploring the futures of those left behind. *Left Behind* does not discuss the future per se; rather, it *enacts* it in narrative form. The use of fiction allows both authors and their readers to explore their future, imagining in narrative form their responses to the world, along with possible outcomes. The novels enact identity, imagining various evangelical responses to their ongoing confrontation with modernity. I emphasize plural *responses,* as the novels do not advocate just a single response, but rather explore in literary fashion a number of possibilities.

The novels, moreover, despite ostensibly depicting future events—events which Christians in good standing hope to avoid—discuss the present much more than the future. Why do the authors devote so much energy to describing a world that will ultimately not matter to believers? Although a mythical Tribulation may await those unfortunate enough to be "left behind," prophecy believers already are, in a very real sense, the ones left behind by bewildering social, cultural, and economic changes. *Left Behind* addresses their struggles and their tribulations in the here and now, as the texts desperately try to transform the marginal cultural status of conservative evangelicals into one of unique privilege.[56] LaHaye and Jenkins seek to turn the tables: prophecy believers left behind in contemporary American culture attempt to demonstrate that others, and not themselves, are ultimately the ones who will be left behind when God, representing a different standard of value, judges humanity. Prophecy believers may or may not escape in the Rapture, but in the meantime they remain earthbound and must contest their fragile evangelical identity against the hostile forces of modernity.

In sum, contemporary prophecy believers face an anxious and uncertain future. Trapped within the rapidly growing networks of the global economy and new communications technologies, believers must stake a place for themselves and their traditional values in a world that is often hostile to such rigid definitions of identity. The *Left Behind* novels depict protagonists who struggle against the symbolic evil in their midst, striving to hold onto some semblance of their evangelical identity and values.[57] The novels read, in a sense, as blueprints for answering such fundamental questions as, who are we? and, what are we becoming? LaHaye and Jenkins's answers may appear disconcerting to outsiders, but they offer prophecy believers a comforting vision both for this world and the next.

The Broader Significance of Left Behind

The previous section offers reasons why the novels may appeal to evangelicals and prospective believers: those on or near the "inside." But why should they matter to anyone else? Can we not simply ignore them as the cultural products of cranks and irrelevant malcontents, or as the symptoms of a fever that will break soon enough? The short answer is definitely "no." The novels may tell us more about American culture as a whole than many observers would care to admit. Historian Paul S. Boyer is a major exception, and his text, *When Time Shall Be No More,* has already established itself as a classic in the field. Boyer notes the more incredulous aspects of prophecy literature, of course, citing it as "chaotic, endlessly gullible, and nearly illiterate."[58] He does, however, direct his analysis beyond the peculiarities of the genre and expresses amazement that the symbol of Antichrist can continue to articulate "so many highly charged contemporary concerns."[59] Scholars, he writes, would be wise not to overlook "this protean and sometimes surprising belief system."[60] Moreover, Boyer suggests—despite numerous reservations—that prophecy belief may represent a "theology of the people."[61] Boyer summarizes the importance of prophecy literature, directly addressing for a wider, nonevangelical audience what one might call the "so what" factor:

> What Christopher Hill wrote at the end of his study of Antichrist theories in seventeenth-century England applies equally well to prophecy belief in modern America: "In one sense we have been exploring a trivial blind alley in human thought: but at all points it trembles on the brink of major intellectual issues."[62]

As Boyer recognizes, prophecy literature may appear banal to outsiders, but observers are ill-advised to overlook its cultural significance, especially when so many Americans either take it quite seriously or have at least encountered some form of it. Clearly, beneath the bizarre, supernatural plots, something important is happening. The most important step for an outsider seeking insight into the texts is the cultivation of empathy. This is, admittedly, a difficult task. Nonevangelical readers will likely find the novels offensive in numerous ways. To understand the novels and their runaway popularity, however, one must find the means to put aside—if just for the moment—the most offensive aspects of the texts and ask why they appeal so much to so many people.[63] The *Left Behind* novels communicate answers in uncertain times; and, even if one finds such answers wanting, one should not ignore the fact that many Americans apparently do find them satisfying.

The immediate aftermath of 9/11 potentially made available to many Americans the kind of empathy necessary for a measure of insight into the apocalyptic mood of the *Left Behind* novels.[64] Media theorist Mark C. Taylor describes the existential uncertainty unleashed by 9/11:

> Crossing the police barricade at Canal Street and walking past the courthouses and city hall toward Ground Zero, you enter an uncanny world that is both completely familiar and totally strange. Though street signs and landmarks remain unchanged, axes of orientation no longer line up as they once did. It is not just the absence of people and traffic or the haunting silence; something else, something palpable yet far more difficult to articulate is loose on the streets.[65]

Everything seemed to change on September 11, 2001. While one could not immediately pinpoint the differences, a palpable heaviness surrounded everyday activities. Officials encouraged Americans "to go back to business as usual," yet the public seemed to understand intuitively the difficulty of such a task. Even thousands of miles from Ground Zero, where the physical "axes of orientation" remained unchanged, people seemed disoriented, with many waiting for inevitable aftershocks. Eventually, the rituals of civil religion stirred the healing process, and baseball resumed play amid patriotic displays, ceremonial pomp, and comforting words from public officials.

Yet the uncanny menace which Taylor called, paradoxically, both "palpable" and "difficult to articulate," remained. It was a sense of evil unlike anything experienced during the Cold War years, when the enemy had a more recognizable face. This enemy, although given names by government officials, was much more insidious. It moved in networks, as Taylor pointed out, not unlike our own. A number of observers claimed that American culture had created the problems it now faced. Whatever the cause, it did seem evident that the terrorist menace represented the underside of the New Economy and our dreams of NASDAQ-driven profits and endless economic growth. Moving in amorphous cells and virtually invisible to our defenses, the terrorists threatened not so much our external borders but our internal sense of security, calling into question our roles as inhabitants of a suddenly vulnerable secular city, returning religion—at least for a brief moment—back to the public square.

I thought I grasped evangelicalism, especially prophecy fiction, sufficiently to understand the apocalyptic mood so critical to the texts and films. Yet I did not realize until 9/11 just how much I did not see, how much I had yet to understand. The events of 9/11, in other words, opened for me an empathy into the texts that was previously unavailable. I understood intellectually the appeal of prophecy novels, but I never really *understood*. Two days later it occurred to me that the events of 9/11 had created for many if not most Americans a palpable sense of apocalypse. For days and weeks after the tragic events, the *Left Behind* novels suddenly made much more sense. I did not agree with their perspectives culturally, politically, or otherwise, but I gained a better understanding of why the texts held such dramatic appeal for evangelicals and those who, while not quite evangelicals, could sympathize with their worldviews. For several days and weeks, I suspect, most Americans had access to this kind of insight into what might otherwise have seemed like yet another banal conspiracy theory. If one wishes to understand the *Left Behind* phenomenon and its cultural impact, one need only remember that uncanny feeling experienced after 9/11. Perhaps, that feeling, like the nebulous threat which evoked it, has never really gone away.

As tempting as it has been to place the texts in a neat little box and dismiss them as the paranoid musings of a lifelong activist and a literary hack, I have found the novels richer and more ambiguous than I had previously considered. The *Left Behind* novels both anticipate and reflect the anxieties that have become important in recent American culture, especially since 9/11. With the uncertainty surrounding the identity of potential enemies and the sense of powerlessness this has wrought, Americans have struggled to put a face on the enemy. This has not been without consequence. Far from existing in the realm of fantasy, the American response to the insecurity of 9/11 has paralleled in uncanny ways the world depicted in the *Left Behind* series. Our world has grown obsessed with security. Terror alerts leave us wondering when the next strike will occur. Experts threaten to comb through library records attempting to identify potential enemies. The use of duct tape and plastic sheeting threatens to seal our homes—literally and figuratively—against a menace we cannot even locate. Granted, some response to the insecurities of the modern age is called for, both within the *Left Behind* universe and without. The question is whether such responses will alleviate tensions or simply promote additional insecurities.

Ironically, this seems like the kind of world LaHaye and Jenkins advocate in their novels. Protagonists attempt to answer the uncertainty triggered by the Rapture with a quest for security and a renewed sense of stability. As the world faces a unique challenge from an elusive enemy, however, the very act of identifying the enemy and remedying the anxieties may in fact provoke the crisis we most fear. The novels, during times of crisis, may do more than reflect American anxieties; the climate of doubt and uncertainty they foster may spill out from the evangelical subculture and influence an American populace already shaken by quasi-apocalyptic events. The *Left Behind* series with its insistence on "internal security" may ultimately encourage a kind of "infernal security." Our own obsession with security in an era when friends are increasingly difficult to discern from foes may have similar consequences. Although this text discusses prophecy believers, one cannot divorce them and the problems they perceive from the larger American culture which sustains them and incorporates their anxieties. The line between the evangelical prophecy subculture and the American mainstream is not always easy to draw, especially during times of crisis.

Such ambiguities trouble those attempting to make sense of the novels and their unprecedented success. Critics struggle to find a language with which to understand the phenomenon. The July 1, 2002 issue of *Time* offered an insightful if long overdue account of the pop culture fascination with the *Left Behind* franchise. Nancy Gibbs, author of the feature article, raised more questions than answers, however, despite her attempts to make sense of it all. Part of the difficulty may have arisen from the limitations of her "cultural toolkit," the set of cultural understandings that people take from their own experiences and attempt to utilize—often with less than admirable results—on different subcultures.[66] Gibbs opens by placing prophecy belief on the margins of rationality:

> What do you watch for, when you are watching the news? Signs that interest rates might be climbing, maybe it's time to refinance. Signs of global warming, maybe forget that new SUV. Signs of new terrorist activity, maybe think twice about that flight to Chicago.
>
> Or signs that the world may be coming to an end, and the last battle between good and evil is about to unfold?[67]

Gibbs then, paradoxically, ties the *Left Behind* phenomenon and its tenth installment, *The Remnant*, into the post-9/11 spirit of uncertainty and existential unease, transforming the anxiety from a limited, evangelical one into something more widespread. She notes that 9/11, like other significant historical shocks, increased the awareness of apocalyptic portents in the mainstream culture, spilling over from Christian bookstores and into the living rooms of ordinary Americans. She also cites a recent Time/CNN poll that indicates 59 percent of Americans believe that the events depicted in Revelation will come to pass. The author extrapolates, justifiably, that Christian fiction, especially the *Left Behind* series, is making an impact on mainstream American culture. The novels depict anxieties that may not be marginal after all.

The ambivalence Gibbs displays exposes the confusion caused when evangelical language overflows its own media and infiltrates mainstream dialects. Analysts such as Gibbs display a solid grasp of the rudiments, but they invariably attempt to filter such language through a secular framework that positions prophecy believers as comically misguided. Gibbs, however, to her credit, seems unwilling to dismiss the phenomenon easily. Her ambivalent observations lead one to suspect that despite her attempts to read the popularity of the *Left Behind* novels using older modes of interpretation, she may be unsatisfied with the results. The *Left Behind* series appeals to an increasingly large percentage of Americans, Gibbs informs us, even if she cannot decide whether prophecy believers belong on the fringe or in a troubled mainstream still recovering from the shock of 9/11. Such a difficulty emerges when one attempts to superimpose static understandings over a dynamic and elusive phenomenon that exists for many not as a separate culture, but as a fiber that has woven itself into the fabric of American religion and culture more pervasively than many observers realize.[68]

Historian George M. Marsden refers to evangelical prophecy belief as a kind of "folk piety" which periodically overflows its banks into communities not necessarily keen on prophecy belief.[69] Nathan O. Hatch underscores this sentiment, noting that the frequent revivals within American evangelicalism have tended to resemble populist movements—rejecting hierarchies and elites along with blind adherence to doctrine—trusting instead the wisdom of the common folk to interpret the Scriptures on their own.[70] This has allowed religious entrepreneurs, along with entrepreneurial beliefs, to flourish in American culture just outside of the mainstream. Prophecy belief—if one believes the many polls such as the aforementioned Time/CNN one—easily seeps out into the mainstream of American popular culture, much to the chagrin of denominational leaders. Granted, what emerges is never a pure form of dispensational prophecy belief. Emotionally charged beliefs, however, tend to travel much more easily than closely reasoned doctrines, and I suspect that the despair, anxiety, and uncertainty that characterizes the *Left Behind* series does make it through to many in the mainstream, even if readers never quite master the nuances of dispensational theology. Boyer observes this "cross-over" phenomenon in his study of Cold War prophecy attitudes, a trend which has continued into the post–Cold War era.

Moreover, one must also take a more careful accounting of who prophecy believers are and where they live, as recent scholarship has begun to do. Granted, one finds concentrations in the South, but temporally and spatially, evangelicals have moved into the liminal spaces of the American middle class, entering perhaps the ultimate tension zone in American culture, suburbia.[71] Planted amid an endless sea of asphalt and strip malls, punctuated occasionally with "master planned" lakes and golf courses, such zones represent a battleground for American cultural values. Significantly, LaHaye and Jenkins, unlike fellow novelist Frank Peretti, do not place their novels within idyllic but embattled small towns. The action in the *Left Behind* novels occurs in suburbs and sprawling cities among middle-class protagonists who could be described as yuppies. Put differently, LaHaye and Jenkins could have chosen to place the headquarters of their fictitious evangelical resistance movement anywhere from Houston to Nashville to Jacksonville, Florida. But they chose instead a suburban Chicago Bible church. This demonstrates not only some wishful demographic thinking on the part of the authors, to be sure, but it also reflects the fact that evangelicals are making inroads outside of their traditional strongholds in the rural Bible Belt of the Deep South.

The suburbs, moreover, offer an ideal position to reach others who might have similar spiritual needs, even if they have not found conservative evangelicalism the answer just yet. Denizens of the American middle class seek to communicate an image of material bounty, although their consumption patterns—if one analyzes the parade of spiritual self-help books and fulfillment guides that perennially top the *New York Times* Best Sellers—display a quest for spiritual connectedness and ultimate meaning.[72] Evangelical prophecy belief thrives in such tension, identifying adversaries while providing simple yet meaningful answers that address a broad range of issues for both current and prospective believers. The friction produced by its interactions with competing religions/spiritualities forces evangelicalism to update its messages constantly, allowing it to corral its share of spiritual seekers.[73]

Evangelicals also share a basic American penchant for mass consumption of entertainment and status products. Granted, they may seek Christian alternatives in music, books, and films, for example, and may even patronize explicitly Christian businesses, but their basic patterns of cultural participation remain similar to the mainstream if occasionally parallel. Historian R. Laurence Moore remarks that "it is, in fact, difficult to wander through these bookstores and imagine any aspect of popular culture that has been left uncloned."[74] My point, however, is not to indict evangelical culture for any lack of originality, but to suggest that even evangelicals who fancy themselves "in but not of the world" may be much closer to the world than they would care to admit.

Indeed, their close relationship to the modern world is undeniable. The novels ostensibly depict a mass exodus from a world hostile to evangelical identity. Yet year after year the Rapture does not come. Prophecy believers, for better or for worse, appear here to stay. The novels function on one level, however, to facilitate accommodation more than they promote escape. They look to a simpler time, perhaps because references to a mythical past marked by moral purpose may help readers to imagine their transition into a future characterized by marked uncertainty. The novels may thus offer adaptation tactics, encouraging readers to imagine possibilities in one of the few modes of language open to such vivid imagery—the apocalyptic. But the authors also attempt—especially toward the end of the series—to violently separate themselves from the world, to purify themselves against the cultural contaminants of modernity. Evangelicals, however, are already too extensively implicated in modernity to make escape a viable option. Any attempt to separate from the world—symbolically or otherwise—may do irreparable damage to the very identity they seek to protect.

Finally, I predicate my reading of the *Left Behind* series on the assumption that the novels represent narrative creations—treasure troves of evangelical ideas. Literary theorist Paul Ricoeur suggests that novels, as narratives, often exceed the bounds of what their authors intend.[75] The novels take on a life of their own. LaHaye and Jenkins ostensibly describe a salvation drama, in which characters must defend their status as evangelicals and accept God in their lives before it is too late. Prophecy believers, however, do not approach the novels the way a scholar does, looking for tensions and break points that indicate something of wider interest. They *experience* the texts. The struggles of the protagonists reflect their own struggles. Neither the authors nor their readers need, in other words, to express the meanings of the texts outside of their mythological framework. Prophecy believers understand the mythological language in which the novels are written on an immediate level. Unfortunately, such language is like any other with which outsiders are unfamiliar—it may appear as so much nonsense. Clearly, the *Left Behind* phenomenon matters; something important is happening. I seek to decouple the central themes in the *Left Behind* series from their mythological trappings and put them into conversation with the observations of cultural theorists, who will likely be more familiar to readers in an academic setting than Tim LaHaye and Jerry Jenkins.

LaHaye and Jenkins create a narrative space in which their visions of the future and its possibilities can be explored in a time much like our own. This has the dual effect of giving readers insight into contemporary developments, along with tactics for altering them. The reader can acknowledge such texts as future-oriented, while still experiencing them as intense reflections of contemporary and not merely future concerns. Even those who expect to forego the Tribulation must still face the issues presented in the texts. For the evangelical reader, the Tribulation is both now *and* yet to come.[76]

In sum, LaHaye and Jenkins create an imaginary world, one that while not identical to our own, offers alternative possibilities. Most of these suggest different ways of constructing identity in a globalizing world perceived as unfriendly to such particularistic notions of religious and cultural identity. What appears on one level as escape, in other words, can also be seen as adaptation or even accommodation, from a different perspective. Nevertheless, a fine line exists between an open and flexible understanding of the apocalypse, and a hardened one that forces believers to fit the strictures of ancient prophecies, undermining their dynamism as evangelicals along with their human dimension. If prophecy believers insist upon certainty and fixed identities in a world often characterized by ambiguity, they may create the Beast they seek to avoid—not a Beast external to them, but one that emerges from within their own fears of the present and attempts to re-create a mythological past. The *Left Behind* series, while it leans closer to a fatalistic outcome, nevertheless contains numerous tensions and uncertainties. These tensions, when read through the question of cultural identity, provide the focal points of this text.

First, however, I offer the reader a brief description of the figures and themes important to the historical development of evangelical prophecy belief. Those familiar with this part of the story may wish to begin with chapter 2, using chapter 1 as a glossary. Others without such specialized knowledge will likely find the following section helpful in their quest to understand the theological underpinnings of the *Left Behind* series.

1

Signs of the Times

The Dispensational Background of Evangelical Prophecy Belief

In most cases the terms for the "last days" or "end times" refer to a period that may encompass no more than seven to ten or so years. We cannot pinpoint it more accurately because we are not certain how much time will elapse between the Rapture, which ends the church age, and the beginning of the Tribulation, begun by the signing of the covenant between the Antichrist and Israel (Daniel 9:27; see also chapter 13). Some prophecy scholars think it will just be a matter of days, but some estimates go as high as fifty years. . . . We are confident that if that writer were living today he would shorten his estimate to about one to three years.[1]
> —Tim LaHaye and Jerry B. Jenkins,
> *Are We Living in the End Times?*

It was the worst of times. It was the worst of times.[2]
> —Tim LaHaye and Jerry B. Jenkins, *Nicolae*

Prophecy writers such as Tim LaHaye and Jerry Jenkins organize the meaning of history around the notion that God deals differently with His people in different epochs called "dispensations." The first five dispensations concern prophecy writers the least, and few devote more than a passing mention to them. The action heats up during the sixth dispensation, known as the "Church Age." It is then that God temporarily shifts his attention away from His chosen people, the Jews, and onto the Gentiles. Beginning with the destruction of the Second Temple in 70 C.E., the Church Age strikes prophecy writers as a period during which God works most mysteriously, almost as if pressing the pause button on His cosmic stopwatch. Christ can return and start the apocalyptic clock ticking again at any time, yet no one knows—as prophecy writers are fond of repeating—"the day or the hour." Believers must simply watch and wait. And watch they do, searching for signs of the times that potentially indicate the cosmic clock will soon start again. Prophecy writers claim that Biblical prophecies will soon be fulfilled, and plenty of signs will be given for the watchful, until Christ returns to rapture away His most loyal believers. Then, the world will endure seven years of torment and woe known as the Tribulation, when people will get one last, painful chance to choose the path of goodness and light. This chapter briefly outlines the basic ideas of dispensational prophecy belief and introduces the mythical seven-year period during which most of the events of the *Left Behind* series take place.

Darby and Dispensationalism

One cannot attribute the development of dispensational prophecy belief to a single figure or even a series of figures. The process is much more complicated. Nevertheless, for the sake of brevity and to reach the issues most essential to this project most expeditiously, I have organized my background discussion of prophecy belief around a few key figures of undeniable importance. The list begins with an Irishman named John Nelson Darby. Darby (1800–1882) was born into a prosperous merchant family—his father sold naval munitions during the Napoleonic Wars—and was thus able and expected to pursue a respectable career. Well-educated, Darby graduated from Trinity College with honors, read law at the Kings Inn in Dublin, and prepared himself for a career as a barrister. His theological avocation quickly turned him from law, however.[3] After a flirtation with numerous Bible societies and conferences in Dublin, Darby sought and attained ordination at the new Anglican parish of Calary in 1825.[4]

Historian Timothy C. F. Stunt describes Darby's experience with the "Irish Reformation" as a brief one, however, as his archbishop soon confused loyalty to the king with Protestant piety, calling for oaths of allegiance from prospective converts in 1827.[5] Darby responded angrily but remained with the church. Nevertheless, his ongoing conversations with evangelical friends and their discussions of the work of the Scotch-Anglican turned dissenter Edward Irving and his colleague Henry Drummond, combined with Darby's field experience, turned him against ecclesiastical hierarchies and their alleged soteriological significance and toward a doctrine of grace.[6] According to such a belief, each individual related to God through Christ, rather than an ecclesiastical structure. Likely as a result of such experiences, Darby inserted an anti-institutional flavor into his dissenting movement, a suspicion of hierarchies and mediators that still influences contemporary prophecy belief.[7] His experience in the Anglican Church also convinced him of humankind's inherent propensity to evil and the need to place an emphasis on the infallibility of the Scriptures rather than institutions, which were, after all, populated by humans capable of error.

None of these developments in isolation inspired Darby to develop his prophetic worldview, but their effects were cumulative. The prophecy conferences sponsored and hosted by Henry Drummond from 1826 to 1830 at his Albury Park estate in England were definitely influential, as delegates there outlined many of the positions that Darby would later synthesize into dispensational belief. These included several critical points, most notably the belief that the Jews would soon be restored to Israel and that the present age was destined not to end in the progressive achievement of universal happiness—as some millennialists believed—but would instead continue to deteriorate until Christ returned—at any time.[8]

Somewhat more controversial was the possibility of a secret, pre-tribulational Rapture during which Christ would appear only to believers—hence, the aspect of secrecy—and whisk them to safety, returning again only after the seven years of the Tribulation, this time visible to everyone. Arthur Wainwright traces the idea of the Rapture back to the sixteenth-century English prophet Joseph Mede, while Paul S. Boyer places the idea on American soil, beginning with the seventeenth-century Puritan divine Increase Mather.[9] While such figures, along with many of the delegates to Drummond's prophecy conferences, probably toyed with the idea of the Rapture, it was left to Darby to popularize the new belief.[10] Darby based the notion of the Rapture on 1 Thessalonians 4:17, "Then we which are alive and remain shall be caught up together with them in the clouds, to meet the Lord in the air: and so shall we ever be with the Lord."[11] Darby read this verse as indicating the literal ascent of believers to "meet Christ in the air."[12] This fit well with Darby's conviction that Scripture should be read literally whenever possible, rejecting "spiritualized" accounts.[13]

Darby's increasingly radical views led him to disaffiliate with the Church of England in 1834. The break was not sudden, however, as he had been meeting since 1830 with a number of like-minded dissenters and even regular Anglicans in Plymouth, England. The result of this loose congregation and its spin-off groups became known as the Plymouth Brethren,[14] and finally the Exclusive Brethren or simply the "Darbyites," once Darby disaffiliated from the Brethren in 1849.[15] Once shorn of any hint of denominational affiliation outside of his own small flock, Darby wove together his various influences, emphasizing God's successive dealings with humankind in a salvation history divided into unique segments. The result, from which the term "dispensationalism" derives, divided history into seven different dispensations, each beginning with a Covenant between God and humans, and each ending with the violation of the Covenant and the subsequent outpouring of divine judgment.

Such philosophies of history were not new. As historian Sidney Ahlstrom notes, "The idea of successive divine dispensations is, of course, immemorial, being implicit in the very terms Old and New Testament."[16] Most historians, however, including Boyer, trace dispensationalism's intellectual antecedents back to the twelfth-century Calabrian prophet-monk, Joachim of Fiore (~1135–1202).[17] Joachim's formula, simply put, divided history into three distinct ages, corresponding with the Father, Son, and Holy Spirit. Each of these personages acted in a particular "status," beginning with the status of the Father or of Law. This status ended shortly before the appearance of Christ, corresponding to the end of the Old Testament. The New Testament, coming shortly after Christ's death and resurrection, signaled the beginning of the status of Grace under the Son.[18]

Each of the first two statuses—note historians Marjorie Reeves and Warwick Gould, following the work of historian Herbert Grundmann—corresponded to a Biblical Testament. Another status remained, however, but Grundmann emphasizes that it was not to be another Testament. Rather, the status of the Holy Spirit ushered in a spiritual understanding of the previous two dispensations, one that spiritualized, but did not discard, previous truths.[19] Such spiritual truths required "spiritual men," monastic figures like Joachim who would come into full understanding of the previous texts, without writing another Testament. This new status nevertheless retained a historical character. It was not the end of history but represented a historical phase, corresponding inexactly to the ages associated with the first two statuses. Joachim divided these periods into generations, but noted that what constituted a generation in one phase altered within and outside of each status.[20] Although Joachim's subsequent readers revolutionized this final status as eliminating the social hierarchies, inequalities, and injustices characteristic of the previous two statuses, Joachim himself apparently never drew this conclusion.[21]

The complexity of Joachim's thought permits only a short introduction, but one can draw several similarities to Darby's dispensationalism. First, Joachim's periodization of salvation history corresponded to Darby's in the belief that God deals with humans in different ways in different periods. Moreover, although antinomian heresies persisted in the wake of both movements, neither dispensed totally with the Old Testament law but merely insisted upon its reinterpretation in light of new understandings. Second, both men placed great emphasis upon the value of generations, which has given subsequent prophecy dabblers plenty upon which to speculate. Finally and directly related to the second issue, neither man insisted upon setting dates for "The End." The End was indeed coming, but no one could know the day or the hour. Grundmann discusses Joachim's perspective:

> Joachim was not a prophet of the End in the sense of announcing an end to history—such speculation lay well outside of the boundary he believed he could reach with his methods of thought. He nevertheless did not doubt that the mundane world would indeed come to an end, but when this would be, "only God knows."[22]

Contrary to popular wisdom, Darby's dispensationalism also opposed rigid date-setting. That is, although one cannot speak of Darby's final dispensation as a replication of Joachim's status of the Holy Spirit, both viewed their end-stages as penultimate to a final act known only in its exact timing and content by God. For Joachim, this reluctance to "set a date" may have been a gesture to the ecclesiastical and temporal leadership of his time—after all, apocalypticism, then as now, always carries the potential for disruptive political influence. Darby, by contrast, probably sought to avoid the opprobrium collected by such popular date-setters as the American William Miller, who twice predicted the Second Coming of Christ, first in 1843, and again on October 22, 1844.[23] Embarrassing failures such as those of Miller may have further dissuaded Darby from setting dates, but they did not convince his successors to avoid the foolishness of date-setting. Although most prophecy believers have proven reluctant to "name the hour," this has not prevented a few intrepid souls from trying.[24]

Dispensationalism, like Joachim's three ages of history, unfolds in considerable detail—detail which, if allowed to unfold in all of its complexity, would take me well beyond my present focus. Nevertheless, I can note the relevant highlights. According to Darby's American interpreter Cyrus I. Scofield—the definitive authority on dispensationalism after Darby who also sharpened Darby's scheme considerably—history could be divided into seven divisions, each called a dispensation.[25] Each division corresponds to different ways God works in the world, with each dispensation containing its own covenant and subsequent judgment when humans inevitably violate the terms of the covenant.

The first dispensation was *Innocency*, referring to the prelapsarian, Edenic paradise of Adam and Eve. Second, humankind moved into the dispensation of *Conscience*, which spanned the gap from Adam and Eve's expulsion from the Garden of Eden until the Great Flood. Following the Flood, God promulgated a covenant with Noah, opening the period of *Human Government*. God's promise to Abraham marked the start of the *Promise* dispensation, while the Mosaic covenant followed, signaling the dispensation of *Law*, which Moses received on Mount Sinai. This covenant stood in force until the appearance of Christ, and ended with his crucifixion, inaugurating the dispensation of *Grace*, or as it is more often called, the *Church Age*. The seventh and final dispensation, which will follow the dispensation of Grace, but not immediately, encompasses the millennial reign of Christ on earth or the *Kingdom Age*.[26]

Humankind presently finds itself in the Church Age. And, unlike previous dispensations, its precise timing appears mysterious to prophecy writers. Part of this difficulty involves reading the apocalyptic portions of the Scriptures as prophetic of future events, which requires careful explanation when attempting to reconcile why the first-century apostles and believers apparently thought Christ would return in their generation. As it turns out, however, at least according to Scofield, those who read Matthew 24:34, as indicating that Christ had to return in the first generation, were mistaken—as were, by extension, the first apostles, a rather perilous conundrum for an avowed Biblical literalist. Scofield's "proof" verse reads: "Verily I say unto you, this generation shall not pass away, till all these things be fulfilled." The ambiguity of "this generation" allowed centuries of Church fathers, and, more recently, textual critics, to assume that Matthew 24:34 referred to either a historicized or false eschatological hope.[27] Scofield and the dispensationalists, however, called into question such interpretations, avowing that the promised Second Coming remained in the future.[28]

But why had God waited so long to end the present dispensation? Darby answered with the notion of the "Great Parenthesis," or a cosmic cooling-off period, in which God suspended his overt activities on earth for a period of unpredictable duration.[29] First, however, one must see this "Great Parenthesis" in its larger context. This period encompassed what the ancient Hebrew author of the Biblical book of Daniel called the "sixty-ninth week" of a total of seventy. The first seven weeks (calculated by dispensationalists as years) marked the period between God's promise and its fulfillment with the rebuilding of the Temple in Jerusalem after the Babylonian Captivity. Furthermore, the next sixty-two "weeks of years," or 434 years, spanned the time from the rebuilt Temple until the arrival of Christ. Yet one mysterious week remained. Daniel 9:26 discusses this missing seven-year period:

> And after threescore and two weeks shall Messiah be cut off, but not for himself: and the people of the prince that shall come shall destroy the city and the sanctuary; and the end thereof *shall be* with a flood, and unto the end of the war desolations are determined.[30]

It is important to note that early interpreters of dispensationalism such as Darby and Scofield recognized that no precise date for the end of this cosmic pause could be determined, leading Scofield to comment, "Verse 26 is obviously an indeterminate period."[31] The rest of Scofield's note on Daniel 9:26 gave license to many future generations of Bible prophecy commentators, with most referencing Matthew 24:36, "But of that day and hour knoweth no *man*, no, not the angels of heaven, but my Father alone." No one could know the day or hour, but by reading the "signs of the times," prophecy speculators could get a general idea, one that invariably indicated their own generation. Finally, this seventieth week, when it finally does arrive, will encompass what evangelicals refer to as the "Tribulation," a seven-year period of suffering for those left behind after the Rapture of the true believers. Dispensationalists point to Daniel 9:27 for an explanation:

> And he shall confirm the covenant with many for one week: and in the midst of the week he shall cause the sacrifice and oblation to cease, and for the overspreading of abominations he shall make *it* desolate, even

until the consummation, and that determined shall be poured upon the desolate.

More will be added to the discussion of the Tribulation momentarily, but first a return to the immediate historical context of dispensationalism and its reception will provide additional insight.

For Darby, as previously noted, the world was not getting better, but instead growing increasingly wicked. Men and women could do nothing to forestall God's imminent judgment. This message was antithetical to the (largely) optimistic, antebellum evangelical spirit, but generations after the Civil War found Darby's message much more meaningful, especially given the challenges of Darwinian evolution, textual and higher criticisms of Biblical sources, rapid industrialization, along with accelerated immigration, and a general sense of social upheaval and unrest. Darby toured the United States extensively promoting his message,[32] but massive success was left to urban revivalists like Dwight L. Moody. Moody, who helped popularize Darby's message, believed that since divine judgment loomed, his only recourse as an evangelist was to "toss out a lifeboat" and save as many souls as possible.[33] Moody's revival success also allowed him to endow a permanent institution, the Moody Bible Institute (1886) in Chicago, Illinois, where dispensationalism could be studied and its views propagated.[34] Perhaps more important, he founded Moody Press, the imprint of choice for generations of prophecy writers.

In addition to Moody's crusades, two other factors proved crucial to the American reception of dispensationalism. First, a string of prophecy conferences inspired by the example of the Englishman Henry Drummond took place across the Midwest and Northeast. James Brookes organized the first pre-millennialist conference on the North American side at Niagara-on-the-Lake, Ontario in 1875. Although the attendees espoused a variety of pre-millennial perspectives, the dispensational view, complete with the pre-tribulational Rapture, quickly increased its persuasive hold over the delegates.[35] Subsequent "Niagara Conferences" proved highly effective at propagating the new eschatology and spawned other, more explicitly dispensationalist conferences like the one in 1878 at Trinity Episcopal Church in New York City.[36] The *New York Tribune* subsequently printed 50,000 copies of the proceedings, and the event generated numerous additional publications.[37] In addition, the Bible conferences, and those responsible for organizing them, contributed to the founding of several Bible institutes, including The Bible Institute of Los Angeles, or BIOLA, in 1907.[38]

On an individual level, Cyrus I. Scofield (1843–1921) arguably represents the most important figure in the spread of dispensationalism among conservative North American Protestants. Boyer refers to Scofield as a scandal-ridden drunk who abandoned his wife in Kansas. Imprisoned in Missouri for forgery, Scofield experienced a prison conversion and became quite interested in Darby's ideas, especially as presented by James Brookes. After leaving prison Scofield took numerous jobs, serving as a pastor, an editor, and a Bible conference speaker, among other occupations.[39] Scofield is best known, of course, for the annotated Bible that bears his name, *The Scofield Reference Bible* (King James Version), originally published in 1909. Published by Oxford University Press and still in print, Boyer estimates that it may have already sold well over ten million copies.[40] Even this number is probably too small, since sales of religious texts have historically been underestimated.[41] So important was Scofield's work, in fact, that one still hears the jingle, "My hope is built on nothing less / Than Scofield's Notes and Moody Press."[42] This is an exaggeration, to be sure, but only a small one.

On the actual pages of his edited Bible, Scofield placed his commentary beneath the King James translation, making it identical in font to the original text. Moreover, he cross-referenced the entire Old and New Testaments to offer the reader the strong impression that the Bible was a cohesive whole designed around the truth of dispensational theology. The typical reader, who probably already revered the words themselves as inerrant, no doubt incorporated Scofield's notes, making his work indistinguishable from that upon which he commented. The result remains the single most important carrier of dispensationalist ideas, even after nearly a century.

Hal Lindsey and the Further Popularization of Dispensational Prophecy Belief

Bible colleges and seminaries helped to ensure the survival of dispensational belief among pastors and teachers during the early and middle portions of the twentieth century.[43] Still, dispensationalism was poorly understood among the rank and file of evangelical believers, remaining a largely academic movement owing to the legendary complexity of its historical periodizations. It lacked, in short, a popularizer who could translate its arcane constructions into a simplified theology that would exhibit tremendous popular appeal among anxious masses of American readers. Hal Lindsey—with assistance from writer Carole C. Carlson— became that popularizer. A journeyman who once worked as a tugboat captain on the Mississippi before attending the hotbed of dispensational theology—Dallas Theological Seminary (DTS)—Lindsey found his calling in prophecy belief, honing his folksy mannerisms and clever wordplay working as an evangelist among college youth. He published his first prophecy manual in 1970, *The Late Great Planet Earth,* and its success was instant and unmistakable.[44]

Lindsey, a reader of the dispensational luminary Charles Ryrie and a student of the venerable prophecy scholar John Walvoord at DTS, took the arcane and complicated aspects of dispensationalism and simplified them for the masses, producing a slick paperback that fit well with the work of other mid- to late twentieth-century prophet figures such as the psychic Jeanne Dixon and "the sleeping prophet" Edgar Cayce. Lindsey surveyed the religious marketplace and delivered what a large segment of the American population—and especially college students and young adults—apparently wanted to read after the uncertainty and radicalism of the 1960's, to say nothing of the accelerating rates of social, economic, and cultural change. Lindsey was not a perfect student, but he did what his teachers could not or deigned beneath them: he made dispensational ideas a staple of American culture. Hence, much of what counts as prophecy belief in the contemporary United States can be traced through Hal Lindsey's further refinement of Scofield's interpretations of dispensationalism.

Lindsey, a man for his times, added several new twists, however. First, he reasserted the anti-institutional bias that lurked within dispensationalism from Darby's earliest pronouncements, through the work of Cyrus Scofield and Clarence Larkin—the latter famous for his complex but instructive prophecy charts[45]—and framed this prophetic trajectory over prophecy believers' fears of a rapidly changing world. Most of these anxieties, when examined more carefully, were related to the phenomenon of globalization. Most immediately, Lindsey observed that nation-states were becoming increasingly interdependent and seemed to be losing a significant measure of their autonomy—surely a development that would pave the way for the rise of the Antichrist.[46] Moreover, the more progressive branches of American Protestantism continued their flirtation with ecumenism, and many evangelicals believed that theological liberals were surrendering too much of their Christian identity. Mergers sometimes followed, folding struggling denominations into larger, seemingly more viable unions. Whatever the reasons given, Lindsey attributed such unions to the machinations of Satan himself.[47]

Lindsey also worried about currencies and the threat that money—an abstract representation of national sovereignty and even collective and personal identity—would be monopolized and merged. Lindsey pulled together all of these tensions and summarized them as the evangelical fears of "One-World Government," "One-World Religion," and the "One-World Currency."[48] All of these one-world developments, Lindsey claimed, were to be read as signs of the times pointing to the soon return of Christ to rapture the Church, followed by the Tribulation.

Moreover, for many years prophecy writers, including LaHaye and Jenkins, have considered these developments as indicative of the rise of the "Beast system," otherwise known as the ominous "New World Order," controlled by secret organizations such as the Council on Foreign Relations (CFR) and the Trilateral Commission.[49] Thus, when President Bush spoke of the "New World Order" in 1991, prophecy writers became understandably alarmed. *Left Behind* even takes special note of Bush's ill-advised statement. The Antichrist—Nicolae Carpathia—exclaims that "with the end of the Cold War in the 1990's, however, your new president, Mr. Bush, recognized what he called 'the new world order,' which resonated deep within my young heart."[50]

In addition to implicating political and economic changes, however, Lindsey also fed evangelical suspicions of new technologies, many of which had nefarious usages. Lindsey writes, "We have increased in technology so rapidly in the past few years that our grandfather's heads would be spinning at what we take for granted."[51] For Lindsey, the rapid growth of technology and knowledge "has not brought mankind one step further toward solving the basic problems of love, security, and true happiness."[52] Instead, new technologies have helped to introduce a global economy from which escape is no longer possible. Lindsey continues:

Do you believe it will be possible for people to be controlled economically? In our computerized society, where we are all "numbered" from birth to death, it seems completely plausible that some day in the near future the numbers racket will consolidate and we will have just one number for all our business, money, and credit transactions. Leading members of the business community are now planning that all money matters will be handled electronically.[53]

If one posits, following Karl Marx, that money represents a "third" unit that provides a common measure or an abstract standard by which to evaluate the worth of different objects—say, apples and oranges—one can ascertain Lindsey's concern with issues of economics and personal identity. The same type of process that reduces objects to a standardized scale of value might also reduce humans to a number. Much more will be added to this theme later, of course, but all of this culminates with the ultimate objectification and dehumanization of the world's citizens through the assignment of the Mark of the Beast, without which one cannot participate in the new global economy. For those left behind after the Rapture, the choice will be simple: either take the Mark and its dehumanization and forced identity—accepting the "Beast system" in all of its aspects—or starve. Again, although Lindsey was not the first dispensational writer to mention the Mark, he made discussion of it palpable and trendy for laypersons.[54]

Lindsey also refined another of dispensationalism's crucial tenets: its attitude toward the Jews and the restoration of Israel. Rather than exhibiting anti-Semitic attitudes—at least overtly—dispensationalists such as Lindsey actively promoted Zionism and other philo-Semitic causes.[55] This owed less to an outpouring of altruism than a dispensational assumption that Israel continued to play a vital role in God's eschatological drama. The seventieth week prophesied in Daniel could not ensue until the Jews had been restored to their ancient homeland. Prophecy writers commonly cite Matthew 24:32–33 as their "proof text":

> Now learn a parable of the fig tree; When his branch is yet tender, and putteth forth leaves, *ye* know that summer *is* nigh. So likewise ye, when ye shall see all these things, know that it is near, *even* at the doors.

Lindsey interprets this parable as indicating that in the End-Times, Israel, the "fig tree," will return from exile.[56] When David Ben-Gurion announced the modern state of Israel on May 14, 1948, prophecy speculators believed they finally had the proof they had long sought. And, when Israeli forces retook much of Jerusalem during the six-day war of 1967, the event energized the prophecy community and enhanced the motivation and potential market for a prophecy manual such as Lindsey's.

Dispensational belief leaves its adherents at this point, watching for "signs of the times." Scores of prophecy writers insist that God's prophetic time-clock restarted with either the foundation of modern Israel in 1948 or Israel's recapture of Jerusalem in 1967. But many others, including Lindsey, caution that while these events may signal the End, the traumatic events of the seventieth week will not begin until the signing of a seven-year peace accord between the Antichrist and Israel. Secular scholars have often mistaken the Rapture as the apocalyptic trigger. Prophecy writers, however, make it clear that while important, the Rapture has little to do with triggering God's apocalyptic timetable; the Rapture merely removes believers. It does not signal the beginning of the Tribulation.[57]

The Seven Last Years: A Brief Outline of the Tribulation

LaHaye and Jenkins place their narrative almost entirely within the seven-year period known as the Tribulation.[58] Inaugurated by Antichrist's deceptive peace treaty with Israel, the Tribulation neatly encapsulates the majority of the events important to dispensationalists. Those "left behind" will experience a greatest-hits compilation of almost every conceivable plague and disaster. Prophecy believers read Revelation and related Biblical texts as a virtual play-by-play of the horrors to come. Of course, texts like the *Left Behind* novels encourage such readings, taking the seemingly allegorical language of Revelation and transforming it into a literal set of predictions for the immediate future. The upshot, of course, is that LaHaye and Jenkins warn their readers that time is running out and God is losing his patience. Those who fail to embrace the evangelical message immediately will soon suffer the seven long years of torment and woe known as the Tribulation.

Indeed, while the *Left Behind* series features an element of *Schadenfreude* taken to cosmic proportions, LaHaye and Jenkins also write their novels for those unfortunates who are left behind and who will hopefully find the books and learn the error of their ways before it is finally too late. This theme dates back to the earliest, widely available evangelical fiction (~1970) but has intensified in recent years. Moreover, VCRs and other video-recording technologies have made the notion of leaving behind a videotaped sermon even more enticing. Several prophecy writers, including Tim LaHaye and Jerry Jenkins, have already produced their own tapes, commercially available now but much more relevant during the Tribulation.

The tapes often begin with a measure of self-congratulation and a general air of "we told you so." Then the speakers explain what believers must do to find salvation during their season of torment. When the tape ends, the believer will presumably drown in self-reproach and finally accept the Truth. *Left Behind* protagonists, including Rayford Steele, Chloe Steele, Buck Williams, and Pastor Bruce Barnes, in fact, attribute an almost magical significance to the videocassette left by their senior pastor Vernon Billings.[59] In *Left Behind,* everyone who views the tape eventually acknowledges its truth and receives salvation, while those limited to the propaganda of mainstream media have a tougher go. Technology, it seems, plays a potentially salvific role during the Tribulation.

Outside the realm of VHS and DVD, however, the waiting continues. Although prophecy believers know that the Tribulation cannot begin until Antichrist signs the seven-year treaty with Israel, they nevertheless look for signs of the times. Such signs indicate the general time frame of the Rapture and may include, notably, a failed Russian invasion of Israel. Most of the signs are more generic and involve the usual suspects of rampant sin, disobedience, sexual perversity, and war. Prophecy writers use key verses from across the Bible—not just the sections ordinarily cited as prophetic—to convince readers that the world is nearing its conclusion. Prophecy writers present readers with exhaustive lists of verses and events that must coalesce during the last days. These consist of carefully selected Biblical proof texts, juxtaposed with creative readings of current events. 2 Timothy 3:1–7 and Matthew 24:4–12 are among the most commonly cited scriptures. 2 Timothy 3:1–7 reads:

> This know also, that in the last days perilous times shall come. For men shall become lovers of their own selves, covetous, boasters, proud, blasphemers, disobedient to parents, unthankful, unholy, without natural affection, trucebreakers, false accusers, incontinent, fierce, despisers of those that are good, traitors, heady, high-minded, lovers of pleasure more than lovers of God; having a form of godliness, but denying the power thereof: from such turn away. For of this sort are they which creep into houses, and lead captive silly women laden with sins, led away with divers lusts, ever learning, and never able to come to the knowledge of the truth.

To this comprehensive yet vague summary of sinfulness, prophecy writers add Jesus' admonitions from the Olivet Discourse in Matthew, often known as the "little apocalypse."[60] The disciples, curious about the last days, ask Jesus for specificity. He answers them in Matthew 24:4–8:

> Take heed that no man deceive you. For many shall come in my name, saying, I am Christ; and shall deceive many. And ye shall hear of wars and rumours of wars: see that ye be not troubled: for all *these things* must come to pass, but the end is not yet. For nations shall rise against nation, and kingdom against kingdom: and there shall be famines and pestilences, and earthquakes, in divers places. All these are the beginning of sorrows.

Difficult as it may seem, prophecy writers consistently find ways to adapt these verses to their time, and not to a future period of even greater significance. Overlooking the historical record of such unfulfilled expectations, writers continue to believe *their* time has witnessed the ultimate in sinful behavior. One prophecy writer, in particular, Robert Bragg, glosses the two cited passages word-for-word, using each deviance as a section heading to prove the proximity of the End.[61] Most prophecy writers, however, use more subtle techniques. LaHaye and Jenkins, for example, distinguish between what they consider legitimate signs and those that are merely imagined.[62] Although they do not provide indubitable proof, the authors cite the increase in *deception,* among other End-Times phenomena. Noting the rise of "false christs" and "cults," LaHaye and Jenkins point to such tragedies as the "People's Temple" massacre in Guyana in 1978, the fiery demise of the Branch Davidians in 1993, and the suicides of the Heaven's Gate saucer-sect in 1997. Groups like these, the authors emphasize, promise much but deliver only more deception. "Deception," they write, "will continue to increase as the end times approach."[63] New technologies and mass media augment the possibilities of deception. The believer has but one recourse: to "Know Your Bible!"[64] Although false prophets will arise at an exponentially increasing rate, believers must do a complete background check on alleged prophets, cross-checking their pronouncements with the literal word of God found in the Bible.

LaHaye and Jenkins also insert a few warnings about earthquakes and plagues, but their next focus lies with war, indeed, the new, "special kind of war."[65] Such a war will be fought on a global scale and will involve many accompanying signs. The authors cite World War One for its special combination of global war, plagues, and massive earthquakes. Although these signs do not point to the imminent End, LaHaye and Jenkins suggest they signal, like a woman's labor pains, that the time is almost here.[66]

The first significant event of the last-days, however, could be the prophesied Russian invasion of Israel, supported by Islamic nations, especially Turkey. This prophecy has undergone many revisions through the years, as changing geopolitical alignments have made certain scenarios more plausible. Regardless of the exact identity of the belligerents, prophecy writers have traditionally focused on Ezekiel 38–39, which talks of an unholy alliance consisting of Gog, Magog, and Gomer, who sweep down upon Israel in an attempt to seize its riches. LaHaye and Jenkins trace Gog and Magog to Russia, Gomer to Turkey, with the Islamic countries also participating in the End-Times axis of evil.[67] All of these nations will descend upon Israel while its allies bring nothing but diplomatic protests to its aid. God, however, will intervene and destroy the invading hordes. Moreover, their weapons will burn for seven years— a strange prophecy—but one the authors insist can be taken literally since Russian armaments will contain lignostone, a highly flammable, coal-like substance.[68] This event must occur before the Tribulation, and probably even before the Rapture, since it will take seven years for the weapons to burn—the length of the Tribulation.

LaHaye and Jenkins also date the Rapture before the onset of the Tribulation, although they briefly acknowledge the possibility of a mid-tribulational rapture. They dismiss this theory, however, which is held by such prophecy writers as Mary Stewart Relfe, famed in evangelical circles for her work warning against bar code technology.[69] Of even greater interest, the Rapture may occur weeks, months, or even several years before the onset of the Tribulation.[70] As we read in the epigraph to this chapter, however, LaHaye and Jenkins insist that the Rapture will not tarry too long after the destruction of the invading Russian, Turkish, and Islamic armies.

When it does happen, the sudden disappearance of the Church will offer Antichrist another chance to deceive the world. LaHaye and Jenkins suggest that his mouthpiece, the liberal "One-World" church, will claim that as in the times of Noah, God has again eliminated the wicked, that is, evangelicals, from the earth. In *Tribulation Force*, Archbishop Peter Mathews explains to Buck that "they opposed the teaching . . . I fear they have been separated as chaff from wheat. Yet those of us who remain should be confident in our standing with God as never before."[71] For the more scientifically oriented, LaHaye and Jenkins suggest that Antichrist will blame UFOs, excessive atmospheric ionization triggering nuclear destruction, or massive electrical discharges such as lightning. In any event, Antichrist will cover up the true nature of the disappearances.

The total removal of the Church, along with the intense anxiety and panic that follow the disappearances, will pave the way for Antichrist's ascent, as the world will seek easy answers and unity in a time of unprecedented tragedy. Nevertheless, the restraining power of the Holy Spirit will remain to assist those left behind, and the Two Witnesses, commonly identified as Moses and Elijah, will preach from the Wailing Wall in Jerusalem and evangelize and save 144,000 "sealed Jews," who will then convert almost a billion to Christ in what LaHaye and Jenkins call a "soul harvest."[72] Grace will not be cheap, however, since such Tribulation Saints will face almost certain martyrdom.

The Tribulation begins when Antichrist signs a seven-year peace covenant with Israel, a compact that also allows Israel to rebuild the Temple, despite the presence of the Islamic Dome of the Rock.[73] God's judgments will pour forth soon after this diabolic pact, divided into three sections. LaHaye and Jenkins, through the voice of their fictional Pastor Bruce Barnes from *Left Behind,* discuss the three segments of divine retribution:

> The first twenty-one months encompass what the Bible calls the seven Seal Judgments, or the Judgments of the Seven-Sealed Scroll. Then comes another twenty-one month period in which we will see the seven Trumpet judgments. In the last forty-two months of the seven years of tribulation, if we have survived, we will endure the most severe tests, the seven Vial judgments. That last half of the seven years is called the Great Tribulation.[74]

The seven Seal judgments, discussed in Revelation 6 as they are revealed to the prophet John of Patmos, begin with the legendary "Four Horsemen of the Apocalypse," the discussion of each represents one Seal. The first, the rider on the white horse, goes forth and conquers the earth. This rider, of course, represents none other than the Antichrist. Antichrist, however, appears as a benevolent conqueror, and much of the world remains blind to his true nature. LaHaye attributes this lack of discernment to the world's gradual conditioning, or brainwashing, to the reality of a One-World government, symbolized by acceptance of the United Nations. He writes:

> Some of the wealthiest foundations in the United State [*sic*] are doing everything humanly possible to brainwash the population through television and other mass communications with the idea that the only solution to the world's problems is the United Nations.[75]

The second Seal brings forth the red rider, representing nations of the world who rebel against Antichrist bringing forth global war and death. Famine accompanies the black rider, while the fourth Seal unveils the "rider on the pale horse," who symbolizes the mounting reality of death during the Tribulation. John sees with the opening of the fifth Seal many martyred saints, while the sixth Seal witnesses a massive earthquake.[76] The seventh Seal, most enigmatic of all, initially brings forth silence and then introduces the seven Trumpet Judgments.

Corresponding to Revelation 8–9, the Trumpet Judgments turn oceans to blood, usher in massive hailstorms, poison a third of the world's water with wormwood, and blot out the sun, at least for a brief period. The fifth Trumpet unleashes an additional array of Satan's minions, along with a five-month torment of stinging locusts, an all-time favorite theme of prophecy writers.[77] The locusts, however—which according to LaHaye and Jenkins are, upon closer inspection, anthropomorphic and pesky little demons empowered with the ability to speak—will only sting those who "have not the seal of God in their foreheads."[78] As the authors put it, they are "madly conflicted beings."[79] Most strikingly, Revelation 9:6 demonstrates the intensity of the suffering, "And in those days shall men seek death and not find it; and shall desire to die, and death shall flee from them." At the sound of the sixth Trumpet, fallen angels will be unleashed to kill a third of the surviving population. Again, however, only those who continue to deny God's authority will suffer.[80] Literal to the End, LaHaye and Jenkins portray the fallen angels in *Assassins* as 200 million fiery horsemen, visible only to the faithful.[81] The seventh Trumpet marks the midpoint of the Tribulation and will include the slaying of the Two Witnesses, along with the assassination and subsequent resurrection of Antichrist, who from that point forward will be "indwelt," or possessed by Satan, recently cast down from heaven.

The seven Vial judgments, or "Bowl Judgments," corresponding to Revelation 15–16, will occur during the latter half of the Tribulation and will feature painful boils for those who have taken the Mark of the Beast, along with more seas and rivers turned to blood. The fourth Vial intensifies the sun's power, scorching those without the sunscreen of God's mercy. The fifth Vial will bring more darkness, while the sixth Vial will dry up the Euphrates River, permitting the Kings of the East—presumed by LaHaye to be the Chinese and their allies—to cross into the Middle East and meet their judgment and doom at Armageddon.[82] The seventh Vial will pour forth the remainder of God's wrath, causing the greatest earthquake the world has even known, along with more giant hailstones. Additionally, the "One-World" church, also known as the "Harlot," will meet its final judgment.[83] All that will remain of the Great Tribulation will be the incredible bloodbath known as Armageddon, followed by the glorious return of Christ to establish his millennial kingdom on earth.

All of these judgments correspond to Antichrist's increasing wickedness and defiance, followed by God's wrathful responses. In spite of these cosmic interruptions, however, Antichrist continues his quest for total world domination. Contemporary prophecy writers posit this evil-doer of the last days as the head of a "New Rome," a final world empire more terrible and powerful than any preceding it. Prophecy writers look to Daniel for their metaphor. King Nebuchadnezzar of ancient Babylon explains his terrifying dream in Daniel 7:7, 8:

After this I saw in the night visions, and behold a fourth beast, dreadful and terrible, and strong exceedingly; and it had great iron teeth: it devoured and brake in pieces, and stamped the residue with the feet of it: and it *was* diverse from all the beasts that *were* before it; and it had ten horns. I considered the horns, and, behold, there came up among them another little horn, before whom there were three of the first horns plucked up by the roots: and, behold, in this horn *were* eyes like the eyes of a man, and a mouth speaking great things.

Prophecy writers equate this fourth beast with Antichrist and his revived Roman Empire. Televangelist Jack van Impe summarizes these sentiments, writing in the same breathless style he employs on his television program, "Jack van Impe Presents":

Since 1957, we have witnessed an amalgamation of Western nations in the form of the European Economic Community or "Common Market." The movement began when Belgium, France, Italy, Luxembourg, the Netherlands, and West Germany joined together in economic alliance. In 1972, three additional members—Denmark, England, and Ireland— were received. Then, January 1, 1981, Greece became the ratified tenth member. Wow! How many toes? How many horns? How many king- doms represented by the ten horns? How many nations now holding membership in the Common Market?[84]

Evangelist Chuck Smith adds, "This confederacy of ten nations is related to the Roman Empire because each nation in the EC was once part of the old Roman empire."[85] John Wesley White, a close associate of Billy Gra- ham and his popular crusades, inserts a word of hair-splitting caution, however, noting that EC membership may appear in excess of ten. But one must differentiate between senior and associate members.[86]

LaHaye and Jenkins offer a more nuanced interpretation, but one with even less documentation for their speculations. Nevertheless, their view has achieved a higher profile than the older EC solution, chiefly due to the popularity of their writings. In a nutshell, LaHaye and Jenkins indict the shadowy Council on Foreign Relations (CFR) and cast suspicion upon the "Club of Rome Conferences." Among other things, the Club of Rome Conferences allegedly proposed a One-World government divided into ten units, each with a seat on the U.N. Security Council. These ten units, or "horns," would correspond to specific geographic regions and report, ultimately, to Antichrist.[87] They summarize their findings:

> We are rapidly approaching—indeed, we are already on the brink of—a time when the world will be divided into ten regions whose leaders form a one-world government. This, in the name of world peace. Who could oppose that? Only Christians who know their Bible and know that this is the predicted world condition just before the Antichrist comes to power.[88]

Moreover, the merging of political and economic powers will be matched by similar developments within liberal Christianity, culminating in the World Church, or "Mystery Babylon," a mix of Satanism, New Age mysticism, liberal Christianity, and just about anything nonevangel- ical. LaHaye and Jenkins write, "If Babylon is the mother of all false religions and Jerusalem is the mother of true faith (since Jesus Christ was born, crucified, and resurrected there), then Rome is the mother of an unholy mixture of the two."[89] All of these false religions, combined with secular humanism, will bring forth the "Great Whore," or the World Church.[90] Although evangelicals have traditionally associated the Catholic Church with this movement toward the One-World religion, La-Haye and Jenkins make certain that liberal Protestants also take prominence in its hierarchy.

This unholy union begins to break apart at the midpoint of the Tribulation, during the seventh Trumpet judgment. The assassination and resurrection of Antichrist marks the turning point of his reign on earth. Whereas before the midpoint he appears as a benevolent dictator, after his resurrection and revival he becomes Satan incarnate and reveals himself as the temperamental and decidedly unpleasant "Man of Sin." His death also shatters the illusion of world peace and global harmony. Revelation 13:3 speaks again of the Beast, "I saw one of his heads as it were wounded to death." This addresses Antichrist's mortal wound, prophecy writers agree, although the exact circumstances remain unclear. Arthur Bloomfield, author of *How to Recognize the Antichrist,* apparently does not recognize how he will be killed, stressing that he "will be killed in a mysterious way . . . neither in anger nor in battle."[91] Novelists describe a dramatic event, usually televised, at which misguided Christian subversives inflict the deadly injury. Whatever the cause of death, however, his death is legitimate. Robert Bragg underscores this conclusion, stating that "the Greek meaning of the word wounded is 'slain to death'"[92]

This becomes crucial since Satan must counterfeit every act of Christ, just as Satan, the Antichrist, and another important character, the False Prophet, compose an unholy Trinity that corresponds to the Father, Son, and Holy Spirit. Hence, Antichrist—the master parodist—must also die and be resurrected; although as Satan, in contrast to Christ, he resurrects *himself.*[93] Satan indwells the body of Antichrist, having been recently cast out of heaven, and arrives filled with wrath since he knows that "he hath but a short time."[94] Taking no time for convalescence and recovery, Antichrist, now Satan, moves to consolidate his empire, breaks his covenant with Israel, desecrates the Temple, and destroys the spiritually inept World Church—demanding instead worship only of himself.[95]

Yet Antichrist's miraculous recovery and illustrious exploits are not enough to secure him universal acceptance. Like a politician who finds himself down in the polls, Antichrist realizes he might have an image problem. He requires a makeover of ultimate significance. Satan responds by calling upon hell's version of a spin doctor to market the Beast: the False Prophet. The False Prophet shares many of his master's capabilities, but, as prophecy writer and novelist Salem Kirban describes him, "The false prophet will never attempt to promote himself. He will never become an object of worship. He will do the work of a prophet in that he directs attention away from himself to the one who he says has the right to be worshipped (the Antichrist)."[96]

False Prophet's astute marketing campaign begins with a highly convincing showcase of Antichrist's miraculous powers, along with his own penchant for producing signs and wonders on behalf of his master. Prophecy writer Leon Wood notes, "These displays will serve as deceiving credentials, which will convince even those who should know better . . . to become followers of this wicked person."[97] False Prophet also creates an "Image of the Beast," capable of speech, and places this image in the Temple for all to see, including those watching on television. Kirban writes, seemingly overestimating the gullibility of the masses, that "when people see this miracle they will fall down and worship the Antichrist believing him to be Christ."[98] Those who refuse to worship the idol will be executed.

Moreover, False Prophet will demand a much more visible and corporeal sign of obeisance. He will require everyone to take the Mark of the Beast either on the right hand or forehead. Anyone caught without the Mark will be unable to participate in the new Beast economy and will also be executed should they continue to resist. Revelation 13:16–17 discusses the Mark, "And he causeth all, both great and small, rich and poor, free and bond, to receive a mark in their right hand, or in their foreheads: And that no man might buy or sell, save he that had the mark, or the name of the beast, or the number of his name."[99] False Prophet will require, in other words, that loyal subjects surrender their will to Antichrist or face economic disempowerment and eventual death. Those who maintain alternative identities, such as the many Tribulation Saints, will be forced underground by the restricted economy. Such a system will allow Antichrist to track the movements of his subjects, becoming the ultimate Big Brother. Many of these technologies are already in place, as prophecy writers like Mary Stewart Relfe point out. A potential Antichrist could already monitor his citizens through fiber optic-based televisions, prophecy writers assert, while credit and debit cards would provide instant tracking of one's moves, financial and otherwise.[100] LaHaye and Jenkins agree with their predecessors, adding that in the New World Order with its cashless society, identity and the freedom of the individual will be most at stake, a development Antichrist and his cronies will take great pains to deny:

> The serious drawbacks of such a system, of course, will not be mentioned. The chief loss will be the death of freedom. Once the government has mandated a cashless society, it will have total control of purchasing, labor, wages, and everything else. Financial control of the people translates to total control.[101]

Recent trade agreements, the authors emphasize, such as the North American Free Trade Agreement (NAFTA) have pushed the world even closer to a One-World system dominated by international bankers.[102]

LaHaye and Jenkins add an interesting twist to their emphasis on individual freedom, however, noting that Antichrist will require individual assent, as individuals will need the moral capacity to freely choose the Mark. They write, "Scripture makes it clear that receiving the Mark of the Beast is no accident but the result of a deliberate *choice* [emphasis added] made during the Tribulation."[103] They summarize their position that "the Bible is quite clear that a person *cannot* take the mark of the Beast accidentally. In fact, it will become the external sign of a deliberate decision to give one's *self* [emphasis added] to the devil."[104] Once one takes the Mark, the decision will be irreversible. God may pardon almost any sin, but this one will merit eternal damnation. Taking the identity of the Beast will doom one to an identical fate.[105]

The implementation of the Mark will help complete Antichrist's Beast economy, but he will not have much time to play the market. Once Antichrist fully deploys his Beast economy, God will respond with his harshest judgments yet, the seven Vial or Bowl judgments. These judgments will only intensify Antichrist/Satan's frustrations and desire for power, and his empire will collapse amid discontent and rebellion. He will meet the rebels, along with his allies, on the battle plain of Armageddon, where Christ will intervene, condemning those who continue to reject him. Revelation 19:20–21 addresses the fate of Antichrist/Satan and his followers:

> And the beast was taken, and with him the false prophet that wrought miracles before him, with which he deceived them that had received the

mark of the beast, and them that worshipped his image. These both were cast alive into a lake of fire burning with brimstone. And the remnant were slain with the sword of him that sat upon the horse.

Thus ends the Tribulation. With this background in place, we are now prepared to take a closer look at the *Left Behind* novels and the cultural tensions they demonstrate.

2

Reluctant Rebels
The Left Behind Novels and the Politics of Evangelical Identity

The growing coalition of pro-moral Americans is a sleeping giant that is gradually awakening to the realization that it has largely ignored the electoral process for decades. Unless it asserts itself and elects pro-moral people to office, America in the twenty-first century will be a humanist country, for the morals and philosophy of the public-school system of today will become the moral philosophy of our nation, in twenty to thirty years.[1]
　　　　　　　　　　—Tim LaHaye, *The Battle for the Mind*

The political activism of fundamentalists and Pentecostals has struck some observers as an anomaly. They asked: are not most of them pre-millennialists who see the near approach of the Rapture followed in seven years by Armageddon? Why should they care who governs the mass of mortals who are doomed to extinction? Anyone who has studied the logic of strict predestination as it affected the work ethic of seventeenth century Puritans knows that trying to find logical connections between theology and behavior is risky business.[2]　　　　　　　　—R. Laurence Moore, *Selling God*

Historian R. Laurence Moore cannily notes that the political actions of prophecy believers do not always fit the seemingly rigid limitations of their theologies. Prophecy writers have found a number of creative ways to circumvent the fatalism inherent to the dispensational End-Times narrative. The *Left Behind* novels demonstrate that LaHaye and Jenkins are no exceptions. Their novels may read on one level as thoroughly escapist fantasies, but political issues saturate the pages. This revelation should come as no surprise when one notes that the intellectual force behind the series, Tim LaHaye, is a seasoned political and cultural activist, having served on the board of Jerry Falwell's Moral Majority. LaHaye also founded his own conservative organizations, the now defunct American Coalition for Traditional Values, Family Life Seminars, and the shadowy Council for National Policy (CNP), among other ventures.[3] And, for many years before he helped Jerry Jenkins pen the *Left Behind* series, he wrote extensively on political and cultural themes. At the same time, he authored numerous volumes treating subjects as diverse as marriage counseling, psychological temperament profiling, and, of course, End-Times prophecy. LaHaye has obviously found a way to balance End-Times prophesying with more mundane topics that suggest that while believers may not expect to hang around much longer, they do want to make the most of the time remaining. This also means that although Antichrist will inevitably arise, signaling the End of the world as we know it, LaHaye believes that evangelicals maintain a responsibility to defend their values and identities as long as possible, while also providing a wholesome witness for the unsaved.

The *Left Behind* series demonstrates the authors' commitment to make a difference in their world even as the End approaches. Twelve novels is a long time to wait for an imminent End, even if one cynically assumes that the longer Christ delays his return, the richer his heralds become. Specifically, all of the action within the novels takes place in the Tribulation—that unavoidable future time of woe and torment. Yet the protagonists behave as if they can make a difference, even if they only save a few more souls. Nevertheless, this requires cultural intervention. It requires the exercise of a degree of power unavailable to previous protagonists in evangelical prophecy novels during their seasons of trial. It requires, in other words, politics. Even dispensationalism, arguably among the most fatalistic of prophecy scenarios, does leave some room for improvisation. This seems reasonable enough. Try as they might to escape, prophecy believers remain part of *this* world, and not the next. If believers have to stay for a while, they might as well make themselves comfortable.

Still, LaHaye's position suggests a measure of reluctance to enter the political arena. It has not been easy for him to discard the (a)political assumptions that predominated among conservative evangelicals for much of the twentieth century. LaHaye decided to enter the fray, he tells us, because evangelical values have been threatened by the rampant growth of a nefarious philosophy known as "secular humanism." I will detail what LaHaye means by secular humanism in the pages that follow, so a brief definition will suffice here. LaHaye writes, "Simply put, humanism is man's attempt to solve his problems independently of God."[4] For too long sinful humans have ignored the wisdom of God revealed in the Bible and have sought their own answers. Inevitably, such solutions have led only to chaos and destruction, LaHaye informs us.[5] The only way to stem the tide of humanism, LaHaye suggests, is for conscientious believers to enter the political arena. This is an ironic move, given that prophecy believers have tended to avoid taking political matters into their own hands precisely because God, after all, remains in control. LaHaye nevertheless believes that evangelicals must engage the humanists or risk losing their evangelical values in advance of the Tribulation, during what LaHaye calls the "pretribulation tribulation." The Tribulation, in other words, is both now and yet to come. The outcome of God's prophecies remains inalterable, but the End has not arrived just yet. LaHaye discusses this phenomenon:

> That tribulation is predestined and will surely come to pass. But the pretribulation tribulation—that is, the tribulation that will engulf this country if liberal humanists are permitted to take total control of our government—is neither predestined nor necessary.[6]

Literary theorist Stephen D. O'Leary's *Arguing the Apocalypse* offers insight into how LaHaye and other prophecy writers have found ways to insert political rhetoric into what would otherwise seem like a fatalistic genre.[7] O'Leary focuses mainly on the question of rhetorical strategies. "How do such texts persuade?" he asks throughout his study. "What special knowledge do they impart, and how do they allow the reader to gain a better understanding of their faith, the world, and their place within it?" Apocalyptic narratives have answered these questions for many millennia, O'Leary argues. Apocalyptic narratives make palpable the otherwise nebulous forces that bedevil people in their daily lives. An effective apocalyptic narrative helps explain why evil happens, along with how and when God will render judgment, and what, if anything, believers can do in the meantime. The texts persuade by providing urgent, relevant answers to those in dire need of a firm foundation upon which to base their lives. Successful apocalyptic rhetoric addresses the experiences of its readers and promotes the expectation of imminent change, sometimes even encouraging the faithful to play vital roles in bringing forth a world more pleasing to God.

O'Leary reads apocalyptic narratives through two basic frames of interpretation: the comic and the tragic. Briefly summarized, the comic frame understands life and history as open ended. The world may be changing rapidly, but humans retain some space for maneuvering as long as the ultimate End tarries. As O'Leary puts it, in the comic frame, "the drama of the End is continually re-enacted and experienced in the present while the End itself is delayed."[8] Moreover, the comic frame carries a prophetic meaning in more than one sense. It predicts future events, yes, but it also addresses humans as fallible beings who are responsible for making a meaningful difference in their world, even if, in the final analysis, decisive change always lies just on the other side of eternity.[9] The tragic frame, in contrast, forecloses all human freedom in a deterministic move that reduces humans to "code breakers."[10] The only point of human existence is to decode God's plan and carry out God's wishes. The tragic apocalypse thus leads to an unwholesome fatalism along with a loss of moral responsibility. If God has ordained certain events to pass, resistance is pointless and probably also sinful.

Evangelical prophecy novels written during the 1970's, for example, generally fit O'Leary's fatalistic, tragic framework more closely than they do his more open-ended, comic one. Protagonists in novels such as Salem Kirban's *666* seem to have been unenthusiastically inserted into the text, as if Kirban recognized that a minimal storyline might enhance the readability of his interpretation of Bible prophecy.[11] Characters passively watch the grand drama of the apocalypse unfold around them. They oppose Antichrist, of course, but for the most part appear trapped in a cosmic tragedy much larger than themselves. In contrast, the *Left Behind* novels, along with the novels of Frank Peretti and the recent work of Larry Burkett, among others, introduce characters who must deal with an End that tarries much longer than they expect.[12] The result is often a perspective closer to O'Leary's comic frame: the denouement might seem ultimately fixed, but the protagonists recognize that they must temporarily swallow their despair and struggle against Antichrist, doing much more than running for the nearest underground shelter.

Anthropologist Susan Harding offers additional insight, suggesting that such a revisioning of prophetic interpretation that permits the reintroduction of political concerns opens a "crack in the postmillennial window."[13] Traditionally apolitical after the infamous Scopes Trial in 1925, conservative evangelicals have reemerged into the political spotlight.[14] As pre-millennialists (those who expect Christ to return before the Millennium), dispensational prophecy believers have been reluctant to participate in political affairs. Post-millennialists, by contrast, suggest that Christ will return only after humanity has ordered its affairs sufficiently to permit Christ's return.[15] Granted, pre-millennialists such as Tim La-Haye have not suddenly switched to the opposing camp. As Harding claims, however, the perpetual delaying of the End has opened a crack in the window, allowing evangelicals to again engage the world (and slip closer to the post-millennial position). The ultimate End remains fixed, but believers can accomplish much in the meantime.

Political activity, as O'Leary and Harding suggest, also includes the quest for power through the deployment of rhetoric. Apocalyptic narratives attempt to persuade readers that the times demand immediate and profound action. What is more, evangelical leaders such as Jerry Falwell have not succeeded exclusively through their appeals to specific moral outrages, Harding notes.[16] Instead, Falwell and others have used the language of apocalypse to suggest, quite ironically, that *not* engaging the political arena might threaten their evangelical identity. Withdrawal or escape is not the answer. Evangelicals need to make the world safer for themselves and their fellow believers. Only then can they fulfill their commandment to win more souls for Christ before the heavenly trumpets signal the Rapture of the believers and the beginning of the irreversible Tribulation.

Harding suggests, in others words, that political involvement has, over time, become more consistent with the soul-winning logic of dispensational prophecy belief. Believers probably cannot save the world, but they might win a few more souls if they manage to stop or even reverse the disappearance of Christian values from American public life. Describing the thought of televangelist and political activist Jerry Falwell, Harding writes:

> He argued that unless born-again Christians acted politically they would lose their "freedom," religious and political, which was what enabled them to spread the good news at home and abroad, that is, to fulfill Bible prophecy.[17]

Prophecy writers play a dual role here: they describe in narrative form specific initiatives carried out by evangelical activists, while also attempting to rally believers to keep up the good work, graphically describing the menaces believers face and the forms of engagement still required to vanquish them. Immediately prior to the *Left Behind* series, one finds overt political activism most prominently displayed in the 1980's prophecy fiction of Frank Peretti. His first two novels, *This Present Darkness* and *Piercing the Darkness,* both feature legions of soul-stealing demons who like to congregate near public schools, progressive churches, new age retreat centers and think-tanks, and especially universities. Peretti depicts in narrative fashion the leading political concerns of the New Christian Right. Peretti worries most about education. According to Peretti's novels, demons control university professors, who train misguided educators and future leaders, while also shaping reprehensible public school curricula. Peretti understands that one must not only fight the battle at the ballot box but also at the school board.

Peretti's emphases in his fictional writings reflect evangelical concerns in real-life. Sociologist William C. Martin devotes a chapter to the "culture wars" in public education, for example, in his work on Christian Right politics. Martin notes especially the 1974 Kanawha County, West Virginia "textbook war." Evangelical activist Alice Moore, a school board member, led the opposition to a set of textbooks that attempted to introduce a multicultural curriculum. She rallied resources from across the nation and finally won a partial victory when the board agreed to review the textbooks. But the assembled crowds wanted much more. Several schools were firebombed, and shootings were not uncommon. Even the textbook supporters struck back with violence of their own. The genie would not return to the bottle.[18]

Peretti's fictional battles have more in common with the Kanawha County incidents than just a struggle over curriculum, however. Martin notes that in 1974 Kanawha County included at least two major demographics: the urban dwellers of Charleston, and the rural Appalachian coal-miners.[19] Religion may have sparked the conflict, but the transitional nature of the region no doubt exacerbated it. Increasingly forced to leave behind the seemingly unchanging expanses of pasture lands and small towns, the rural residents of Kanawha County found themselves in a liminal position between the past and a future arriving far too rapidly. The textbooks represented the vanguard of urban, middle-class values and challenged the cultural isolation of the rural residents. Peretti repeats this theme. Protagonists fight demons in small towns embattled by the encroachment of urban values and unwanted cultural change. Ultimately, angels help the town residents restore their threatened values, and the community symbolically purges its demons. Peretti's novels demonstrate that prophecy believers, like the rural populace of Kanawha County, find themselves locked into a period of rapid change, facing the potential loss of time-honored values. Peretti, along with LaHaye and Jenkins, seeks to insulate and protect the evangelical community from the ravages of cultural change.

LaHaye and Jenkins incorporate all of Peretti's concerns, but give the forces of darkness a specific label: secular humanism. If evangelicals allow the humanists to win, they will be hampered in their quest to spread the Gospel message and win more souls for Christ before it is too late, negating a critical aspect of their evangelical identity. Thus, for LaHaye and Jenkins, along with Peretti, believers must get involved if only to defend a cultural climate favorable to conservative evangelicals; and, it follows that the best defense may be a good offense. God controls the ultimate outcome, so when the End finally comes, it will not matter what believers do. But LaHaye, Jenkins, and Peretti make it clear that politically awakened believers must learn to help themselves in the meantime.

Indeed, conservative evangelical Protestants—whether or not directly motivated by the calls of Tim LaHaye and other evangelical leaders— have reentered the political arena in recent decades. Beginning in the 1950's but intensifying in the mid-1970's, conservative evangelical political activity has focused on issues important to evangelical identity and culture, including opposition to legalized abortion, opposition to the Equal Rights Amendment and gay rights, support for parochial and home schooling, and a reformation of public school curricula, among many other issues. This upsurge in political activity has resulted, LaHaye suggests, from the evangelical response to the threats posed to the evangelical way of life by secular humanist ideologies. Conservative evangelicals, however, have faced a learning curve in the political arena. They have not always understood the nature of the beast, so to speak, and have had to work from the ground up to cultivate political savvy. Evangelicals have also discovered that politicians are often gifted with the ability to promise much, while delivering only token, symbolic goods.[20]

This is not to say evangelicals have been without significant influence, of course. They have learned quickly how to play the political game.[21] Nevertheless, their overt impact has largely been limited to single-issue politics. Moreover, evangelicals have been reluctant to tackle structural ills, preferring to work with solutions dealing with individuals, a stance consistent with their theological assumptions. Finally, while leaders such as Tim LaHaye, Jerry Falwell, Pat Robertson, and Ralph Reed have found ways to steer around the limitations of their prophecy beliefs, they have not totally overcome the despair and fatalism implicit in the dispensational schema. Prophecy belief may not stop evangelicals from engaging in political activity, but it does complicate matters.

Let us not forget that prophecy believers like Tim LaHaye have reentered the political arena because they have sensed their evangelical values and identities under threat from ominous developments within the mainstream culture. It is a cultural politics, mainly, that concerns prophecy believers. Yes, Tim LaHaye has found ways to include such Reaganesque themes as "peace through strength" and a strong military in his platform, but these have emerged largely from cultural concerns.[22] The Soviet Union was, after all, an "evil empire" to prophecy believers that suppressed Christianity and fostered atheism, and it is significant that Reagan made his "Evil Empire" speech to appease evangelicals at a meeting of the National Religious Broadcasters.[23] Evangelical political activity— especially that of Tim LaHaye—has emerged first and foremost from a sense that evangelicals are slipping further on the scale of cultural disempowerment.

This chapter discusses evangelical political concerns as depicted in the *Left Behind* novels and in the other writings of Tim LaHaye. First, I explore the rhetorical significance of evangelical prophecy belief, examining how it may influence American political and cultural attitudes, taking a close look at issues raised by academic readers of prophecy literature. Second, I examine the nonfiction writings of Tim LaHaye, exploring how his earlier work helps illuminate the specific cultural and political attitudes expressed in the *Left Behind* novels. Finally, I show that the kind of political rhetoric deployed in the novels resembles the language of nineteenth-century American Populism, a series of movements that owed much to the evangelical spirit. The use of a populist approach allows LaHaye and Jenkins to appeal to a broader readership. An examination of nineteenth-century American Populism, however, also reveals that such rhetoric has a tendency to take discontent and strip it of its political efficacy, essentially functioning as a social safety valve to let off steam. Nevertheless, apocalyptic rhetoric, in and of itself, may play a significant role in shaping the cultural attitudes of prophecy believers and perhaps many in the American mainstream. LaHaye and Jenkins, along with other recent prophecy writers, may do more than simply reflect real-world trends; they may also play an important role in reshaping the way their readers view the world by alerting them to ominous cultural developments.

The Rhetorical Force of Prophecy Belief

The cultural marginality of prophecy believers, combined with renewed political involvement, may have serious consequences under the right circumstances both for themselves and for the American mainstream. Prophecy belief tends to cast complicated issues into absolute terms, bypassing carefully reasoned considerations. Intellectual historian Paul S. Boyer works with this premise in his study of American prophecy belief, *When Time Shall Be No More*. Boyer includes a wide-ranging discussion of prophecy belief and political attitudes. His discussion of prophecy believers and the potential impact of their beliefs on American attitudes toward nuclear proliferation, for example, proves especially interesting.[24]

As the work of O'Leary and Harding suggests, however, political activity often assumes subtler forms. Boyer shares their premise that prophecy belief may serve as a powerful language of political persuasion. While conservative evangelicals actively seek cultural change, opposing homosexuality and equal rights for women, for example, it would be misleading to depict them as calculating Machiavellians on large-scale policy issues such as nuclear proliferation. As Boyer admits when addressing the issue of whether prophecy belief results in any direct political impact, "The question is difficult, the evidence is sketchy."[25] Furthermore, Boyer, addressing prophecy belief during the Cold War era, writes that "my own sense is that the connection between grassroots prophecy belief and nuclear-weapons policy, while real, was subterranean and indirect."[26]

As Boyer demonstrates, prophecy writers like Hal Lindsey devoted a great deal of effort during the 1970's and 1980's to showing how God approved of a conservative foreign policy. Highly nationalistic, prophecy writers occasionally stepped outside of the limitations of dispensational belief during the Cold War to give the United States an End-Times role that was simply untenable from within their own apocalyptic understandings. Boyer nevertheless warns that "one must be careful not to view postwar prophecy belief as merely a theological rationalization of Cold War ideology that exalted virtuous America, demonized the wicked communists, and gloated over Russia's approaching doom."[27] Boyer's caveat has considerable merit. But I would go a step further. Prophecy writers have no doubt proven overzealous in their nationalism, both during and after the Cold War. I suspect, however, that while their pronouncements have been influenced by nationalistic or other mundane, political sentiments, they have mainly followed theological rather than primarily political imperatives. I note again Harding's point that political action among prophecy believers may stem from a sense of cultural disempowerment which threatens their evangelical values. When prophecy believers feel threatened, they may latch onto the first prophet or political philosophy which promises to rectify their situation. During the 1980's, the prophet was Ronald Reagan.

Evangelical supporters of President Reagan gave him much symbolic capital, even if he ultimately rewarded them with only symbolic gestures. In many cases, prophecy writers had anticipated Reagan, making his policies, in retrospect, appear more plausible to believers. Lindsey, for example, tapped into the anti-Soviet sentiments rampant during the Cold War in *The Late Great Planet Earth*.[28] He made a blunt comparison between Russia and the End-Times enemy of Israel, Gog—the invader from the north:

> How could Ezekiel 2600 years ago have forecast so accurately the rise of Russia to its current military might and its direct and obvious designs upon the Middle East, not to mention the fact that it is now an implacable enemy of the new state of Israel?[29]

Lindsey managed to justify, using dispensational interpretations of the Scriptures, what would become key components of Reagan's foreign policy, even including China, Arab countries, Africa, and communist Eastern European states in his axis of evil. It might seem as if Lindsey was a dupe for conservative foreign policy interests. After all, Russia played an all-too-convenient role in his prophecy scenario. His writings, moreover, continued to dovetail nicely with Reagan administration policies a decade later.[30] Like Boyer, however, I doubt that Lindsey or his readers were interested in political outcomes in isolation from religious motives. Nuclear warfare might hasten the End. And if prophecy writers could equate Russia with Gog, surely this proved the End was near. If anything, the relationship between the newly invigorated evangelical voting bloc and elite conservative policymakers resulted from a marriage of convenience. But each partner may have harbored quite different motives.

Boyer notes that Reagan eagerly spoke of prophecy belief—taken directly from Lindsey whom he evidently admired—as early as 1971. Boyer quotes Reagan from a dinner address delivered to California legislators:

> Ezekiel tells us that Gog, the nation that will lead all of the other powers of darkness against Israel, will come out of the north. Biblical scholars have been saying for generations that Gog must be Russia. What other powerful nation is to the north of Israel? None.[31]

Reagan's prophetic claims bear a striking and alarming resemblance to those of Lindsey.

During his presidency, Boyer points out, Reagan and some of his chief advisors often displayed a rather dualistic understanding of public policy issues. Besides Reagan's own "evil empire" speech, his secretary of the interior James Watt declined to engage pressing environmental problems because he believed that Christ would return soon, making human intervention a waste of effort.[32] More disturbing yet, Reagan's secretary of defense Caspar Weinberger acknowledged that he had read the book of Revelation and affirmed its contents, claiming that "time was running out."[33] As problematic as these developments were, however, and with the ever-present worry that the line between church and state was disappearing, Boyer focuses on the big issue: the Bomb. Specifically, Boyer suggests that the rapid arms buildup of the 1980's, combined with Reagan's persistent flirtation with apocalyptic belief, offered up a potentially volatile combination.

Prophecy believers, Boyer suggests, may have a powerful motivation to oppose nuclear disarmament, even if they do not seek to hasten Armageddon through direct human intervention.[34] Boyer does not suggest the likelihood of the latter, but he raises quite justified concerns about the fatalism inherent in evangelical apocalyptic literature and nuclear proliferation run amok. Prophecy believers would have no reason to oppose such a buildup. First, if the world did ignite in nuclear destruction, believers might assume they would be raptured, spared the horrors of nuclear holocaust. Moreover, God might even use nuclear technologies as part of his End-Times plans. Hal Lindsey made just such a claim, interpreting Bible verses to indicate God's advanced knowledge of and fascination with nuclear fission.[35]

Notably, historian Grant Wacker disagrees with Boyer's assertion of a connection between prophecy belief and public policy. Wacker writes:

Yet surely the most striking feature of prophecy belief is precisely the op-
posite: how impotent it has been as an instrument of public policy. Consider the Reagan years, when many high-ranking officials, including the
secretary of the interior, the secretary of defense, and the president himself all identified themselves as firm adherents. Nuclear holocaust did
not ensue, the cold war thawed, Israel lost the ear of the president, and
the U.S. government continued to spend hundreds of billions on social
reconstruction. . . . Indeed, one of the most striking characteristics of the
vast majority of prophecy believers has been the contrast between the
militancy of their rhetoric and the law-abiding regularity of their daily
behavior.[36]

Wacker makes a number of important points, especially his observation
that rhetoric does not necessarily lead to action, especially regarding the
nuclear issue. Yet one cannot overlook the unprecedented arms buildup
that accompanied Reagan's tenure as president. Boyer's point, as I understand it, is that prevailing attitudes among prophecy believers helped
make the defense buildup seem like a reasonable move. What such an at-
mosphere lacked was a spark. Despite Wacker's distinction between
rhetoric and behavior, Boyer's claim that prophecy belief influences public opinion (and indirectly public policy) remains an important one. As
Boyer offers, "the evidence is sketchy," but it nonetheless remains quite
suggestive.

Susan Harding makes more explicit Boyer's otherwise subtle distinction between overt political action and a form of rhetoric that influences
political attitudes—itself a kind of political action or political language—
in the broader sense. Harding finds cause for concern not in the more obvious ways suggested by those suspicious of evangelicalism for its purported threat of large-scale political action, but in the rhetorical strategies
deployed by prophecy writers. Prophecy statements, she claims, do not
reflect reality, but instead attempt to "constitute reality." This is a politics
of a different sort, but one no less contestable or problematic. By attempting to alter the frame through which Americans read current events,
prophecy writers attempt not so much to force particular solutions to the
world's ills, as much as they try to reframe the grounds upon which such
policy determinations are based.[37]

Apocalyptic language may encourage Americans, especially prophecy
believers, to reshape the way they view the world and its problems.
Prophecy writers appeal to Biblical narratives as sources of plausibility,

which may influence the many conservative evangelicals who regard the Bible as authoritative. If a public policy issue of secular origin happens to fit reasonably well within such rhetoric, the combination can bring forth significant changes in how prophecy believers understand public policy. Or, as Boyer puts it, "When prophetic interpretations of world realities converge with those of secular opinion molders in government and the media, the result can be an ideological groundswell of enormous power."[38] Whether or not secular leaders actually believe such religious ideology remains unclear, perhaps even dubious. But the importance of this question retreats as one considers the potential alliance of two different ways of understanding the world: the marriage of secular policymakers and prophecy writers. Each group potentially gets something they want. Prophecy writers seek either the fulfillment of prophecy or enhanced cultural protection to spread their message while time remains. Policymakers require passionate justification for their policies, which prophecy writers often provide in abundance. It is potentially a marriage made in heaven—or somewhere else—depending on one's perspective.

Tim LaHaye and the Battle for the Mind of Evangelicalism

One can find the political views that LaHaye and Jenkins espouse in the *Left Behind* novels featured in greater detail in the earlier work of Tim LaHaye. LaHaye, as the intellectual force behind the series, has written prodigiously for several decades on a number of themes, but has saved his most passionate prose for what he describes as a fatal attraction on the part of the global elite to a nefarious philosophy known as "secular humanism." LaHaye discusses the threat of secular humanism in a series of books that includes *The Battle for the Mind, The Battle for the Family, The Battle for the Public Schools, The Hidden Censors,* and *The Race for the 21st Century.* Although I draw my observations from all of these texts, I have organized my discussion around LaHaye's principal work on secular humanism, *The Battle for the Mind,* published in 1980.[39] Borrowing heavily from evangelical thinker Francis Schaeffer's *How Then Shall We Live?* LaHaye claims that the hearts and minds, along with the sovereignty of the American people, are under threat from a small but highly influential cabal of international elites he calls secular humanists. Elsewhere, LaHaye provides a useful definition of secular humanism:

Secular humanism is the philosophic base of liberalism and is easily defined. I call it a Godless, man-centered philosophy of life that rejects moral absolutes and traditional values. It makes man the measure of all things rather than God. It is usually hostile toward religion in general, with a particular hatred toward Christianity. I consider this worldview to be the most harmful, anti-American, anti-Christian philosophy in our country today. Most of society's current evils can be traced to secular humanist thinkers or liberals whose theories originated in that philosophy.[40]

Unless someone alerts the public to the dangers of humanism and the masses of American Christians heed the warnings, LaHaye opines, secular humanists will lead the United States and the world into an era of unprecedented immorality and sociocultural chaos.

LaHaye sounds the alarm in *The Battle for the Mind*. The title reflects his conviction that secular humanists deploy subtle methods. Secular humanists achieve their aims not through the direct exercise of power but through flooding the minds of people, especially children, with humanist propaganda.[41] Consistent with his thesis, LaHaye begins with a layman's discussion of neuroscience. Similar to pop psychologists such as Maxwell Maltz (*Psycho-cybernetics/Pulling Your Own Strings*), LaHaye emphasizes that the mind, and by extension the body, are highly malleable. He offers an anecdote, "One man I know, who went to his doctor because his heart was racing, discovered that fears in his mind caused his body to simulate a heart attack. By learning to govern his fears, he was able to control his heart."[42] But there are limits. LaHaye manages to maintain an essentialist position when arguing that gender traits are ingrained, pointing out that in a recent study "boys and girls from primitive cultures" gravitated to toys appropriate to their gender.[43] Although not all brain functions are malleable, LaHaye nevertheless argues that humans can "regulate far more of them than they realize."[44]

Humanists recognize this, of course, and use our two most vital senses—sight and hearing—to influence our thoughts. "Millions of parents," LaHaye writes, "have already lost their children's minds to rock stars, atheistic-humanistic educators, sensual entertainers, and a host of other anti-God, amoral, and antiman influences."[45] Second, humanists also work on the emotions. LaHaye describes what he calls the "emotional center": "This seat of your emotions is located behind your forehead and between your temples. Rather than being heart shaped, as romantics tend to visualize it, in reality it is walnut shaped."[46] Humanists attempt to influence the emotional center by flooding the media with pornography and violence, inflaming the passions of sensitive souls, especially youth. LaHaye, however, offers a method for counteracting the humanist assault, "Here is a healthy rule of thumb to follow, when you recognize wrong or harmful feelings: Examine what you have been seeing and hearing lately and how your mind has been thinking. Feelings are not spontaneous; to control them, you must first control your mind."[47] Humanists also influence the third and most important aspect of our mind: the will. Humanists, LaHaye believes, by subtly flooding our minds with images and harmful thoughts, make it difficult for us to take control of our lives. By influencing these three interdependent aspects of the brain, humanists seek to gain total control over our minds.[48]

Secular humanism, LaHaye explains, has its roots in ancient Greek philosophy. The teachings of the apostle Paul, who considered humanism "the wisdom of man," helped squelch humanism for approximately 1200 years before the Dominican theologian Thomas Aquinas revived it in the thirteenth century. In a dizzying display that demonstrates more haste than erudition, LaHaye skips forward to the Renaissance before quickly tying humanism to the radical philosophies of the French Revolution. Finally, LaHaye indicts the nineteenth-century German philosophers Georg W. F. Hegel and Friedrich Nietzsche and concludes with twentieth-century existentialists along with the educational philosophies of John Dewey.[49] Although his treatment of intellectual history is breezy and not always coherent, LaHaye makes it abundantly clear that he reserves his most damning indictments for contemporary intellectuals, who inherit and extend the ideals of their humanist forebears—along with public schools and universities—for the loss of "traditional American values."

LaHaye identifies five interdependent influences of secular humanism on American culture, what he calls "The Five Basic Tenets of Humanism." They are atheism, evolution, amorality, autonomous man, and the socialist one-world view. The first two tenets are straightforward. Atheism is "the foundation stone of humanist thought" and teaches "the belief that there is no God."[50] Furthermore, atheism replaces God with the deification of humans. The second tenet, evolution, places humans at the center of the universe, a universe without absolute, moral values. The third tenet, amorality, takes advantage of evolutionary thought by freeing humans from all Biblically derived responsibilities, allowing individuals to "do their own thing," so long as no one else gets hurt. The fourth tenet, autonomous man, conceives the human as an "autonomous, self-centered, godlike person with unlimited goodness and potential—if his environment is controlled to let his free spirit develop."[51] Furthermore, La-Haye writes that "one of the worst sins of man (according to humanists) . . . is inhibiting the liberty and freedom of another to express himself."[52] Finally, humanists seek to establish a "socialist one-world view" that will bring the world together under the aegis of the United Nations and its subsidiary bodies.[53] Obviously, the threat of socialism has subsided considerably in recent years. Still, LaHaye indicts the humanist understandings that he believes undergird socialist ideals, so he has not had a difficult time updating his model.

LaHaye presents the threat of secular humanism to his readers and includes a jeremiad. A humanist victory is not inevitable if the sixty million Christians in the United States rally behind candidates representing traditional values. Those people whom LaHaye names the "sleeping majority"—narrowly evading the specter of Richard Nixon's "silent majority"—must awaken to reclaim the United States for God.[54] LaHaye presents his jeremiad:

> The growing coalition of pro-moral Americans is a sleeping giant that is gradually awakening to the realization that it has largely ignored the electoral process for decades. Unless it asserts itself and elects pro-moral people to office, America in the 21st century will be a humanist country, for the morals and philosophy of the public-school system of today will become the moral philosophy of our nation, in twenty to thirty years.[55]

LaHaye's warning takes the familiar form of apocalyptic speech. Unless believers participate in the electoral process now, humanists will seize the reins of power irreversibly—at least prior to Christ's return.

LaHaye also understands, however, that many of his evangelical and fundamentalist colleagues will resist such a call. He devotes special and not always cordial attention to them. He writes:

> My godly pastor echoed the unwise advice of many Christians during the early 1940's, when he taught, "Politics is a dirty business. Rather than getting involved in politics, we Christians should stick to preaching the gospel and let the nice, civic-minded people run the country." As a result, for forty years the American Humanist Association, the Ethical Cultural Union, and the American Civil Liberties Union, and other hu-

manist groups have backed their humanist candidates in both parties, gaining the strongest representation in our government.[56]

Conservative Christians, LaHaye believes, must overcome their traditional distaste of politics and become engaged—now. And, in the unlikely event his readers may have missed his main point, LaHaye concludes *The Battle for the Mind* by quoting Dante, "The hottest places in Hell are reserved for those who, in times of moral crises, maintain their neutrality."[57] LaHaye, it seems, leaves little room for hesitation or compromise.

Besides LaHaye's obvious concern with secular humanism, the theme that keeps reemerging throughout his published writings is a fear that Americans are losing control of their values and institutions to clandestine elites. Secret plots and underground organizations have wrested control from the majority of Americans, a majority that still clings to traditional (Christian) values. But they will not constitute a majority for long if such organizations as the Council on Foreign Relations (CFR) and the Trilateral Commission have their way. LaHaye describes the threat:

> When one reads CFR and Trilateral Commission documents and analyzes the writings of CFR and Trilateral Commission members, it is clear beyond any reasonable doubt that these two organizations are actively seeking to destroy our nation and establish a ruthless world dictatorship—to be run by them.[58]

Such secret organizations threaten evangelicals and their values, LaHaye believes. LaHaye appears ambivalent, however, about how to confront such groups. Believers may be losing power, but do Christian activists merely attempt to clean up the cultural mess or do they take on the nefarious groups responsible for America's cultural decay? LaHaye does not provide a clear answer. He obviously calls believers to do *something*. Christians can form watchdog groups to police the media, they can fight pornography, and they can even provide alternatives in media and entertainment products. Still, it remains unclear whether they can (or indeed want to) banish the secret societies allegedly responsibly for the world's ills. The specter of secret, empirically unavailable organizations responsible for the world's ills provides all-too-convenient adversaries for LaHaye. He will obviously have an easier time propagating his values and building his organizations if he can convince his readership that a large, clandestine, and dangerous threat exists. The larger the perceived threat, the logic goes, the larger the apparatus required to combat it. Still, La-Haye remains ambivalent about what to do with the additional cultural clout he would gain from building alternative Christian organizations. He seems to urge believers to resist manifestations of evil, while suggesting that God will ultimately destroy structural evil in His own time. Either way, LaHaye and Jenkins continue to struggle with this issue in the *Left Behind* series.

The Politics of Left Behind

On first glance, LaHaye and Jenkins depict a salvation drama that would seem to permit little room for political action. After all, the die has been cast and the fate of the world shifts to God's hands during the Tribulation. Or does it? Keep in mind that those who become believers in the novels, after all, are left behind a long time, encouraging political activity. LaHaye and Jenkins open what Harding calls the "post-millennial crack in the window." They create protagonists who challenge Antichrist and his forces, even as they proclaim their own powerlessness, and they do have power. Their empowerment owes, at least in part, to their secret, Gnostic knowledge of what lies behind current events. Believers, equipped with such secret knowledge, can see through Antichrist's conspiracies. They know something he does not. Empowered by knowledge, protagonists in *Left Behind* transform their despair into an often successful series of challenges against Antichrist. The End remains fixed, but believers maintain a responsibility to grapple with the forces of darkness on the grounds set forth by their own understanding of the Apocalypse. Finally, the *Left Behind* novels, remember, do not only describe a future world, but they also describe the struggles of believers in the present world, offering a suggestive framework for the enactment of the present during what LaHaye calls the "pre-tribulation tribulation."

As with Hal Lindsey, LaHaye and Jenkins try to keep their political aspirations consistent with their theological underpinnings, even if their policies strike one as amazingly congruent with those of hard-line conservatives—especially on cultural issues. They do not advocate political accomplishment for its own sake, in other words. They have objectives, which they make evident in their texts, but these objectives cannot be permitted to override the limitations placed on believers by God's End-Times plan. LaHaye and Jenkins must again strike a delicate balance be-

tween activism and piety. They attempt to negotiate such tension by focusing mostly on individualized solutions consistent with their dispensational beliefs. This allows them to avoid structural entanglements, for the
most part. But it also may also complicate matters, creating unintended
consequences and contributing to the ephemerality of their political accomplishments.

Historian Michael Kazin in his work on nineteenth-century American
Populism labels such an emphasis an "ironic focus on the individual."[59]
Dispensationalists such as LaHaye and Jenkins respond to evil, more
often than not, by focusing on individuals rather than institutions. If individual humans are inherently sinful, it follows that human institutions
will be sinful, too. Yet most conservative evangelicals, despite occasional
forays into public policy, focus on saving individuals rather than institutions, since sinful humans, and not their organizations, lie at the root of
human evil. LaHaye and Jenkins, while wary of institutions, pursue instead the more palpable and immediate questions of individual morality.
They seek to create a moral universe favorable to spreading the Gospel as
widely as possible before Christ returns to clean up the rest of the terrestrial mess. Thus, despite tossing tantalizing nuggets into their novels condemning global capitalism, environmental depredation, or other large-
scale ills, the authors appear most comfortable handling complicated issues on an individual, moral level, as I point out in the following brief
treatment of race and gender issues in the *Left Behind* novels.

Sociologists Michael Emerson and Christian Smith in *Divided by Faith*
point out some of the unfortunate consequences of the evangelical focus
on individuals rather than social structures. Emerson and Smith argue
that evangelicals often ignore institutionally based and structurally supported poverty, racism, and sexism. Specifically demonstrating the problems of evangelical assumptions vis-à-vis racism, Emerson and Smith suggest that evangelicals genuinely seek to heal the racial divide, provide
equal opportunity for all, and eliminate poverty, but they want to do so
at the individual level, remaining oblivious to the institutional basis of
these problems. According to Emerson and Smith, evangelicals typically
see racism as a problem among individuals that can be corrected through
better one-on-one relationships and communication, rather than as a serious flaw in American culture than cannot be corrected with such easy
answers.[60]

Hence, the authors conclude that many evangelicals, while basically
benevolent in their outlook, remain profoundly naive regarding the root

causes of racism and in a sense prolong and exacerbate the problems of institutional racism. Emerson and Smith refer to this as the problem of "racialization." Racism has become more covert, institutionalized, and "invisible to most whites."[61] Evangelicals, because of their belief in free will and equal opportunity, tend to blame individuals and cite moral defects for conditions which have a much more pervasive, institutional dimension. Thus, their theological assumptions tend to undermine their otherwise genuine attempts to address questions of racism in contemporary American culture.

The *Left Behind* series reflects many of the tensions Emerson and Smith find in their study. This occurs in spite of the authors' obvious attempts to make their novels reflect the diversity of American culture along with that of global Christianity. Nevertheless, the *Left Behind* novels display an ingrained suspicion of cultural outsiders, a condition to which the protagonists appear oblivious. As literary critic Amy Johnson Frykholm points out, the *Left Behind* novels tend to marginalize characters of nonwhite ethnicities, sometimes calling into question their status as believers, even when they bear the Mark of Christ.[62] One finds this most clearly illustrated in the case of Albie, a pilot of Arab descent, who assists the remnant believers in every conceivable way but still falls under suspicion. Interestingly, in book six, *Assassins,* LaHaye and Jenkins begin adding a preface to each novel that includes the names of key characters and their status as either "believers," "the undecided," or "the enemies"—a sort of salvation scorecard that would seem to help believers sort out any confusion about who plays for which team. But in the preface to *The Mark,* the authors add a fourth category, "Professed Believer," for Albie. Albie accepts the evangelical teachings, affirms their truth, and receives the miraculously bestowed Mark of Christ, yet he still falls under suspicion because of his Arab origins. Similarly, a Chinese character, Chang Wong, is depicted as bearing *both* the Mark of the Beast *and* the Mark of Christ. A not so subtle xenophobia enters the text, as the authors struggle with whether to admit cultural outsiders into the ranks of believers in good standing. Ultimately, they do, but not before subjecting the "others" to a period of suspicion and reduced status within the group.

As Frykholm also notes, this suspicion extends to women as well, especially women who resist traditional gender roles.[63] The novels belittle the homosexuality of the treacherous Verna Zee[64] and call into question the loyalty of Rayford Steele's second wife, Amanda Fortunato. Hattie Durham, flight attendant and temptress extraordinaire, becomes a perpetual traitor to the Tribulation Force. She falls in love with Antichrist and has no other ambition than to bear his child. In this case, family values are trumped by prohibitions against copulating with Evil. She has the baby, but it is stillborn, with horrible birth-defects. Even otherwise loyal women such as Chloe come under censure for not following rigidly delineated gender roles. Indeed, Frykholm finds The Cult of True Womanhood valorized throughout the novels, which relegate women to largely supporting roles.[65] The authors' attitude toward women is not monolithic, however. They do accord women such as Chloe additional responsibilities as the novels progress. For example, Chloe takes over one of the Tribulation Force's most important operations, the commodity cooperative. Yet when she gives birth to a son, she becomes a "stay at home mom." LaHaye and Jenkins ultimately affirm "traditional" values.

Besides addressing questions of individualism and morality, however, the *Left Behind* novels discuss such large-scale enemies as the United Nations, global capitalism, and the increasingly pervasive influence of new technologies, especially improperly implemented technologies. Yet the authors approach such issues in a paradoxical, individualized manner. Global capitalism, for example, is obviously a structural concern, yet the imperatives of prophecy belief force the authors to personify the otherwise vague networks of global capitalism, attempting to reduce structural concerns to a more familiar language of individualism and immorality. Bad people, not unjust social structures, are responsible for human suffering. LaHaye and Jenkins must offer their criticisms of global capitalism and new technologies with care. Although they indict global capitalism and new technologies for facilitating the rise of Antichrist, leading to the enslavement of the globe, they also know that they must develop a language that offers criticism without threatening structures. They do not seek to bite the invisible hand that feeds them. The language they deploy in the *Left Behind* series, interestingly enough, resembles the language of nineteenth-century American Populism.

Left Behind and the Populist Trajectory

The popularity of the *Left Behind* franchise recalls mass movements from American history that while ostensibly different, offer enough similarities to make comparisons fruitful.[66] For example, one can encapsulate many of these themes—at least for the sake of clarity and brevity—into another phenomenon endemic to American culture: populism. Populism, like most -isms, represents a polyvalent category, one to which writers often refer with imprecision, as historian Michael Kazin laments. Kazin notes that populism has become a catch-all term for almost any blip on the radar of popular culture, "from Bruce Springsteen to Rush Limbaugh to loose-fitting cotton trousers."[67] He nevertheless seeks to rehabilitate the term and its historical context of providing hope for the politically disempowered. Although discussing numerous populist characteristics, he suggests that a spirit of protest against anyone who would deny "the rights of individuals against the state" assumes central importance.[68] Another historian of populism, Lawrence Goodwyn, concurs, writing that "at bottom, Populism was, quite simply, an expression of self-respect."[69]

The *Left Behind* novels fit the rudiments of such a definition, especially if one considers that "the rights of individuals against the state" need not involve a literal, political protest but may also take on existential or even religious overtones. Populism with a "P" describes a particular historical movement of economic and political cooperation among frontier farmers in the late nineteenth century. Although it failed as a political force, its restless energy has influenced later movements of often quite different character, all of which have sought to articulate the core elements that lent Populism its mass appeal. Such movements have invariably sought to return a sense of empowerment to the "common" people, whether one understands the latter, like Kazin, in economic terms as "the producers" of material wealth,[70] or as Goodwyn suggests, as those seeking personal and cultural autonomy, along with a measure of self-respect.

Historically, nineteenth-century American Populism developed as a grassroots response to the excesses of post–Civil War industrial capital and its captains. Kazin traces its formation to an uneasy yet intertwined pair of intellectual strands. The first emphasized key secular leaders, including Thomas Jefferson and his valorization of personal freedom, democracy, and hard work; Andrew Jackson with his opposition to the eastern banking establishment; and Abraham Lincoln for his humble origins, hard work, and integrity.[71] The second strand inherited a moral emphasis from the evangelical revivals associated with the Second Great Awakening (~1800–1840).[72] The Second Great Awakening as a historical phenomenon included a series of large-scale revivals in the northern cities, the southern and western frontiers, and just about everywhere in between.

Although one can observe commonalities from the revivals—they shared a concern for salvation with a denunciation of pervasive sinfulness, including intoxication, promiscuity, and general dishonesty—one finds disagreement among historians on the ultimate meaning of the Second Great Awakening, owing in no small measure to regional, class, and denominational differences. Historian Paul E. Johnson argues, for example, that the revivalist Charles G. Finney—whatever his spiritual intentions—functioned as a hired gun for nascent capitalists in industrializing cities such as Rochester, New York. Finney brought a spirit of evangelical revival but also helped to instill potent values among the working classes that made their work and leisure habits much more amenable to the capitalist spirit.[73] Nathan O. Hatch, however, notes that whatever their ultimate outcome on a functional level, nineteenth-century revivals tended to have an antinomian and populist flavor, appealing to the disenfranchised—economically, culturally, or otherwise. Hatch also compares the populist sentiments of the revivals (and, by extension, the popular pieties of contemporary evangelicalism) with late nineteenth-century Populism, writing that "in their passion to communicate with and mobilize ordinary people, to challenge them to take responsibility for their destiny and to educate themselves, these movements [American Christian] resemble a mass democratic movement such as Populism."[74]

Hatch's suggestion is indeed perceptive. Like Populists to come, those who championed the revivals, which collectively made up the Second Great Awakening, placed their trust in pioneering individuals rather than sedentary structures, also preferring local control of their affairs to centralized domination by condescending elites. Methodist circuit riders, for example, eschewed the economic security typically associated with settled ministries and surrendered their livelihoods—and, often, their lives—to bring the Gospel to the hinterlands.[75] Upstart religious leaders such as Alexander Campbell wrote bracing parodies of elite clergy, while the revivals as a whole tended to cast suspicion on all elites within American society: spiritual, governmental, or business.[76]

Moreover, the character of the revivals, alongside the beliefs promoted by them, emphasized an individualistic ethos consistent with the hardships of the frontier. Rowdy, weeklong camp meetings—the staple of the western revivals—offered lonely pioneers an opportunity for community, wholesome and edifying entertainment, and perhaps salvation, even if distilled spirits sometimes mixed with the Holy Spirit, and Christian love occasionally gave way to the lusts of the flesh. Indeed, as camp meeting lore puts it, "more souls were begot than saved."[77] Regardless of their excesses, however, the rough-and-tumble spirit of the meetings, along with the larger phenomenon of the Second Great Awakening, fostered a climate of distrust toward learned elites and traditional bearers of power. The revivals, Hatch argues, helped to democratize American religion and culture, opening up a confusing welter of possibilities in the young republic, also encouraging the powerless to rise up and challenge the educated and powerful aristocracy.

Just as importantly, the revivals helped swell American church membership to record levels, making it seem, more than ever, that the United States had become a truly Christian nation.[78] Such high levels of evangelical church membership in the early nineteenth century, along with the radical spirit of democracy fostered by the revivals, provided a backdrop for another key trait of Populism: nostalgia. Populists, whether eastern trade unionists, western miners, evangelical reformers, or Farmer's Alliance members,[79] accepted the notion of a simpler and morally secure time that had collapsed due to the rampant greed and vice of the emerging industrial capitalist elite. Whether one emphasized the plight of urban workers, the mounting debt of farmers suffering from restrictive monetary policies, or the increasing immorality of the urban masses, Populists held in common the ideal of a golden age that combined the Jacksonian reverence for the free, democratic individual, with the moral fervor characteristic of the Second Great Awakening. Sociologists Rhys Williams and Susan Alexander concur, suggesting that Populism had a "priestly subtext" that called for a return to a golden age of American republicanism.[80]

The empirical existence of such a golden age is dubious. Still, the decades-old memory of a more pious and activist era helped spur people of divergent economic and cultural backgrounds to struggle against the injustice in their midst. Ironically, however, their lionization of individualism along with a concomitant resistance to sustained structural action may have hamstrung their efforts. With the notable exception of a brief period of radicalism within the Farmer's Alliance—an 1880's movement among Texas farmers that sought to create cooperative networks among farmers to better facilitate the sale of their produce along with the purchase of raw materials—Populist uprisings compromised their quests for justice with a distaste for building the institutions that might have allowed them to sustain their reform efforts beyond a generation or two.[81]

The *Left Behind* novels include many of the themes associated with nineteenth-century American Populism, including a suspicion of moneyed elites, a passion for moral issues, an "evangelical" spirit that lends such disparate concerns an energetic and urgent emphasis, and a nostalgic longing for a time when the United States was a Christian nation ruled by goodly people and values.[82] But the series also contains the contradictions of its forebears. LaHaye and Jenkins hedge their indictments of capitalism, allowing them both to support capitalism with enthusiasm while emphatically protesting individual capitalists. The authors differentiate between capitalism as a means of distributing resources, and individuals such as bankers—especially international financiers—who have used "the system" to their own selfish ends. Hence, the *Left Behind* novels, like the Farmer's Alliance a century ago, can suggest the creation of cooperative networks independent of the capitalist elite without venturing into Marxism or challenging core social values. The *Left Behind* series, despite its hostility toward "the system," still tends to describe itself as a collection of personalities centered on Antichrist and his CEO, Satan, rather than as a fundamentally unjust amalgamation of social structures.

This "ironic focus on the individual," as Kazin points out, marks one of the reasons populist movements have appealed to so many people without ever changing their social realities too radically.[83] Nevertheless, populist movements have proven remarkably effective at addressing the anxieties of those Americans who apprehend cultural change with alarm. Raising suspicions against wealthy bankers and intellectuals and valorizing the "common man," populist movements have historically deployed a "language of hope," as Kazin calls it, reimagining the world with an urgent desire to change it.[84] Movements deploying the language of populism have indeed brought about modest change, but not before their grander visions have been co-opted—and confiscated—by other organizations, often political parties.[85] Despite the seemingly unavoidable reality of co-optation, the populist imagination has also served another important function: to empower individuals with a sense of understanding changing times and with it the hope that life remains meaningful. The *Left Behind* novels play such a role, appealing to economic, political, and, most important, existential concerns.

The populist language of LaHaye and Jenkins encourages believers to grapple with forces that would otherwise seem outside their control. It appeals to the anxieties of prophecy believers concerning the spread of global capitalism, the withdrawal of religion from public life, the spiraling growth of new technologies, rampant immorality, and the general movement toward globalization. It also serves to accommodate prophecy believers to the realities of a rapidly changing world, along with motivating them to undertake changes. But the religious imperatives of the *Left Behind* series, along with a related sense of nostalgia, would ostensibly appear to undermine the ability of the authors to motivate believers to undertake sustained, structural action against what they perceive as social evils. The populist language of the *Left Behind* novels maintains a tension between the needs of individuals and a desire to bring about more profound changes. Ultimately, the series stumbles along the faultline created by such tension, alternately encouraging readers to engage the world, while at the same time complaining much about structural problems without offering anything more than the hope of miraculous interventions when pressed for solutions.

Put differently, populist language—undergirded by the individualist assumptions of conservative Protestant religiosity—becomes problematic when it encourages adherents to vent their frustrations without solving the underlying structural causes of human suffering. As such, populism can serve as an all-too-convenient vehicle for "letting off steam," but without structural reforms, the language of populism takes grassroots protest and renders it ineffectual. Part of this owes to the sense of nineteenth-century Populists (and many contemporary Americans who use populist language) that resources are not necessarily scarce. The economy is not a closed one but is instead imminently capable of producing still more consumable goods. As historian David M. Potter points out, expressions of American populism have often resembled millennial movements, shunting aside pressing social problems by hoping for an imminent solution through economic expansion, technological advancement, or any other mechanism that allows people to hope for a better tomorrow through quasi-miraculous deliverance without engaging the source of present ills.[86]

For a brief period, the language of populism found in the *Left Behind* novels may encourage believers to remain hopeful and active in the world. Dispensationalism, however, is a fundamentally pessimistic worldview. What happens, for example, when the economy does not expand or when technology cannot deliver higher standards of living or cures for new diseases—at least not fast enough? What happens when believers realize that resources are indeed finite? One option would involve social justice: in this case the quest for the more equitable distribution of resources. But this is not possible from the dispensational perspective. Only an infusion of energy from outside the economy can salvage the human experiment. The world is doomed without Jesus. Only His imminent, miraculous return can save the world from its serious problems whether environmental, social, or economic. Evangelical political activity stems from a desire to maintain or even expand the ranks of the saved. But it also takes the form of a despair which is neither an absence nor a renunciation but rather an active, expansive sense of pessimism concerning the ability of human societies to save themselves without supernatural help. Finally, those who advocate social justice—who attempt to solve global problems ethically and not supernaturally—immediately come under suspicion. From the perspective of the *Left Behind* series, economic systems, new technologies, and even religions, while at times useful, ultimately become false idols standing in place of the only one who can restore balance and return humankind to a time of peace and plenty. Anyone or anything that attempts to supplant the salvific role of Jesus reeks of Antichrist.

Conclusion

In this chapter I suggest that the rhetoric of prophecy belief fosters evangelical political activity not only on a more obvious level, but also as an attempt by prophecy writers to reshape the way believers view their world, winning the "battle for the mind," as Tim LaHaye calls it. Yet it would seem that prophecy writers have encouraged political involvement, despite their own theological injunctions against such entanglements. Dispensationalism—the philosophy of salvation history I detailed in the previous chapter—discourages involvement in "the world." Nevertheless, LaHaye and Jenkins appear to have found a way around the limitations of prophecy belief and have developed rhetorical strategies for winning the hearts and minds of Americans during the "pretribulation tribulation."

LaHaye and Jenkins have, in effect, hurled a brick (or a series of bricks) through what Susan Harding calls the "post-millennial window," opening up a space for political activity this side of the Rapture. Nevertheless, they retain the knowledge that human action cannot save the world, but believers can help create a culture more favorable to their beliefs, making it easier for them to retain their evangelical identity and win more souls for Christ before the *real* Tribulation arrives. After all, if humanists have seized control of the country through insidious techniques of mental manipulation, should not clever believers be able to fight back using the same tactics? Tim LaHaye certainly thinks so. His politics may take more obvious turns, but his pre–*Left Behind* writings indicate that he believes future political battles will be won or lost by the way people imagine their world, long before they reach the ballot box. If humanists have filled the media—and, by the extension, the hearts and minds of everyday people—with their propaganda, it is up to believers to offer countermeasures, to engage "the battle for the mind." And the authors have found no better means to wage their imaginative campaigns against their humanist adversaries than through the suggestive pages of their best-selling *Left Behind* novels, texts which utilize the vehicle of prophecy belief to suggest how evangelicals can reverse the humanist tide and defend their evangelical values and identities.

Prophecy belief taps into the anxieties many Americans feel vis-à-vis the rapid technological, economic, and cultural changes experienced since the advent of the twentieth century. Despite obvious advances in recent years toward a more activist stance, however, an "ironic focus on the individual" continues to hamper the efforts of prophecy believers to make a sustained difference in their world. In this sense the apocalyptic language of the *Left Behind* novels resembles that of nineteenth-century Populism, organizing discontent at the grassroots level with limited prospects for bringing about meaningful changes. Put differently, LaHaye and Jenkins not only suggest ways to defeat the humanist menace; they may also drown discontents in apocalyptic language, neutralizing such concerns by reducing them to questions of individual moral failures rather than attributing them to structural ills. Using the language of populism, the *Left Behind* series appeals to basic human discontents in the Information Age, but may render them ineffectual, *perhaps even exacerbating underlying tensions.* Unlike the basically innocuous policies of their nineteenth-century predecessors, the *Left Behind* novels also advocate a politics by omission—a blessed despair that awaits miraculous intervention.

Thus, a third, subtler form of political rhetoric exists in the *Left Behind* novels. Prophecy belief cultivates attitudes toward contemporary life. Such attitudes, while not overtly political, still have profound political implications. Apocalyptic literature, we must recognize, always features a political dimension. The *Left Behind* novels contain not only the more obvious forms of political activity, as this chapter has discussed—

both in terms of policy pronouncements and subtler forms of rhetorical suasion—but the novels also contain elements that are potentially more elusive and problematic than even the aforementioned methods might indicate. Dispensational prophecy belief, even the relatively activist version found in the *Left Behind* novels, invariably contains the seeds of despair.

On one level, the novels may encourage believers to sort out the uncertainties in their lives, encouraging them to make sense of what often seem like chaotic cultural developments. This theme—by now a familiar one in this text—is that of accommodation. One finds another strong thread in the *Left Behind* novels, however—especially the final ones—that promotes a reactionary response to contemporary culture along with a desperate quest for absolutes and certainties that is anything but inconsequential. This attitude of despair may, in the final analysis, represent the novels' most potent influence on contemporary American culture. In apocalyptic narratives such as the *Left Behind* series, one is either "with us or against us." Dispensational prophecy belief, taken to its logical conclusion, eliminates the middle ground. In the End, we must all choose sides, something not always practical in an increasingly interconnected world in which those sides are often ill defined. Protagonists, ultimately, cannot challenge the root causes of evil in society; they can only treat the symptoms and hope for miraculous intervention. This attitude, what one might call a politics of fatalism or despair—along with the many ways prophecy believers are already too intertwined with modernity to escape it—form the cornerstones of the remaining chapters.

3

The Emergence of the
Network Culture/Beast System

This recent tragedy [9/11] will be used by many as an excuse to give "Big Brother" type enthusiasts an excuse to strip the coveted personal freedoms enjoyed by Americans to allow in the name of "national security" the right to impose more government restrictions on us. . . . The American people will trade personal freedom for national safety, setting the stage for a "one world order" governed by you know who.[1]

—Tim LaHaye, "The Prophetic Significance of Sept. 11, 2001"

I am convinced that the technological developments of the last half-century are creating conditions for a revolution as profound and far reaching as the industrial revolution. Information and telematic technologies are recasting the very social, political, economic, and cultural fabric of life. . . . What is emerging is a new *network culture* whose structure and dynamics we are only beginning to fathom.[2]

—Mark C. Taylor, *The Moment of Complexity*

Within the economy of speculative theology, death does not discredit God but is actually the climax of divine self-realization. Through a kenotic process, God's transcendence becomes an immanence in which the divine is *totally* present here and now. . . . When there is nothing beyond the sign, image is all.[3]

—Mark C. Taylor, "Discrediting God"

Infernal Security

September 11, 2001 had no direct prophetic significance, Tim LaHaye tells us, yet he believes that world leaders responded to the tragedy much as they would to an event of much larger magnitude, something like the Rapture. During the Rapture, millions, if not a billion or more Christians will suddenly vanish when they go "to meet Christ in the air." Those left behind will clamor for answers and a sense of stability. They will seek a "return to normalcy" as President Harding once phrased it, but like the crowds he addressed, weary of global conflict, they will not find it. A charismatic figure will nevertheless emerge from almost total obscurity to charm the world and gain its confidence, encouraging people to believe that they, and not the departed, represent God's chosen few. "We must disarm," he will say, "we must empower the United Nations, we must move to one currency, and we must become a global village."[4] He will require emergency powers for his idealistic plans. Political leaders under pressure from impatient citizenries will acquiesce. Under the guise of benevolent dictatorship he will bind the world together as never before, uniting governments, economies, currencies, and religions to form his *Beast system*. Only when his plans have been laid in stone will many realize his true identity and tire of his repressive culture of surveillance and total control. But it will be too late. There will be no escape from the Beast.

The apocalyptic scenario deployed in the *Left Behind* novels has changed surprisingly little since Cyrus I. Scofield, Clarence Larkin, and other early twentieth-century dispensationalists described its basic contours.[5] Key players have changed over the years, corresponding with geopolitical and cultural shifts—to be sure. The basic framework of dispensationalism, however, has remained remarkably steady. Thus, while the details have changed over the past several decades, the more gifted prophecy writers have demonstrated an uncanny knack for matching the dispensational scenario with current events, rising to prominence through their ability to render newspaper headlines and long-term cultural trends meaningful within a prophetic framework. Such writers identify what their readers find most problematic about modernity, revealing evil where others see only circumstance, and illuminating a conspiratorial order of demonic powers that others view as the spontaneous—if not necessarily random—expression of complicated forces.

The list of notable contemporary prophecy writers begins with Hal Lindsey, of course, who popularized the arcane ideas of his dispensationalist teachers at Dallas Theological Seminary in the 1970's, becoming an instant superstar among prophecy believers. Tim LaHaye and Jerry Jenkins attained Lindsey's lofty heights of popularity in the 1990's with their remarkable aptitude for translating amorphous and complicated cultural developments into a language of personal and cultural wickedness familiar to evangelicals. They have transformed potentially meaningless information and uncertainty into a knowing recognition of good and evil only available to those granted the gift of discernment.[6] With God, believers become privileged knowers, carrying answer keys to the bewildering events of the world's last days. Without God, however, one lacks the ability to see Satan's machinations for what they really are, making it almost inevitable that one will become trapped in Antichrist's technological webs.

The emergence of the network culture may seem like a logical consequence of the development of global capitalism, for example, but to prophecy believers it represents the work of Antichrist. The world is rushing headlong into disaster, according to such views. The explosive growth of new information technologies, free trade agreements, corporate mergers, and an expanded role for the United Nations will indeed carry profound consequences whether for good or for ill, but prophecy believers *know* that such developments will only play into the long-simmering plans of Satan. Moreover, peace initiatives, notably in the Middle East between Israel and her Arab neighbors, have come under special prophetic censure. The Antichrist will, after all, deceive the world by bringing a false peace to the turbulent Middle East. The road to hell, it seems, is indeed paved with good intentions, at least according to the *Left Behind* series.

This chapter explores what cultural theorists Manuel Castells and Mark C. Taylor have called the "network culture," briefly framing the economic and cultural conditions to which prophecy writers have adapted their enduring if subtly shifting apocalyptic scenarios. I begin with a somewhat abstract discussion of the network culture and networks, before discussing the Internet and its brief history to help make the notion of network culture more palpable. I then discuss what LaHaye and Jenkins consider the rise of the Beast system, demonstrating that they share many observations in the *Left Behind* novels—albeit on a mythological and decidedly pessimistic level—with secular and more sophisticated cultural critics. While the latter believe contemporary developments signal the emergence of the network culture, for example, LaHaye and Jenkins instead recognize the machinations of Antichrist and the arrival of his dreaded Beast system. The final section shows how the *Left Behind* protagonists respond to the network culture/Beast system, building elaborate counternetworks of resistance that increasingly come to resemble, ironically, those of Antichrist.

Nodes and Hubs: The Emergence of the Network Culture

The network culture began to emerge just after World War II. Decentralized and global, the "system" appeared less a monolithic enterprise operated by a secret cabal wielding total control—always the favorite of conspiracy theorists—and instead developed a more complicated structure based in networks. The transformation did not occur instantly, of course. Just as the Cold War appeared most prominent, a new order began to take shape, reflected in everything from art and architecture, to economies and national governments less dependent upon industrial production and more geared toward information processing. Although such factors have become so intertwined as to discourage analysis based upon an assumed determinism of any one aspect, technology, especially advances in information processing, has proven a key player in the development of network culture. Such transformations, however, have required more than a technological capacity; they have also required favorable social and political factors to make use of new information technologies. Technology did not bring about the emergence of network culture, but it did allow long-simmering tendencies within various aspects of Western culture to accelerate their development and merge synergistically with related strands.[7]

The result cannot be contained by the dual Cold War understandings of wealth and power as concentrated either in centrally planned state economies (Soviet Union and satellite countries) or capitalist systems propelled by industrialists and entrepreneurs (United States and "Western" economies). Something more complicated and pervasive has emerged. Manuel Castells, in offering five points to describe what he calls the "Information Technology Paradigm," also hits many of the key characteristics of the network culture—or, as he prefers to call it, the network society. First, Castells argues that new information technologies "act on information," making information the most valuable raw material for postindustrial economies. This means that information as a commodity and the subsequent processing of information assume primary significance in the network society.[8]

Second, Castells notes that technology (and, by inference, information) has become pervasive in its influence, shaping "all processes of our individual and collective existence."[9] Technologies do not determine contemporary life, Castells adds, but do influence it to a great extent. Third, networks, according to Castells, continue to grow and evolve into ever greater levels of complexity and pervasiveness, with definite benefits for those inside such networks and disadvantages for those outside. Persons and cultures "wired-in" to the global economy, for example, benefit, while those left behind suffer. Moreover, Castells believes that the "switchers"—those who control media empires and the flows of finance capital—concentrate power in the network culture, as they determine who shares the benefits of new technologies and who does not.[10]

Fourth, networks, in order to sustain themselves and grow, must remain flexible. As Castells puts it, "What is distinctive to the configuration of the new technological paradigm is its ability to reconfigure, a decisive feature in a society characterized by constant change and organizational fluidity."[11] The ability to remain flexible, or to create additional flexibility, also enhances the exercise of power, although Castells adds a caveat, writing that "flexibility could be a liberating force, but also a repressive tendency if the rewriters of the rules are always the powers that be."[12] Flexibility and disorder, in other words, create tremendous opportunities for those able to tolerate the ambiguities of contemporary life, especially those who thrive on such upheavals. In addition, I must mention the organizational logic of network culture, although Castells does not include it among his five points. Nevertheless, Castells devotes much of his book, *The Rise of the Network Society,* to the discussion of organizational questions, thus it seems logical to mention it here. Basically, Castells notes that rigid hierarchies have given way to more flexible, *decentralized* networks, since the latter are inherently more flexible and responsive to rapidly changing conditions.[13]

Fifth, technologies tend to converge. Castells writes that "micro-electronics, telecommunications, opto-electronics, and computers are all well-integrated into information systems."[14] Additionally, one can infer from Castells's discussion of the convergence of technologies that information networks themselves tend to converge, ultimately participating, to use the example of the individual networks that have together formed the Internet, in a World Wide Web.[15] Finally, Castells notes the more concrete example of corporate megamergers, a phenomenon familiar to even casual observers of the financial pages. The proliferation of new information technologies, along with the loosening of rules by regulatory agencies, has encouraged such developments.[16]

Along with Castells, Mark C. Taylor makes the emerging network culture a focal point of his work, briefly describing it as "a revolution as profound and far reaching as the industrial revolution. Information and telematic technologies are recasting the very social, political, economic, and cultural fabric of life."[17] Taylor's description may strike one as breathless hyperbole; after all, we can observe historically the significance of the Industrial Revolution(s) from afar, a luxury which the present situation does not permit. Nevertheless, we can see indications of profound transformations all around us. The collapse of the Berlin Wall and the disintegration of communism in Eastern Europe provide dramatic examples. For decades the emerging network culture had eroded the symbolic supports upon which the Wall had been built. Networks, Taylor suggests, carrying their payloads of information across the border, had already undermined the Wall, making its fall anticlimactic from an analytical standpoint—an indication of the emergence of network culture but not an event that in itself hastened the fall of communism.[18]

Now that we know—in the abstract—what network culture is, we must ask "what is a network?" Networks, simply put, embody the logic of network culture. A network is a *specific mode of interaction* among decentralized, constituent parts that together form the network. A network does not have a central core that dictates its operations as more hierarchical systems have.[19] Such avoidance of centralization enhances its survival. Whereas a hierarchical system becomes vulnerable if its core comes under attack or collapses, a network can sustain itself because its parts—often called "nodes"—form the network through their own interactions. Order emerges not by fiat, but through the spontaneous interactions of interconnected nodes that resemble a web. If one part of the web gets destroyed, alternate paths will still be available.[20] Whether one speaks of telecommunications networks, transportation networks, or even interpersonal networks, a central point is not required for the successful operation of the network.[21]

But how, one might ask, have such networks developed? What is their *purpose*? Neither question has a straightforward answer. Networks do not appear to have developed by design, and those who envisioned protonetworks probably did not know just how pervasive they would become. One could speak in terms of *function*, but *purpose* proves a troublesome category, especially since networks have transcended their original designs. For all practical purposes, then, networks have "self-organized"—more products of chance than intelligent design.[22]

Taylor, borrowing insights from complexity theory, believes that networks form at the "tipping point," "far from equilibrium." Simply put, the tipping point represents the moment when a culture straddles the line between rampant, destructive disorder, and a moment of creativity that feeds upon unrest and allows new possibilities to emerge. Such moments foster growth, so long as cultures do not become either too rigid, resisting change and seeking equilibrium, or too chaotic, embracing change faster than they can accommodate it.[23] They must negotiate a delicate balance far from equilibrium. The *Left Behind* novels, to name a particularly germane example, attempt to negotiate this tension and transform cultural discomforts and uncertainties into an invigorated form of popular evangelicalism. The advent of the network culture represents a transformative moment for prophecy believers. Too much or too little willingness to change may result in the loss of their cultural identity.

The Internet represents perhaps the most universal and easily recognized example of the network culture. Thus, a very brief discussion of the Internet follows, both because LaHaye and Jenkins feature the Internet prominently in their novels, *and* because the Internet (or the World Wide Web in its most recent and popular manifestation) serves as a convenient metaphor for understanding networks. The Internet appeared almost as a postscript to mid-twentieth century geopolitical and economic developments. It came about not because someone envisioned e-mail and the dot.com boom several decades ago.[24] Rather, it gained its initial impetus because American defense officials realized that hierarchical, centralized systems might prove vulnerable in the event of attack or might fail at a critical moment due to hardware, software, or human error. If the center collapsed, the effects might domino throughout the system. A strike at a critical operations center might disable defensive capabilities. Hence, American defense officials recognized the tactical significance of a decentralized communications network capable of linking strategic sites, or nodes, with less risk of interruption. ARPANET (Advanced Research Projects Agency Network), as it became known, ultimately linked thousands of computers in a network with no control center. Blocks of information could be broken up into "packets" and transmitted from node to node, which the receiving computers would then reassemble according to the transmitted protocols. If one node was destroyed, the packets would simply find another path. If the receiving computers detected missing packets, replacements would be forwarded.[25]

The use of ARPANET was initially reserved for the military and scientific communities (especially scientists working on military projects). A number of related networks soon emerged, however, allowing scholars not involved in military or scientific research to benefit from ARPANET technology. Still, ARPANET and its offshoots excluded many computer enthusiasts and even researchers, as the scope of the networks remained quite limited.[26] The task of building a more democratized communications network fell to "hackers," then known not so much as virulent anarchists but rather as computer professionals and enthusiasts, who found ingenious solutions for tapping into network resources.[27]

Fueled by the invention of the modem in 1978—a device that allowed computers to connect to each other using telephone lines—alternative networks sprang up that utilized the logic of networks, if not their underlying infrastructure.[28] Known as CMC, or computer-mediated communication, this process of linking individual computers using modems and telephone connections began humbly.[29] Initially, CMC took the form of simple messaging (e.g., e-mail) between individual users but soon developed into a more complicated system of electronic bulletin boards. Instead of dialing other computers on a person-to-person basis, users connected to remote computers which housed bulletin boards. Users could read their contents, post messages, and interact with other users.[30]

The network infrastructure that began as ARPANET closed in February 1990, only to be replaced by NSFNET or the National Science Foundation Network. In April 1995, NSFNET, too, succumbed to its limitations and the Internet—assisted by protocols that enhanced compatibility among individual networks—emerged in the form of the World Wide Web, which made a comprehensive, interactive network possible. Inspired by the impressive yet unrealized dreams of the 1970's programmer Ted Nelson, the World Wide Web allowed the integration of private networks into a loose, largely unregulated conglomeration. The protocol languages of HTML (Hypertext Markup Language), and HTTP (Hypertext Transfer Protocol), permitted the encoding and transfer, respectively, of information across the world.[31] With the further development of sophisticated web browsers, users could visualize and experience cyberspace through multimedia interfaces, making the World Wide Web an even more impressive, interactive communications network.[32]

Transcending its origins as a Cold War experiment designed to safeguard defense communications in the event of a nuclear assault, the Internet/World Wide Web included by the year 2000, among other things, plenty of shopping, religion, gambling, adult entertainment, and even on-line education.

One can see that the Web provides an almost perfect example of network logic. Awareness of network imperatives has spread beyond the Web, however, and into many aspects of everyday life. Physicist Albert-László Barabási also settles on the Web as a convenient extended metaphor, but his research indicates that network logic can potentially describe the interactions of almost any system.[33] According to Barabási, categories as diverse as Hollywood actors, intercellular communications, the interlocking nature of corporate boards of directors, and even the spread of religious beliefs follow a networking logic. To form a network, power and importance must be decentralized and distributed throughout the network. Again, meaning and power emerge in the network culture not because of a core command structure, but through the interactions of the nodes that constitute the networks.

Nodes are not inherently important, Barabási reminds us, but gain influence by their connectedness. A particularly well-connected node that influences the behavior of smaller nodes becomes a "hub." Just as airlines use a hub system to distribute air traffic, hubs form in networks when certain nodes become especially well-integrated into the network vis-à-vis other nodes. To obtain employment it helps to know a person with "hub" status in interpersonal relationships. Moreover, especially well-networked individuals are more likely to propagate trends such as consumer preferences in music and clothing. Unhappily, "hubs" can also spread epidemic diseases faster than less well-connected nodes. Using the example of the Internet, certain hubs dominate on-line traffic. America On-Line gets more "hits" than a personal website, for example, because America On-Line has more "links." Internet traffic, just like traffic in any network, follows a "directed" pattern from hubs to smaller nodes. Networks may be decentralized, but they still contain points of convergence that wield significant influence.[34]

One can also find numerous examples of the phenomenon Barabási describes among evangelicals. Pat Robertson, host of the "700 Club" television program, interviews celebrities who offer their testimonials of faith with the obvious goal of convincing viewers to follow their example. Similarly, the *Left Behind* series contains constant references to the high status of its protagonists. Ivy-League educated characters work alongside economists, engineers, computer technicians, and airline pilots in the elite Tribulation Force. LaHaye and Jenkins imply that if such high-status "hubs" can accept the evangelical message, ordinary people ought to as well. Finally, even the apostle Paul, who played an instrumental role in popularizing Christianity, may have enjoyed some of his evangelizing success due to his privileged status as a network hub with many social links.[35] In sum, ideas, religious or otherwise, propagate if they are adopted by influential persons who act as hubs. The ideas will then spread, according to Barabási, in a directed manner throughout the individual's social network, which consists largely of lesser nodes which link to the larger hub.

The same network logic that allows the rapid spread of ideas, religious or otherwise, however, also makes networks vulnerable to seemingly inconsequential threats. The global economic network, for example, was threatened by the seemingly minor failure of Thai banks in 1997. The collapse soon cascaded and led to the Asian currency crisis of the late 1990's, a financial panic that debased the Japanese yen and even rocked the Dow Jones Index on October 27, 1997.[36] The failure of an obscure currency such as the Thai baht shook the global economy because the damage occurred in a sensitive area, setting off cascading failures.[37]

Moreover, hackers—understood here not as Web pioneers but rather as stereotypical electronic anarchists—can also use network pathways to interrupt or even shut down portions of the Web by targeting critical nodes. Networks, despite a design that enhances stability, can be threatened if enough critical hubs fall under attack. If one hub—however large—is removed, the network will adapt and reroute communications around the damaged hub. If enough critical hubs are damaged or destroyed, however, the network faces cascading failures which spread throughout the network. Cascading failures represent what Barabási considers the "Achilles' heel" of decentralized networks. If a hub, however inconspicuous, becomes compromised in a sensitive area, the network will struggle to regain stability.[38]

Barabási points out that a completely decentralized network, in which all nodes have an equal number of links—a random network—remains an idealistic dream. Although industrial hierarchies seem to have transformed into more flexible, lateral forms of management, the global networks still have several soft spots. An attack on America On-Line can be deflected or rerouted, but a coordinated assault on the communications hubs may shut down the World Wide Web, if only for a brief but cata-strophically expensive moment. The same networks that promise stabil-ity, can, under the right circumstances, undermine everything connected to the network. Such is the promise and peril of networks. They are de-centralized and less vulnerable to overt assaults, but clever tactical inter-ference can grind the entire system to a halt—at least temporarily.[39]

Despite such dire possibilities, the advent of network culture offers tremendous benefits to those who know how to use network resources to their advantage. The rules of global capital, after all, are not suspended in the network culture. The "rich tend to get richer" due to their superior positioning and understanding of the changing models of organization.[40] Thus, despite the Internet's democratizing potential, it is not a magical technology that dissolves injustice. Nevertheless, even those who choose to oppose such developments benefit from an understanding of networks. As the fundamental organizational logic of contemporary life, networks distribute information and influence to those wired into them. The Inter-net and the concomitant logic of networks increasingly pervade people and institutions so extensively that "de-linking"—removing oneself or one's cultural enclave from the network culture—only intensifies mar-ginal status.

Implications of Network Culture and the Crisis of the Real

As the previous section indicates, LaHaye and Jenkins are not the only observers who hold apocalyptic beliefs (at least in terms of believing in the advent of a new order of rapid change) vis-à-vis contemporary cul-ture. Scholars from across the humanities and social sciences have noted with profound interest the rise of network culture and the changes it has wrought. Sociologist Daniel Bell, focusing on global economies, calls the transformation from societies of industrial production to those domi-nated by *tertiary,* service-oriented economies, "the coming of post-indus-trial society."[41] Castells notes many of the same phenomena as Bell does in his 1976 observations, but also explores in greater depth the cultural consequences of the transition to a postindustrial, or informational soci-ety, especially the potential impact of network society on notions of cul-tural identity.[42] Finally, Taylor, reflecting on the observations of French theorist Jean Baudrillard, among others, contemplates how the rapid changes associated with information culture—or, as Taylor prefers, network culture—will affect persons and cultures and their ability to adapt to rapidly changing conditions. Cultures unable to make the necessary adaptations will suffer or perhaps even perish, Taylor believes. He writes, "Those who are too rigid to fit into rapidly changing worlds become obsolete or are driven beyond the edge of chaos to destruction."[43] Taylor's description aptly fits the predicament of contemporary prophecy believers.

Network culture impacts the contemporary world in a number of ways significant to this study. For example, many aspects of contemporary culture, in a sense, are digitizing—reduced to bits of data—right before our eyes. Recording engineers place intricate symphonies on aluminum discs containing nothing but tiny pits denoting ones and zeroes. Analogously, geneticists attempt to unravel the puzzles of human life by tracing our characteristics to simple chemicals found in infinitely variable combinations along DNA strands. Telemarketers store survey data and purchase records, building databases that suggest our personalities and product preferences. Credit reports have become arguably more important than our personal reputations, as such records determine our ability to obtain credit and loans, and, in some cases, employment.[44] Information, as Castells points out, becomes the most important commodity in the network culture. Taylor, in fact, takes the matter a step further and claims that everything, including humanity, is always in-*formation*.

Taylor's pun suggests several things about the network culture. First, information has become central to our understanding of the world and each other. With the increasingly anonymous nature of contemporary life, we often know others—at least initially—only by the information they or a third-party provides us. Second, the network culture with its fast-flowing information brings forth the possibility of rapid and profound change. Like high waves pounding across a sandy beach, information continuously erodes and reshapes our understandings of ourselves and our cultures. The network culture demands dynamism and flexibility. Permanence is not one of its traits. Not surprisingly, some groups feel "left behind" when their cultural moorings are swept away in the ceaseless flows of information.[45] If information increasingly comes to define identity, cultural groups that choose to resist must seize control of their own self-definitions, in-*forming* themselves—in effect, damming the information they receive from the mainstream. Walls may be ineffective means of protection against the network culture, but resistant groups must still find ways to filter information, keeping enemies out.[46]

Resistant groups must do much more than keep their enemies outside, however. Controlling the enemies within—the seductive voices of modernity—may prove an even more difficult task. It is not necessarily helpful, that is, to depict a rigid dichotomy between "inside" and "outside" when considering the cultural impact of network culture on communities such as prophecy believers. Prophecy believers are already part of the network culture. The enemy, in a sense, is already inside of them. It is not only a matter of filtration, in other words, since information already infiltrates the ranks of prophecy believers, but it is also a question of recognition and integration. Prophecy believers must find ways to interpret and assimilate the dissonant information in their midst without losing too much of their evangelical identity.[47] To this end, LaHaye and Jenkins attempt to help believers sort out the informational glut by offering their readers reassurance and reaffirmation through the examples of protagonists, who successfully navigate the perilous straits of the network culture.

But such a task is enormously difficult. Specifically, LaHaye and Jenkins remind their readers that no matter how chaotic things become, they are, ultimately, not a product of this world, but rather of Christ. It is no coincidence that prophecy writers often speak of a return to solid foundations. Believers strive to build their lives upon "the solid rock of Christ." It is precisely this solid rock, or firm foundation, that the network culture lacks. Life in the network culture requires a measure of trust. But how does one know whom or what to trust? Deception abounds. We lack a foolproof, unquestioned standard against which to measure the value of information. The loss of this unquestioned standard is a side-effect of network culture that not only permits dynamic change but also unsettles people used to taking such matters for granted. Without firm foundations, lacking anything by which to measure reality with total confidence, how can we avoid deception? What, beneath all of the information we receive, do we allow to *inform* us? What, ultimately, is *real*?[48]

"Real" can assume multiple meanings, but for the sake of clarity I will list several examples. Traveling to a distant locale may seem more authentic than watching a television documentary or viewing a slide show. Also, individuals may prefer "face-to-face" dialogue rather than more obviously mediated forms of communication such as e-mail. More significantly, cultural practices and beliefs such as those associated with religions may appear more "real"—that is, more valid foundations upon which to build shared values—than their secular alternatives, at least prior to the onslaughts of the network culture. Analogously, even currencies have begun to lose their centrality as unquestioned symbols of value. Although currency rests upon any number of abstractions now disconnected from perceived sources of inherent value such as precious metals, credit and debit cards move a step further. "Smart money," as the Master Card advertisements tell us, is fast and convenient. It flows much more quickly than its alternatives. Informational flows call into question the real, since what we consider real, along with its foundations, has been absorbed into the accelerating information streams of the network culture.[49] The rapid exchange of information provides the needed knowledge to keep the system moving, while it may also destroy or render mute local cultures, which, unlike abstract flows of information, remain fixed and local, much like the sandy beach pounded by high waves.[50]

The "real," in others words, potentially disappears into the flows of information which undermine its unquestioned foundations. As Castells notes, borrowing and extending the insights of cultural theorists Fredric Jameson and David Harvey, the disappearance of the "real" into an instantaneous and omnipresent network of information flows calls forth a crisis:

> *Timeless time belongs to the space of flows, while time discipline, biological time, and socially determined sequencing characterizes places around the world, materially structuring and destructuring our segmented societies.* Space shapes time in our society, thus reversing an historical trend: flows induce timeless time, places are time bounded.[51]

Put differently, the irresistible force of information overruns the immovable objects of what people have often taken for granted in their daily lives. The logic of global capital appears incompatible with the imperatives of "lived time," or the tendency of human communities to seek stability and firm foundations.

The crisis of the real also affects individuals, who come to be seen less as enfleshed bodies and more as what sociologist David Lyon calls "data-images"—amalgamations of credit reports, survey data, and consumer preferences stored in a decentralized network of computer databases.[52] Similar to the data "constructs" envisioned by cyberpunk novelist William Gibson two decades ago,[53] data-images increasingly come to represent individuals in the minds of government officials, creditors, and marketing agents. They project distinct personalities, aspirations, even sexual proclivities, based upon the available information. The individual—often empirically unavailable and costly to retrieve—increasingly takes a secondary role to data-images for resolving questions of proper identity.[54] It is no accident, then, that identity theft has become one of the most insidious and destructive forms of crime in the network culture. In the in-*formation* age, identity thieves treat the virtual person like the philosopher Jean Baudrillard's simulacrum—a representation that has become, for all practical purposes, more real than the original. When cultural changes have such far-reaching existential effects, religion is also implicated. Not surprisingly, LaHaye and Jenkins have responded to these challenges in their *Left Behind* novels with varying degrees of sophistication, as we will see in chapter 5. Meanwhile, it is safe to note that the authors attempt to recover a sense of firm foundations for their readers.

Taylor questions such a response on the part of LaHaye and Jenkins, noting critically that the "crisis of the real" and the seemingly inexorable logic of global capital have not prevented individuals and cultures from reaching back for secure foundations.[55] The quest for stability accelerates as the network culture increasingly ties technologies, economies, and cultures more closely together.[56] This does not necessarily lead to homogenization, Taylor tells us; if anything, it may lead to more complicated articulations of culture since no one can really know who is steering the ship, even if some passengers remain in first class. Nevertheless, cultures are built upon models of consensus, and as the network logic threatens to undermine consensus, movements emerge to reclaim the lost ground and form cultural islands in a turbulent stream of change. Contemporary evangelicals seek a language to articulate a sense of disconnectness along with an anxiety that their foundations are slipping away.

In sum, Castells and Taylor both regard the emergence of network culture as potentially problematic but nevertheless inevitable. For Castells, the danger looms that the inequalities inherent in industrial society will be passed in accelerated form to network society. Whether one speaks of financial *or* cultural goods, the rich may get richer, and the increasingly fluid and critical nature of information may make it easier for the few to concentrate and isolate it from the many.[57] Taylor, while noting such possibilities, appears more optimistic than Castells. Borrowing insights from complexity theory to explain network culture, Taylor views complexity as a way to explain a system that acts as a whole without totalizing. Such a system, Taylor notes, requires difference and contingency to survive and grow more complex, opening possibilities rather than simply closing them.[58] Nevertheless, difference as a valued aspect of culture remains in jeopardy if cultures refuse to make adequate accommodations to emerging networks and seek instead the stability of foundations, in effect, resisting themselves into obsolescence, or as Taylor puts it: *indifference.*[59]

As Castells suggests, the network culture, built on the backbone of accelerating developments in information technologies, poses a seemingly irreconcilable conflict between the flows of information and capital, and the lived time of individuals and cultures.[60] That is, although capital and information thrive upon instantaneity and omnipresence, cultures remain rooted in more basic understandings of time and space. I would modify Castells's inflection slightly, suggesting the difficulty lies less with a division between dynamic, global forces and virtually static, local ones. Instead, the difference appears as one of adequate adjustment. Local cultures continue to change, but the network culture changes still faster. The logic of network culture centers on instantaneity, which conflicts with the lived time and space of localities, disrupting social rhythms. As with many dualities in the network culture, distinctions begin to blur, and the network culture challenges individuals and cultures to adapt or be left behind.[61]

One World under Antichrist

LaHaye and Jenkins have good reason to tweak their understandings of the system—it just isn't what it used to be. The development of networks, along with the cultural influence networks have come to wield, has also caught the attention of the authors. Tim LaHaye, especially, seems to understand that even prophecy believers must either learn to adapt to emerging technological and cultural conditions or face irrelevance. LaHaye devotes considerable attention in his writings to the rise of the information society and the centrality of networks, also emphasizing the transition from hierarchical to decentralized modes of economic and social organization.[62] In *The Race for the 21st Century,* a venture into social forecasting reminiscent of Alvin Toffler's *Future Shock,* LaHaye writes approvingly of some aspects of network logic, "Having established my first network (the American Coalition for Traditional Values, which set up 435 congressional district pastor-chairmen for the 1984 election), I was fascinated by this futuristic concept."[63] LaHaye, of course, maintains profound suspicion of the network culture, as we will see, but he recognizes that evangelicals, too, must adjust their operational tactics.

LaHaye and Jenkins's mythological account of the rise of Antichrist and his totalitarian system follows a time-honored dispensational formula—for the most part. Antichrist fits the usual criteria: he is young, handsome, articulate, bright, witty, unusually conscientious, and driven to forge world peace; and, most important, he possesses a charisma that makes him much more appealing than the sum of his already formidable traits. Moreover, he traces his lineage to Italy, the heartland of the ancient Roman Empire. Antichrist, among other things, must revive the Roman Empire, keeping his actions commensurate with the prophecies of Revelation. Finally, Antichrist must consolidate his power through the deceitful use of his personal gifts. He is a counterfeit, albeit a convincing one, who feigns omniscience, omnipresence, and even omnipotence—all attributes reserved for God. Using virtual reality technologies and even sleight-of-hand magic tricks, Antichrist attempts to dupe a credulous public through visible signs and wonders.

Antichrist cannot accomplish his tasks alone, however. His False Prophet serves as his aide and spiritual director, while Satan offers inspiration and later possesses the resurrected body of Antichrist after the latter is assassinated forty-two months into the Tribulation period. The false trinity of Satan, Antichrist, and False Prophet corresponds to the holy Trinity of God, Christ, and the Holy Spirit. Together the diabolic trio ushers in the Beast system, a development critical to their infernal success. The Beast system becomes for Antichrist a reliable structure that allows him to consolidate power and govern his kingdom more efficiently. Even Antichrist, it seems, recognizes the benefits of a rational bureaucracy.

The Beast system has several generic attributes which almost all prophecy writers describe. First, Antichrist must convince the world to adopt a one-world currency—a seemingly implausible development. In *Left Behind,* Cameron "Buck" Williams, speaking with his friend and long-time conspiracy theorist Dirk Burton, expresses incredulity at the idea of a one-world currency:

> "Too bizarre. Too impractical. Look what happened in the States when they tried to bring in the metric system. . . ."
>
> "I know, Cam. Your people thought you'd be paving the way for the Communists to take over if you made maps and distance markers easy for them to read. And where are your commies now?"[64]

LaHaye and Jenkins make an easy transition from one time-honored conspiracy theory—the alleged communist takeover—to another one with greater contemporary plausibility. In doing so, ironically, they not only discard the outmoded fear of a communist takeover, but also ridicule it in such a way as to make their current conspiracy musings appear more reasonable. Indeed, throughout the twentieth century, the possibility of a unified currency seemed a remote one, but recent developments, including the introduction of the Euro as a circulating currency in 2001, have made this long-time dispensational bugaboo more plausible.

Moreover, European countries have not been united in their support of the Euro. Some, including Great Britain, have cited economic grounds for their opposition, but cultural identity also plays an important role. The ability to stamp currency with a national insignia bears witness to a nation's independence and identity, with currency functioning as a symbol that a nation-state has some control over its ability to define cultural identity.[65] Prophecy writers have noted this connection; thus, it seems logical that since their narratives discuss cultural identity, they also focus on the issue of currency, and not simply for reasons of economic expediency. The ubiquitous concern with a unified, global currency one finds in prophecy literature suggests a pervasive anxiety among prophecy believers that national units, especially the United States, are surrendering their cultural identities to larger, faceless, and unaccountable entities, also permitting such external forces to shape values—in more than one sense.

Second, Antichrist urges world leaders to put aside petty political and cultural differences and unite in a one-world government, apparently to end many millennia of war and misunderstandings. Antichrist, however, does not act by fiat. His personal power, while quite extensive, is not always overt. He acts through persuasion and the manipulation of circumstances, enhancing his power precisely by not making it obvious. All of the important developments in *Left Behind*, in fact, occur because Antichrist convinces others to come up with *his* ideas.[66] Then, Antichrist "reluctantly" agrees. The unprecedented state of emergency triggered by the Rapture provides one example of Antichrist in action. He takes advantage of the crisis, providing a coordinated plan of action for an anxious and uncertain world. Antichrist stands all-too-prepared to seize the opportunity to promote his platform of unification as an answer to the global threat represented by the disappearance of over a billion people. The world must work together as never before. The problem, of course, is that the same system that promotes global cooperation also allows Antichrist to rapidly consolidate his power. Uncertainty, anxiety, and fear provide the ideal conditions for the rise of evil. Once Antichrist ascends to a position of total control, he considers any identity, any hint of disagreement, and any surge of particularity that denies his authority a threat worthy of immediate eradication. Tribulation-era believers must either face martyrdom or go into hiding.

Third, Antichrist values the importance of religion. Antichrist recognizes that religion plays a vital role in building political and cultural consensus, and he actively cultivates spirituality among his citizens. Specifically, he takes advantage of the twentieth-century ecumenical movements among the world's religions to promote greater cooperation, extracting elements common to all and discarding particularistic truth claims. A cultural Cuisinart of indistinct spirituality results, with a mix-and-match of religious symbols used to foster a cooperative spirit conducive to the development of Antichrist's kingdom.[67] Finally, False Prophet leads the Beast religion and directs worship of the Beast system initially, then later Antichrist himself. But beneath the vague symbolism communicants of the Beast religion worship not just a culture or a person but instead come to deify the technological and cultural processes coterminous with modernity.

LaHaye and Jenkins agree with their predecessors on the basic contours of the Beast system but differ on significant points. For decades, prophecy writers have produced cookbook-style approaches to the Apocalypse, with premeasured storylines ready to serve in formulaic plots. *Left Behind*'s Antichrist deviates from the script in ways I have already outlined, including his unprecedented technological savvy. Most important, however, Antichrist understands global capitalism, and he moves easily within the emerging network culture. Nicolae Carpathia, LaHaye and Jenkins's Antichrist, ascends through the patronage of the global capitalist elite, at least until he turns on them, too. He might be a product and partner of Satan, but international bankers have much to do with his ascendancy. After affirming his belief in "the power of money," Carpathia reveals to journalist and Tribulation Force operative Buck Williams— whom he still considers a loyalist—how he garnered the attention of international bankers and rose to prominence:

> I was a better than average businessman while still in school in Romania. I studied at night, many languages, the ones I needed to suc-

ceed. During the day I ran my own import-and-export business and made myself wealthy. But what I thought was wealth was paltry compared to what was possible. I needed to learn that. I learned it the hard way. I borrowed millions from a European bank, then found someone in that bank informed my major competitor what I was doing. I was defeated at my own game, defaulted on my loan, and was struggling.[68]

Carpathia, as a shrewd networker, nevertheless found an alternative source of finance capital and ruined his competitor. His actions, however, incurred a debt to the world's richest financier, the mysterious and elusive Jonathan Stonagal, who, Carpathia notes with admiration, wields genuine power.[69]

Keeping with his image, Carpathia rises not through an unimpeachable reputation or great personal wealth but through *debt*. "Debt" in German, for example, carries an ambivalent meaning. The German term *Schuld* can translate to "debt," but it also carries the overt connotation of "guilt." Antichrist, quite fittingly, ascends not through goodness but through a debt of guilt he cannot repay. Global capitalists serve as his chief backers and advisors. In fact, Carpathia names financial savvy as the most important criterion for membership in his world government. He seeks people "with good financial backgrounds" when assembling his cabinet of ten kings or regional rulers.[70] In ironic contrast to the sinner's guilt, or debt to God, Carpathia's debts are not forgiven, and his actions draw him into a tighter relationship with his mentor and chief backer, Satan. Carpathia assumes an enviable position among the global elite, but such debts, in the End, are hell to pay.

Carpathia, however, like any successful business executive, distributes his debts throughout the system. He extends favors to supporters, while doling out punishments to those who refuse his patronage. All of this requires a methodology to separate the goats from the sheep. Antichrist needs a system not only to communicate with and control his vast global holdings, but he also requires the means to track citizens and ascertain their degree of loyalty. The Beast system addresses such imperatives. Moreover, information and power must flow unimpeded through the interstices of Antichrist's networks. Nevertheless, in an age of corporate cost-consciousness, Antichrist, too, despite massive financial backing, must pay close attention to the bottom line. Ruling the world is quite expensive. Antichrist must devise a system that allows him to become a global tyrant on a budget. His infernal CEO, Satan, demands corporate accountability.

Antichrist wisely invests in advanced communications technologies which permit him to build his web of deceit. He builds his power not only by using technology to monitor and control his empire, but he also uses technological tools to foster a climate of *uncertainty*. After all, Antichrist's ultimate role in this grand drama is not to compel anyone to choose him or his system. Prophecy writers insist that individuals must exercise a free choice when selecting their existential identities. Antichrist can offer grand rewards or dire punishments, but the only way he can lure individuals away from Christ—hence earn the name "Antichrist"—is through deceptive trade practices. He must use the Beast system to accelerate not only the flow of information and power but also misinformation and deceit. His system fosters uncertainty by casting doubt on the "real" Christ, flooding the masses with more information than they can decipher, positioning himself as the default choice and the only "visible" god. The spiritual survival of those left behind requires faith in the unseen or even the absurd; Antichrist has no such prerequisites.

Despite an initial penchant for totalitarian rule, Antichrist quickly realizes that decentralization makes for more efficient leadership. LaHaye and Jenkins differ from their forebears in their implicit awareness of network imperatives. As I noted in the previous section, centralized systems of power—concentrated and obvious—remain vulnerable to assault. Decentralized systems, in which power is distributed throughout flexible networks, prove more responsive, adaptive, and less vulnerable to internal failure or external attack. This might explain the authors' move to decentralize the Beast system and shift its authority to ten regional kingdoms or nodal points in the network. Previous authors have tended to interpret the "ten-horned beast" of Revelation more narrowly as a ruler who emerges from a ten-member European Community. Supreme Potentate Nicolae Carpathia, however, while remaining true to his Roman origins, spreads power to ten distinct rulers, or subpotentates, across the globe. Literary imperatives force the authors to devote much attention to Carpathia, but smooth operation of the Beast system requires a distributed network that can recover from the assaults of the Tribulation Force.

One could explain such a turn in LaHaye and Jenkins's narrative as a reflection of post–Cold War global developments. Cold War prophecy writers had an easier time identifying evil. Typically Roman Catholic and vaguely communist, evil bore a more obvious face. LaHaye and Jenkins must still find evil within the contemporary world, since dispensational belief and the genre of prophecy fiction require it. But obvious centers of power are harder to find since the end of the Cold War. Reflecting global trends, Antichrist moves his headquarters from New York to New Babylon, rebuilding the ancient city in contemporary Iraq. Despite Carpathia's residency in New Babylon, other world regions, especially North America and Europe, retain their importance. The authors' usage of New Babylon, moreover, indicates not so much a geographical place as it does a metaphor referring to the attempts of humans to revel in the most abhorrent of sins, not the least among them an attempt to deify humanity, thereby usurping the centrality of God. New Babylon as such represents a network hub, even if decisive action typically occurs elsewhere. Evangelical audiences, along with the textual imperatives of an apocalyptic novel, however, require that evil have a more recognizable, individual face.

It seems doubtful that LaHaye and Jenkins possess an advanced knowledge of network theory, although LaHaye's published writings do demonstrate awareness, albeit on a popular level, of the changes associated with network culture. Nevertheless, LaHaye and Jenkins have succeeded to the extent they have been able to observe the complexity of geopolitical developments and reduce much of it to a simple, well-recognized formula. Such a simplified approach has helped the authors craft a broadly appealing, populist message. Their approach may also empower believers to grapple with an enemy they might otherwise fear. Yet the authors' simplified understanding of networks may prove problematic as well. As I discussed in chapter 2, evangelicals often reduce structural evils to a language of individual moral failure. Putting a name on what makes believers so uncomfortable may ease their anxieties for a season, but it may also complicate their adjustments to the emerging network culture and may even trigger counterproductive responses.

Problematic responses, ironically, may emerge from the attempts of believers to adjust to network imperatives. The balance between resistance/adjustment and an excessive resistance that becomes an end in itself remains a delicate one. To survive, believers must emulate aspects of the Beast system they deem fruitful. For example, even the evangelical resistance benefits from a decentralized approach, with the Tribulation Force often mirroring key organizational tactics of the Beast system. The Tribulation Force begins with a more hierarchical structure. As the Tribulation unfolds and Antichrist develops more sophisticated methods of control, however, believers must decentralize or perish. Effective resistance against the Beast system requires not only a more sophisticated articulation of the adversary but also a more mobile and flexible—and less vulnerable—style of opposition. LaHaye and Jenkins do appear to understand this. Economic, organizational, and even meteorological imperatives require Antichrist to build a system that is both leaner and meaner.[71] Successful resistance requires the Tribulation Force to adopt analogous tactics.

Such tactics also tend to ensnare believers deeper within Antichrist's web, however. To resist Antichrist's global network they must build their own webs. Webs, though, seldom remain isolated in the network culture. The possibility always exists that resisters will become so entangled that they will accept the imperatives of the Beast system as if by default. Resistance requires a relationship, on some level, to that which one resists. The overreliance of prophecy writers on technological tools, for example, has not gone unnoticed by academic readers of evangelical culture. Critics have impugned prophecy writers for making information technologies such important aspects of their narratives.[72] But do they have another choice? The problem is not whether one interacts with the network culture; it is precisely how one negotiates such relationships. Engagement carries risk, but escape is not a viable alternative for those left behind.

The Resistance of the Tribulation Force

Network culture is not necessarily original in many of its effects upon contemporary American life. Although the rise of network culture potentially affects a wider stratum with greater intensity than previous instigators of unrest, much can be learned from historical examples. A number of unsettled periods in American history have encouraged doomsday prophets to formulate and spread their troubling prognostications. Apocalyptic attitudes, however, have seldom been limited to a few intensely anxious souls. More commonly, such anxieties about the future have spread throughout American culture, periodically bringing forth what can best be described as a kind of halfhearted antimodernism.[73] Hardly wishing to reject American culture outright, those holding such antimodern attitudes have welcomed changes deemed beneficial while struggling against developments that threaten their settled ways of life. Prophecy believers, for example, want the best of *this* world, but they also harbor significant, lingering anxieties about the future. As I discussed in chapter 2, such anxieties concerning the future often overrun their banks in the traditional prophecy milieu and spill over into the mainstream, especially during times of crisis.

Historian Jackson Lears tracks a similar sense of cultural and personal restlessness that developed among many Americans in the late nineteenth century. Lears notes that a profound ambivalence arose among artists, literati, intellectuals, and middle-class Americans vis-à-vis the emerging world of bureaucratic capitalism. He characterizes the collective anxieties of such Americans as "antimodern." By "antimodern," Lears highlights ambivalence toward, although not outright rejection of, contemporary cultural developments.[74] His late nineteenth-century antimoderns, for example, enjoyed the newfound material comforts of the Victorian era, but also sensed that the cost of such comforts included a loss of their cherished illusions of the autonomous individual, along with dreams of an ultimately meaningful cosmos.[75] In this sense, Lears's nineteenth-century antimoderns share many similarities with contemporary prophecy believers.

Lears notes several factors that called forth the antimodern ethos of nineteenth-century Americans.[76] First, the workplace had become ever more numbing and impersonal. As Marx and Engels so famously observed, capitalism increasingly severed the link between workers and the fruits of their labors. Second, bureaucratic capitalism inserted a complicated, impersonal, and often unresponsive hierarchy between workers and managerial elites. Third, profound economic upheavals accompanied the transition from entrepreneurial forms of capitalism to the highly rationalized, bureaucratic forms. As the workplace became ever more alienating and impersonal, intellectuals and literati fantasized about the allegedly simpler days of yeoman farmers and craft workers. Fourth and perhaps most important, insights from the social sciences called into question notions of autonomous selves capable of free moral decisions. Anticipating the work of provocative twentieth-century evolutionary biologists and philosophers such as Richard Dawkins and Daniel Dennett, respectively, late nineteenth-century social scientists posited complex forces that determined many aspects of human behavior.[77] Determinisms of all sorts suggested that humans did not control their destiny, but instead acted according to manipulative external factors they only poorly understood, if at all.

In addition, such developments, along with the emerging field of Biblical criticism, called into question the validity of traditional Christianity, replacing collective dreams of an ultimately meaningful cosmos with moral imperatives that seemed groundless. Borrowing the terminology of the nineteenth-century German thinker Friedrich Nietzsche, Lears calls this condition "weightless culture." Lears writes, "A weightless culture of material comfort and spiritual blandness was breeding weightless persons who longed for intense experience to give some definition, some distinct outline and substance to their vaporous lives."[78]

This sense of unreality, Lears suggests, prompted anxious individuals to search for the grail of lost meaning and existential foundations. The resultant quests for meaning bore curious contradictions: intellectuals wrote passionately about medieval times, romancing their alleged simplicity and directness. They were violent times, to be sure, but the violence of the Middle Ages—in contrast to the subtler forms witnessed by the late nineteenth century—injected a meaning and purpose to humanity. Death and destruction, in other words, contributed to a sense of vitality. The warrior emerged as a much-valued archetype over against the leisured, bureaucratic office worker. Even more important, warriors took their fates into their own hands, leaving little ambiguity about friends or foes. In sum, Lears suggests that the more Victorian Americans saw themselves as "overcivilized" and powerless, the more they longed to reclaim such power and meaning—at least symbolically—through the image of the warrior.[79]

One finds analogous expressions of such tepid antimodernism mixed with a sense of risky adventurism in late twentieth-century science-fiction, especially productions dealing with the intersection of technology and the human self. Author William Gibson's characters, for example, are high-tech action heroes who work within the interstices of giant supercomputers, struggling, without much success, to reclaim a world more responsive to human needs. The protagonist of Gibson's 1984 cyberpunk novel *Neuromancer,* who is known simply as "Case," actually ends up getting used by one supercomputer against another supercomputer.[80] The sense one gets from this and Gibson's other two novels in his cyberspace trilogy is one of mild cynicism and romantic longing—precisely the traits that match Lear's sense of Victorian antimodernism. Not seeking to turn back, Gibson's protagonists face an inhuman future and must work with the tools of the enemy, ironically, to struggle against it. Their struggle, however, only traps them deeper within the technological machinations of the beast.

The late 1960's British serial, *The Prisoner,* provides an even better example of the antimodern spirit and an occasionally violent struggle against the future.[81] The protagonist, played by actor Patrick McGoohan (who also wrote and produced much of the series, both under his own name and a pseudonym), is a British secret agent who suddenly and inexplicably resigns. The agent, known to the audience only as "#6," is drugged and carried off to a remote seaside town called "The Village." The Village at first seems like a utopia where all needs are provided, and everyone lives in comfort and ease. Beneath its façade, however, The Village is a dystopia where the personal identities of its citizens are progressively stripped away by bureaucratic forces seeking to create a society of virtual automatons. Moreover, no one in The Village has a name, just a number. Number 6 struggles against his "Village" identity and faces a series of trials and tortures each week, contending with Village authorities to retain his personal identity. In the end he finally escapes—or so it seems—killing his masked oppressors to the tune of the Beatles' song, "All You Need is Love." As he reaches London and his old flat, however, the viewer recognizes, with some irony, that he never really escaped The Village at all. Like evangelical prophecy believers who dream of being raptured only to find themselves living in the tenuous world of the Tribulation, #6, whether he recognizes it or not, cannot escape the horrors of The Village so easily.

Left Behind—a hybrid evangelical prophecy/science-fiction/fantasy series of novels—features remarkably similar themes, with protagonists who alternately struggle to escape from and adapt to the network culture. The texts demonize the disorder that results as global trends threaten local cultures, including conservative evangelicalism. Yet characters in the *Left Behind* novels attempt to mount a successful resistance. Unlike the protagonists of previous prophecy novels who remained largely passive in the face of the Apocalypse, LaHaye and Jenkins create characters who find ways to survive and even prosper. They practice what historians have labeled "muscular Christianity," valorizing an active, virile, and occasionally violent activism that seeks to wrest meaning from the confusing morass of the network culture. Lears's description of late nineteenth-century antimodernism—save the reference to industrial capitalism—remains apt for LaHaye and Jenkins's armed resistance:

The fascination with pain of martial antimodernists was one of the early manifestations of an attempt to move beyond the pleasure principle of a democratic, industrial culture. It was a groping for transcendence, an effort to restore some superhuman dimension of meaning to the moral life. But because it was surrounded by spiritual confusion, its purpose remained vague and its denouement unsatisfying. Like other varieties of romantic activism, it often ended in a self-defeating quest for authentic selfhood.[82]

LaHaye and Jenkins's underground resistance movement forms among a handful of Chicago suburbanites who find themselves left behind after the Rapture. Coming from backgrounds deeply immersed in prophecy belief, they quickly realize their predicament. Assembling at the nondenominational New Hope Village Church in Mt. Prospect, Illinois, they form the "Tribulation Force," an all-purpose paramilitary organization, designed to disrupt Antichrist's networks during the fateful years of the Tribulation. The Tribulation Force, and by extension the authors, appears to understand that the rules of engagement have changed in the network culture. Power has become decentralized, and maintaining mobility and the rapid flow of information prove most critical to the success of the insurgents. Although the composition of the Tribulation Force strikes one as too convenient, it nevertheless illustrates the types of expertise and training LaHaye and Jenkins value most in their struggle against Antichrist.

The titular head of the Tribulation Force, Rayford Steele, flies a 747 but also has a knack for operating smaller jets and even helicopters, both civilian and military. As the series progresses, it seems almost every new character can fly a plane. The insurgents never lack medical personnel or supplies, either served by Dr. Charles and a nurse, Leah. Late in the series as the Tribulation Force turns more militant, it seems that new members invariably have advanced weapons training, counting among their arsenal exotic devices that exceed even Antichrist's best armaments. Spiritual advisors include the best and brightest, especially a famous messianic rabbi named Tsion Ben-Judah, who broadcasts the teachings of Jesus and descriptions of God's doomsday plan via the Internet. The group also requires a constant parade of techies, starting with Donny Moore, who builds their original underground "safe house," and includes characters such as Chang Wong who the authors assure us ranks as the brightest computer genius on the planet. Zeke Jr., an oil-change technician turned make-up artist, serves ably as a "master of disguises" and helps Tribulation Force members change their identities at will in a world in which image assumes so much importance. Finally, the Tribulation Force includes a gifted economist, a London School of Economics graduate named Ken Ritz, who doubles as a talented, multipurpose pilot.

The Tribulation Force seems especially obsessed with technology, however. Specifically, protagonists experiment with almost every conceivable mode of Internet communication. Characters communicate frequently via e-mail; Buck Williams publishes an anti-Global Community website; and Dr. Ben-Judah operates an electronic bulletin board and webcasts his lengthy sermons. The authors even display an awareness of Internet security. Each character, dull and profound alike, understands the importance of data encryption, sometimes known as PGP or, more colloquially, "pretty good privacy." If anything, they display a naïve confidence in their ability to keep themselves hidden. Antichrist, after all, controls the global networks and can track all transmissions, at least in theory. To circumvent the obvious contradiction between Antichrist's pervasive networks and the virtual invisibility of the Tribulation Force, the authors again return to what Michael Kazin calls "an ironic focus on the individual."[83] The Tribulation Force deploys several undercover computer operatives, or "moles," within Antichrist's network, attempting to negate his advantages. They place naïve confidence both in their own counternetworks and in the proper placement of undercover agents who routinely manipulate the Beast system. Their focus on individuals acting against powerful structures may serve them textually—to a limited extent as I demonstrate in later chapters—but its wisdom appears dubious outside the realm of prophecy fiction.

In sum, the Tribulation Force values mobility, flexibility, the rapid exchange of information, an advanced knowledge of new technologies, and the clever manipulation of appearances and image. They also recognize that power in the network culture/Beast system no longer extends from a single center or node. When the Tribulation Force initially forms, they operate out of a single safe-house and church building in suburban Chicago. They are a small band, hierarchically linked to the leadership of Rayford Steele. As the novels continue and the Tribulation unfolds, however, they recognize that concentrating power in Chicago threatens their viability. If Antichrist were to raid one location, it would threaten their survival. Echoing the logic of Internet pioneers, the Tribulation Force scatters its operations and communications, making it less vulnerable to assault. As

the world-renowned botanist and Tribulation Force elder Chaim Rosenzweig explains to Rayford, "perhaps the safe house of the future will be
in a thousand places, not just one."[84] LaHaye and Jenkins may believe
that the rise of the network culture paves the way for Antichrist and his
infernal Beast system, but their Tribulation Force does an excellent job of
deploying its logic.

The success of the Tribulation Force depends on its ability to clone
vital components of the network culture—the Beast system it seeks to resist. Operatives require flexibility, the latest technologies, ultramodern
weapons, mobility, and a decentralized organizational logic. They even
recognize the importance of image and the possible benefits of deception
in a world characterized by confusion and uncertainty. Ironically, they
criticize what the network culture makes possible, namely, the emergence
of Antichrist and his Beast system. Yet in resisting it they utilize the same
resources, occasionally outfoxing Antichrist with their own alternative
networks. But what are the consequences of the Tribulation Force's co-
optation of Antichrist's methods? What should one make of its attempts
to work within the network culture to attempt to bring forth again that
which the network culture has already banished? Protagonists seek, after
all, to reclaim firm foundations, something the logic of the network culture does not ostensibly permit.

Conclusion

LaHaye and Jenkins describe in significant detail the inevitable rise of the
Beast system. The Antichrist—a powerful, charismatic leader—will
emerge during the last days to seize control of the world through his personal charm, ungodly talents, and canny manipulation of both people
and new communications technologies. He will then use his Beast system
to unite the world as never before, undermining traditional religious and
cultural values. No one will escape his web, and those left behind to suffer his wrath will face an unenviable series of deceptions. Only those who
cling to Christ as their firm foundation will recognize the machinations of
Antichrist and receive salvation. Bible prophecy, the authors suggest—
which the *Left Behind* series describes in dizzying detail—will offer believers such a foundation against which to measure the reality of life during the Tribulation.

Of course, as I described in the Introduction, the Tribulation has, in a sense, already begun. Theorists of a phenomenon known as network culture describe what LaHaye and Jenkins call the Beast system almost as apocalyptically, albeit without many of the negative connotations sometimes suggested by the term "apocalypse." Rather, cultural theorists such as Manuel Castells and Mark C. Taylor have recognized that significant changes are afoot, changes that will affect all aspects of contemporary culture. Webs of information increasingly link the world together as never before, offering beneficial technologies and economic development but also threatening local cultures that fail to make adequate and timely adjustments.

The *Left Behind* novels reflect the significance of the network culture, albeit on a mythological level, and suggest ways believers can maintain or even enhance their evangelical identity under threatening circumstances. The protagonists attempt to do this by wresting meaning, often forcefully, from the clutches of Antichrist, stepping outside of their sleepy suburbs to engage in risky adventures that resemble paramilitary operations much more than familiar forms of evangelizing. The novels may prove a bit naive in their depictions of a successful evangelical response to Antichrist, but prophecy believers must nevertheless respond somehow to the network culture/Beast system. As Taylor puts it, "The only viable freedom is not freedom from constraints but the freedom to operate effectively within them."[85] Escape is, ultimately, not a realistic option.

4

Technologies of Transcendence
"Beast Religion" and the Deification/Demonization of the Network Culture

The evangelical faith has always had its media pilgrims. Because evangelicals shared with American culture a disinterest in tradition, a faith in technology, a drive to popularize, and a spirit of individualism, they found the media to be helpful conduits for establishing their own institutions and broadcasting their evangelistic messages. But the urge to communicate has not always served evangelicals well.[1]   —Quentin J. Schultze, "Keeping the Faith"

Universal product codes now have 666 built into them. You can't see it (until we show you where to look) but the scanner in your grocery store sees 666 every time. . . . Government agencies can listen in on your phone call and track you via satellite anywhere on the planet . . . within 6 inches. . . . Microchip implants for humans are being tested. . . . International databases now record your every purchase, every transaction, and your medical records. . . . Electronic border identification systems are being erected to keep out dangerous cult members. The definition being used includes "anyone who believes that the Bible predicts that the end of the known world is near."[2]   —Jack and Rexella van Impe, promotional blurb for *The Mark of the Beast*

The prophecy beliefs of Jack and Rexella van Impe no doubt strike many observers as paranoid and incredible. To anyone who has ever lived in the southern United States, however, such ideas will likely seem familiar, if not necessarily plausible.[3] My own experience attests to this. Although brought up in the progressive United Church of Christ (UCC) denomination, I discovered that living in southeast Texas made it difficult to avoid exposure to prophecy belief. Billboards around Houston promoted the usual local celebrities such as auto and furniture dealers, politicians, along with celebrity pastors, whose radio and television broadcasts contained ample references to the last days. Even within my own church, Sunday school teachers would occasionally talk about "signs of the times," including how to recognize the Mark of the Beast. No one would associate the liberal UCC denomination with dispensationalism. Pastors and denominational leaders have alternately despised or overlooked prophecy belief. Nevertheless, many pew sitters in my local church probably knew the work of Hal Lindsey far better than that of theologian Paul Tillich.

Most of my experiences with prophecy belief came not in physical brick-and-mortar churches, however, but came instead via the so-called electronic church. Televangelists regularly bought time on the local channels; and, with the boom in cable television systems around 1980, a number of full-time networks arrived on the scene devoted to the more flamboyant aspects of Protestant religiosity. Jack and Rexella van Impe's program, *Jack van Impe Presents*, while certainty not among the flashiest, has proven highly effective and enduring at transmitting its End-Times message. Usually appearing soon after the late local news, "Jack van Impe Presents" looks like a mixture between a news program and a talk show, complete with a startlingly low-pitched announcer. Jack van Impe reads the headlines, many of which are already familiar to viewers, and gives them an apocalyptic spin, informing his audience why such headlines are signs of the last days. Rexella van Impe, although an excellent singer who often performed on the program in the past, now plays a smaller role, seconding the assertions of her husband and helping to provide an uncannily warm setting for a program pitching the end of the world.

Several ironies surround this and similar electronic prophecy programs. First, the van Impes use the medium of television to persuade their viewers that new technologies are a sign of the End. One can see the signs of Antichrist everywhere, whether in supermarket bar codes, the proliferation of satellite tracking systems, or a rumored supercomputer in Belgium, nicknamed "The Beast," that maintains extensive records on every living soul. Antichrist will use such technologies to build his kingdom, the van Impes inform us, and the technologies need no further refinement. The way is clear for the ascendancy of that master deluder and showman extraordinaire, Antichrist. Yet the van Impes put on a pretty good show themselves, using the tools of their dreaded adversary as an indispensable part of their campaign to alert viewers to the imminent danger posed by Antichrist and his culture of surveillance. This indicates a related irony. Antichrist, of course, uses his infernal devices to monitor and control the world's population. But the van Impes tell their viewers that Christ, too, is watching, and no one knows the day or the hour of his return. Christ will come "like a thief in the night" to rapture those who remain faithful and vigilant. Whether one speaks of Christ or Antichrist, viewers are informed that they are always under surveillance.

God, of course, has no need of Antichrist's sophisticated technological apparatus. God is omnipresent, omniscient, and omnipotent without requiring any bells or whistles, while Antichrist must keep up with the latest technological trends in order to counterfeit God's vital characteristics. Antichrist and his mentor, Satan, even use television to monitor viewers, presumably knowing which viewers watch the van Impes and thus require extra demonic attention. Prophecy writers have picked up on the theme of fiber optics, for example, pointing out the allegedly two-way transmitting capabilities of televisions deploying fiber optic technology. Prophecy writers, including Emil Gaverluk, Patrick Fisher, and especially Mary Stewart Relfe, popularized the idea of two-way televisions during the late 1970's and early 1980's, tapping into an already powerful suspicion of the televisual medium among prophecy believers.[4] Gaverluk and Fisher write:

> There is a pinhead-sized camera lens on the end of the fiber optic which can watch anything taking place in the room. . . . This data is recorded on computers which can collate all remarks pro or con, to implement dictatorial control by any group or individual. The startling thing is that this fish-eye camera lens can still see and record everything, EVEN WHEN THE TELEVISION SET IS NOT TURNED ON.[5]

Not only is the programming sinful, but also Antichrist does not require Arbitron ratings to tell him who is watching. Prophecy writers like Relfe suggest that Antichrist's televisual entertainment will gradually accommodate viewers to his Beast system. Once viewers become part of his network, they will willingly obey the talking heads who act as his high priests, and they will all too eagerly accept the values and behaviors that certify one as a member of his infernal kingdom. By using powerful surveillance tools, Antichrist will gain the ability to monitor his unwholesome flock. Moreover, technology allows Antichrist to enhance his powers of deception. LaHaye and Jenkins remind their readers repeatedly that Antichrist is the ultimate deceiver. Taking advantage of the "crisis of the real" brought about by the advent of network culture, Antichrist uses his infernal Beast system to launch the best marketing campaign imaginable. When knowledge is mediated through images, Antichrist's opportunities for deception multiply.

Televangelists such as the van Impes display a naïve confidence that they can somehow broadcast the message of Christ through a media infrastructure they believe the Beast controls. They continually denounce the evils unleashed through new communications technologies, yet they appear addicted to the potentially large audiences of believers the message may reach. What televangelists seldom, if ever, account for, however, is the influence of the medium itself. They assume that as soon as the red light activates atop God's Panaflex camera that their words—inspired by God—will flow directly to the audience without any distortion. As Quentin J. Schultze, paraphrasing media theorist Marshall McLuhan puts it, "The *medium* of communication shapes the *content* of the messages."[6] Although televangelists assume an immediate connection with their viewers, in reality, the message is always mediated by the networks that carry it. To believe otherwise suggests a naïve faith in technology. The "spirit of the air" may get through, but not necessarily the Holy Spirit.

This chapter tracks technological themes in the *Left Behind* novels, exploring especially how LaHaye and Jenkins depict the importance of new communications technologies. Protagonists, as I have suggested, are caught in a paradoxical position. They know that technology buttresses Antichrist and his dreaded Beast system, yet to resist him they must use his own tools against him. The Tribulation Force takes regularly to the airwaves, knowing that they are playing on borrowed time and on borrowed bandwidth. But they succeed in the *Left Behind* narrative, owing largely to the charismatic appeal of their spiritual leader, Dr. Tsion Ben-Judah. Antichrist, conversely, uses technology to build the infrastructure necessary to consolidate his global kingdom. Ultimately, however, he requires an unwholesome combination of technology and religion to encourage the world to accept his rule. Antichrist's Beast religion serves this role, encouraging citizens to deify Antichrist—and, by extension, the network culture/Beast system.

Tsion Ben-Judah, Superstar

LaHaye and Jenkins express their more optimistic assessments of new communications technologies through the spiritual leader of the Tribulation Force, Dr. Tsion Ben-Judah. Ben-Judah, although quiet, scholarly, and slight of build, rises to stardom shortly after he broadcasts the results of his three-year study on the identity of the Messiah on international CNN. It is a much anticipated event. Even his soon-to-be rival, the Antichrist—Nicolae Carpathia—takes a break from his busy schedule of subjugating the world to tune in:

> Dr. Ben-Judah was so engaging that everyone on the plane had stopped talking, moving, and even shifting in their seats. Even Nicolae Carpathia, despite the occasional sip from his glass and the tinkling of the ice, barely moved. It seemed to Rayford that Carpathia was almost embarrassed by the attention Ben-Judah had commanded.[7]

When Ben-Judah declares Jesus as the Messiah, he immediately catapults himself out of obscurity and into the international limelight. He even receives a congratulatory phone call from one of the Two Witnesses, the Hebrew Bible prophet Elijah:

> "Yes, this is Rabbi Ben-Judah."
> "This is Eli. I spoke to you last night"
> "Of course! How did you get my number?"
> "I called the one you mentioned on the broadcast, and the student who answered gave it to me. Someone convinced her who I was."[8]

Elijah arranges a rally for Dr. Ben-Judah at Teddy Kollek Stadium in Israel and also appears along with his partner, Moses. But Ben-Judah's star burns brightest of all.

Ben-Judah's broadcast predictably makes him plenty of enemies, however, and the Tribulation Force sends Buck Williams—a prize-winning journalist turned commando and undercover operative—to bring Ben-Judah to the relative safety of Tribulation Force headquarters in Mt. Prospect, Illinois. There, computer specialist Donny Moore outfits Ben-Judah with the latest technological hardware, allowing him to establish computer bulletin boards and even webcast his sermons across the world, building "the most powerful Web site in history."[9] Buck asks himself rhetorically, understanding the rabbi's potential impact:

> Was it possible his ministry could be more dramatic and wider than ever? Could he do his teaching and preaching and Bible studies on the Net to the millions of computers and televisions all over the world? . . . His mind was engaged with the possibilities of a ministry for Tsion Ben-Judah that would outstrip anything he had ever been able to accomplish before.[10]

Ben-Judah's Internet broadcasts and written messages convert millions around the world, further enhancing his celebrity status. Since presumably all of the representatives of the electronic church were taken during the Rapture, Tsion Ben-Judah becomes, in effect, the Tribulation's foremost televangelist. In words that could be spoken by televangelists Paul Crouch, Jerry Falwell, or Pat Robertson, Ben-Judah extols the powerful benefits of technology for believers, "I envision thousands of technological experts creating a network of resources for believers, informing them of safe havens, putting them in touch with each other."[11]

Of Ben-Judah's millions of on-line converts, perhaps no one proves more important than computer genius David Hassid, who replaces Donny Moore as the technological guru for the Tribulation Force, after the latter's untimely death. Rayford, working undercover in Carpathia's New Babylon palace, discovers Hassid, who relates his tale of conversion: "But I was so enamored of Carpathia, I immediately applied for service to the Global Community. It wasn't long before I discovered the truth on the Internet."[12] Hassid becomes the palace "mole" for the Tribulation Force, scrambling Antichrist's communications networks. Hassid's role appears implausible, however, to say the least. The authors repeatedly claim that Antichrist has the finest people and machines in the world, yet somehow the Tribulation Force—through proper planning and individual initiative—undermine this most imposing of structures. Hassid explains to Mac, a Tribulation Force pilot, how he turns the tables on Antichrist, monitoring all of his communications without being detected:

> "In one way it's simple. It's another miracle of technology. The stuff is actually being recorded onto a miniature disk embedded in the central processing unit of the computer that runs all of New Babylon."
> "The one people like to call the Beast."[13]

After acknowledging, paradoxically, that Satan is the "prince and power of the air," Hassid admits that although Antichrist's technological prowess scares him to death, he remains confident that he will remain one step ahead of the Beast.[14]

Late in the series the introduction of the Mark of the Beast forces believers to flee to the caves of Petra where they receive supernatural protection. Hassid, however, never makes it, although his even more capable assistant, Chang Wong, does. Chang oversees a staff of computer and communications experts who build the finest computer and broadcast center in the world. This apparatus allows Ben-Judah to reach a global audience at any time and on any channel, a far cry from his humble beginnings in the emergency shelter of the New Hope Village Church. Like the twentieth-century pioneers of the electronic church, Ben-Judah finds it exceedingly difficult to procure airtime through traditional channels, so he buys (or, in some cases, steals) his own, eventually forming his own networks.[15] Moreover, his operatives routinely interrupt Carpathia's messages, substituting Ben-Judah's words for those of Antichrist. The apex of the Tribulation Force's media empire arrives when Tribulation Force operatives, safely hidden deep within the technologically sophisticated caves of Petra, tap into surveillance equipment that allows them to monitor Carpathia's most important cabinet meeting:

> But it was as if selected members of the Trib Force were in the room. Gathered around a big-screen TV deep in the caverns of Petra, Rayford's hand-selected lineup of colleagues watched every moment through the miracle of technology and Chang's expert maneuvering.[16]

Although Antichrist rules "the most technologically advanced regime in history,"[17] the Tribulation Force, through individual initiative and old-fashioned know-how, consistently find the means to undermine him.

The technological sophistication of the Tribulation Force strikes one as odd for a group allegedly heaven-bent on leaving the world behind. The *Left Behind* novels often depict believers as more beholden to technologies than to God or each other. Quentin J. Schultze, extrapolating from his analysis of televangelism, does not mince words in his assessment of a phenomenon analogous to what one finds in the *Left Behind* narrative:

> Contemporary televangelism shares with the national culture a remarkable faith in technology that borders on idolatry. . . . Paradoxically,

contemporary evangelicalism often perceives mass-communications technologies as ways of returning humanity to a better past and thereby guaranteeing a utopian future. In other words, televangelists have appropriated the American myth that sees technology as the vehicle for building a perfect world—in this case a world like that before the Fall.[18]

Schultze's analysis, when superimposed over the *Left Behind* novels, remains prescient, if perhaps a little overstated. Nevertheless, his concerns do appear justified. In the *Left Behind* series one finds a similar drive to deify technology, and this reliance on technology and the imperatives of mass communications tend to make celebrities out of the leaders of the Tribulation Force, especially Tsion Ben-Judah. Second, LaHaye and Jenkins assume that individual believers will somehow find the means to conquer Antichrist, using his technological infrastructure—a dubious proposition. Finally, the Tribulation Force relies on Internet and satellite broadcasting as an efficient means of spreading their resistance movement, along with the Gospel of Christ. But how much of the message gets through? Schultze addresses the basic problem, "Emphasizing technology over communication, and information over understanding, actually makes religious communications more unlikely. No matter how sophisticated the transmitting and receiving equipment, the basic problem of communicating something of value remains."[19] The authors assume that when Ben-Judah's words are digitized, uploaded, and transmitted, viewers will recognize the difference between his product and that of Antichrist. This requires an ironic leap of faith in technology.

One World under Surveillance

LaHaye and Jenkins, however, like their fellow prophecy writers, also take the paradoxical step of demonizing technology. After all, technology allows Antichrist to reduce the world to a global village he can control, using the technological infrastructure bequeathed him by Satan himself— the spirit of the air. Alongside triumphant prose that celebrates the ability of ordinary churchgoers to manipulate sophisticated technology and undermine the Antichrist, the authors insert the usual caveats about this world—at least during the seven years of the Tribulation—belonging to Antichrist. With such an understanding, it is not the Tribulation Force that does the monitoring but Satan himself. He has the whole world in his hands, or at least under his surveillance.

Thus, LaHaye and Jenkins's technological optimism notwithstanding, the genre of prophecy literature still requires them to depict the world as growing worse and more sinful—not a place in which any self-respecting believer would wish to remain. This again appears paradoxical, given the extent to which the Tribulation Force interrupts and occasionally controls Antichrist's infrastructure. The authors must nevertheless convince their readers that life on earth is growing more unbearable. As it happens, however, Antichrist is indeed more powerful technologically, after all. After the Two Witnesses—Elijah and Moses—are resurrected and taken to heaven on live television, Carpathia simply makes the incident disappear:

> David Hassid had reported that he had seen Carpathia's eerie interruption on TV Monday night, but that the incident did not appear on any tapes of the event. And now, no replays of the resurrection appeared on the news.

"'What power,' Mac thought. 'What pervasive control, even of technology.'"[20] Antichrist needs technology to fake the key attributes of God: omnipotence, omnipresence, and omniscience. Using technology, Antichrist can do anything, be anywhere, and know anything happening in his global kingdom. Of the three characteristics, the final one, omniscience, appears most disconcerting to prophecy writers. They understand that in a world governed by Antichrist, *privacy* falls by the wayside, and the individual becomes transparent to the powers of the state. David Hassid, acknowledging the concerns of another Tribulation Force member, Hannah, admits that he worries about his ability to stay hidden from the surveillance powers of the Global Community:

> He believed the only reason she raised the issue was because she cared, and she was, after all, a civilian when it came to technology. But he almost wished she hadn't planted the seed of curiosity in his mind. With every message, every transmission, every phone call, he got the niggling feeling that someone, somewhere could be looking over his shoulder.[21]

Paul S. Boyer finds similar attitudes in his study of prophecy literature. He reads the dystopian musings of prophecy writers like Mary Stewart

Relfe and David Webber and Noah Hutchings as evidence of widespread cultural, even populist, discontent. Mary Stewart Relfe, the author of a self-published best-seller named *When Your Money Fails: The "666 System" Is Here,* serves as Boyer's favorite example of the evangelical fascination with and concomitant fear of new technologies. Boyer does not paint a flattering portrait of Relfe and her readers. Relfe, according to Boyer's portrayal, demonstrates a detailed yet superficial and disconnected understanding of new technologies. Her list of problematic developments includes an urban legend that still circulates widely within evangelical circles: the tale of the infamous Belgian supercomputer nicknamed "The Beast." The supercomputer, allegedly housed in Brussels, maintains comprehensive files on every global citizen. Relfe also notes with alarm the proliferation of bar codes, credit cards, and even the "*" and "#" keys on telephones.[22]

Relfe, Boyer suggests, possesses just enough awareness of technological developments to place them within a preexisting framework that supports a conspiracy theory "almost coterminous with modernity itself."[23] Relfe's descriptions, however, ultimately prove opportunistic and gullible. Boyer cites the example of Relfe's belief in the existence of a device used to vaporize stray animals through cable television lines.[24] Despite finding humor in Relfe's almost incoherent prose and gullible beliefs, Boyer concludes by emphasizing a critical point, "that her books became bestsellers reminds us again that even 'marginal' voices, evocative though they may be of the supermarket tabloids, ought not be too quickly dismissed by those seeking to understand American popular thought as the twentieth century draws to a close."[25] Boyer offers an interpretation of evangelical prophecy fiction that emphasizes its widespread appeal. Such appeal derives largely from a fear pervasive among many Americans who look upon new technologies as threatening developments.

Sociologist David Lyon's account of contemporary surveillance theory provides an insightful resource for understanding the anxiety-laden world of prophecy literature. Lyon—similar here to LaHaye and Jenkins—discusses an interesting paradox. The same twentieth-century developments that stimulated the growth of democracies and permitted greater personal liberties, Lyon writes, also carried with them the price of increasingly extensive networks of surveillance.[26] As societies rapidly grew and urbanized, anonymity proved a double-edged sword. One could forge a new identity, but such flexibility required a surveillance network capable of keeping tabs on citizens—making sure, among other matters, of who they were in order to reduce the risk of fraud. Growing populations meant that individuals required more dependable and objective forms of identification. Urban dwellers may have increasingly felt anonymous and disconnected, but new technologies and bureaucratic practices supplemented the face-to-face conversations that once helped shape human identity with an extensive network of files. One may have lost a measure of intimate contact with family and friends, but one had a new "Big Brother."[27]

Lyon, however, attempts to move beyond the problematic understandings that often accompany discussions of Big Brother. Orwell does retain a place in Lyon's account, but Lyon takes issue with how Orwell's dark prophecy has been received by contemporary commentators who emphasize privacy issues. The quest for privacy emerges as a natural response to the increasing pervasiveness of surveillance technologies, Lyon suggests, but the social atomization that results gives individuals even less control over their environment.[28] The response, in other words, proves even more dangerous than the irritant. The language of privacy isolates individuals from moral responsibility and social interaction, placing them into consumer bubbles in which they can either accept the fruits of consumption or suffer the consequences of their intransigence.

Lyon also finds theorist Michel Foucault's reading of Jeremy Bentham's "Panopticon" highly problematic.[29] Bentham described the Panopticon as a circular-shaped institution that would introduce a more enlightened model for the reformation of deviants than the regressive notions of punishment widespread in early nineteenth-century England. A guard tower stood in the center of the structure, which, along with the use of venetian blinds and lighting effects, allowed jailers to maintain constant surveillance over inmates who were sequestered individually in narrow cells. Everything a prisoner did was transparent to the watchers, at least in Bentham's conception of the Panopticon. Guards could not monitor every cell, of course, but psychologically this proved unnecessary as the prisoners could not see their guards. They did not know when they were being watched. Such knowledge prompted "self-policing," Foucault observes, as individuals never knew with certainty when they might be watched. As a result, prisoners would reform themselves by internalizing the expectations of their keepers, since they never knew when they might be called to account for their misdeeds.[30]

Foucault's account, despite its obvious erudition, misses the mark for Lyon precisely because Foucault allegedly totalizes the power of the

Panopticon, leaving individuals little hope of escaping—or at least modifying—its control over them.[31] Bentham's enlightened prison was never built, but Foucault suggested that the Panopticon has transcended a mere structure and has instead become a grounding principle for contemporary social life. We are all inmates of the Panopticon, in such a view, and unseen elites, governmental or otherwise, potentially monitor our every move—we never know with certainty.[32]

Foucault's pessimism, Lyon offers, emerges from his fundamental misinterpretation of the *theology* of the Panopticon. Similar to many cultural theorists who are either blinded to the importance of religious issues or respond to them cynically within a materialistic framework, Foucault, Lyon believes, overlooks the religious significance of the Panopticon.[33] Bentham professed atheism, after all, and designed his structure to overcome the need for religion as a basis for moral behavior. One could design institutions to inculcate such morals, Bentham argued, without the overt coercion associated with religion. Lyon points out, however, that even Bentham borrowed Scriptural language in the margins of his Panopticon blueprint, ultimately indicating that his new correctional institution might do something other than simply obviate religion—it might also parody it.[34] Foucault overlooks such marginalia, however, and reads the institution solely within a materialistic framework.[35]

For Foucault, Lyon argues—using the example of the Panopticon—values become a product adopted because of fear and *uncertainty* rather than mutual *trust*.[36] Foucault depicts priests as normative agents who operate on fear through the use of the confession, for example, and describes the Panopticon as a secularized extension of a coercive drive for individual transparency. Lyon suggests that such a perspective closes Foucault off to the possibility that values, and by extension personal identities, can emerge from trusting relationships that are not always coercive.[37] Indeed, Foucault's earlier text, *Discipline and Punish,* casts a bleak picture on this account. Yet Lyon's critique of Foucault, while genuinely insightful at times, ultimately goes too far. When viewed in the wider context of Foucault's later work, for example, *Discipline and Punish* reads more like a warning of emerging cultural conditions than a description of absolute, inalterable facts. Foucault's later thought, building upon Greco-Roman models, introduces alternatives to the apparent pessimism of his earlier genealogies of power.[38]

Placing questions of Foucault interpretation aside for the moment, one finds that Lyon heeds Foucault's ironic "warning," and urges his readers to retain the hope that values can emerge from noncoercive relationships of trust, or indeed *faith,* as it becomes for Lyon. Lyon, in a surprising turn for a progressive social theorist, calls upon the ancient Christian thinker Augustine's notion of the "City of God."[39] Citing Augustine, Lyon calls for renewed dedication to issues of justice through an emphasis on moral personhood and an end to "other-denying violence," without reducing persons to autonomous subjects bent on the mastery of themselves and others (a charge often levied against Enlightenment notions of autonomous personhood). Such a condition cannot be attained through power, Lyon tells us, but only through grace—an empirically unavailable gift from the "City of God." Lyon seeks to affirm such a possibility of grace without denying the importance of the material world—a daunting task indeed.[40]

Lyon argues that humans ought to recognize the *possibility* that their personhood derives in part from an "image of God." As such, communities that respect and foster particular forms of identity do not derive, according to Lyon, from an incessant quest for self-isolation or even private piety, but must instead emerge from a renewed commitment to social justice on behalf of others. Persons come to trust one another, which presents not only the risk of betrayal but also offers the hope of more fulfilling forms of social interaction. And, although he hesitates to use the term, he recognizes that his vision, too, has utopian overtones. Given a climate of increasing uncertainty and mistrust of empiricism, however, trust seems like a valid option. Lyon points out the difficulties of a strictly empiricist position in such a cultural climate, and adds that any position—even those derived from empirical observation—has its "baseline" of uncertainty or "given" upon which it builds other propositions.[41] Moreover, Lyon insists that such a position need not derive from an essentially Christian theology, despite his invocation of Augustine. People of all faiths must learn to trust one another in the midst of the often crippling uncertainty that marks contemporary social relationships. Such trust proves risky, Lyon recognizes, but the alternative—a panoptic, atomized culture driven by rampant mistrust and anonymous tipsters—may prove the greater threat.[42]

Like any utopian vision, however, Lyon's "City of Faith" totters on the edge of collapsing into dystopia. Lyon is a social scientist and not a theologian; hence, his stated intent is to provide a more fruitful articulation of critical theory that might make a positive difference. Lyon's insights, when viewed as a critique, do indeed appear helpful. If one attempts to understand his suggestions as theological, however, one quickly encounters the same problems that prompted his critique. Lyon's solutions to the problems of the network culture prove nothing of the sort when read for their face value. One cannot attain the precarious balance he suggests, whether understood as analogous to the nineteenth-century Populist synthesis of faith and social action, or on an individual level through an increased awareness of our "data-images," along with periodic revisions of privacy legislation and consumer activism against the unregulated transfer of personal information. Lyon admonishes us that faith and trust remain critical to contemporary existence, but he cannot articulate a strategy that eliminates the dangers of trust poorly invested. His hope is deferred to an empirically unavailable future, implying that one would be foolish to reify his positions as a way out of a labyrinth that has no escape. Hope remains, along with uncertainty.

Evangelical prophecy writers, too, compose narratives based upon deployment of trust, or, to put it more accurately in this context, faith. Faith always carries the risk of betrayal, however, and what resembles a realized utopia can quickly become something more problematic. Prophecy writers have been extremely reluctant to apply such self-reflection to their own theological positions, of course, but LaHaye and Jenkins have, through their obsession with mistrust and deception, inadvertently opened such doubts. I will explore LaHaye and Jenkins's own answers to the contemporary problem of trust (or faith) in chapters 5 and 6.

I begin instead here with something more immediately relevant to the central concerns of this section—the observation that Antichrist and his Beast system thrive on uncertainty. Antichrist offers to replace the uncertainty characteristic of contemporary existence with assurances of security, in exchange for his citizens' trust. Such trust, however, turns individuals against each other and produces ever greater uncertainty. Antichrist builds a panoptic culture, feeding off of the anxiety and uncertainty of his subjects, but he cannot, he *will not*, offer them any more than temporary assurances. He needs mistrust to build his system, and individuals who eschew risk and eagerly embrace his promises of certainty find themselves trapped ever more tightly within his grasp. But at least they receive the comfort of a fixed identity in an uncertain world. But like everything else Antichrist promises, this too proves, ultimately, illusory.

Thus, one can extend Lyon's observations to evangelical prophecy fiction without significant modification. After all, Antichrist must gain the trust of the world through deception—by appearing to be God. He must copy, even parody, every aspect of God in order to gain not only the trust but also the faith of his citizens. Ironically, if Lyon's observations hold, one finds just such a parodic statement in the Panopticon itself. Lyon writes:

> Recall that Bentham planned his Panopticon as the centrepiece of his aggressively secularist approach to policy. The Panopticon was a weapon wielded in his war against religion. With a social panacea like this prison plan, religion would be rendered redundant. Virtue could be fabricated without reference to religion, the church, theology, or God. Yet paradoxically Bentham's Panopticon retained some religious referents. It was still located in a "theology," albeit a secular one. The Panopticon inspector is a parody of God; the inspector's vision, a play on omniscience or omniperception. He even used a biblical quotation from the Book of Psalms as an epigram to make this point.[43]

One could read the Antichrist of the *Left Behind* novels as a sort of panoptic overseer, bringing to light those who attempt to evade his authority. Moreover, Antichrist and his Panopticon do not destroy religion as much as reinvent it based upon the worship of Antichrist as the new deity. His "secular" theology embraces all but understands none and hides his true intent beneath a web of deception. By controlling networks and information technologies, Antichrist consolidates his power through a "divide and conquer" strategy that focuses citizens' suspicions anywhere but on the sinister source of their misery. Finally, through the use of his panoptic networks of surveillance, Antichrist acquires attributes usually reserved for God. As Lyon observes, the master of the Panopticon achieves a measure of omniscience and omnipresence. Citizens know this and adjust their patterns of behavior to fit Antichrist's expectations. After all, they never know when he is watching. Antichrist thus paradoxically forces his citizens to accept the imperatives of the network culture without the overt exercise of power.[44]

The theorists we have looked at in the last two chapters, notably Barabási, Castells, Lyon, and Taylor, all note the potential downsides of the network culture, although they nevertheless express their views with varying degrees of cautious optimism. More to the point, we have already noted that Lyon detects a quasi-transcendent quality in contemporary surveillance technologies, but many of the others share his observation, also finding an almost deity-like (or demonic) significance to the network culture. Castells, for example, suggests an insidious, "invisible hand" operating beneath the apparent complexity of network culture, claiming that "above a diversity of human-flesh capitalists and capitalist groups there is a faceless collective capitalist, made up of financial flows operated by electronic networks."[45] Extending the religious metaphor, Castells further describes individual capitalists as "incarnated" within the space of capital flows, alluding once again to a quasi-religious understanding of the network culture.[46] Granted, Castells expresses reservations vis-à-vis the rapid development of the network culture, but he also seems to view it as more inevitable than inherently regrettable.

Taylor, in contrast, works within a more personal, existential framework, understanding himself and all of us, ultimately, as incarnations of the World Wide Web.[47] Taylor, like Lyon, calls upon Augustine, combining the human and technological aspects of contemporary selfhood into what he calls a "technological unconscious." The mind, Taylor tells us, recalling Augustine's notion that "the mind is not large enough to contain itself,"[48] has too much information to be contained within the material bounds of one's skull. Taylor embraces a mystical union of sorts with the deity of the network culture and encourages us, ironically, to surrender our dreams of autonomy to a condition that promises unlimited possibility. The network culture progressively effaces the distinctions between humans and their technologies, producing a beneficial codependency that allows both humans and technologies to exceed their inherent limitations.[49] Once the stuff of science fiction, theorists of the network culture including Castells, Barabási, and Taylor observe the merger between humanity and new technologies happening all around us. The *Left Behind* protagonists share a similar ambivalence, both condemning such developments as diabolical precursors to Antichrist, while enjoying the luxuries a closer cooperation affords them to resist Antichrist.

Even as we find ourselves trapped within the network culture, however, uncertainty breaks through the ecstasy to remind us that such unions always remain necessarily incomplete. Taylor's vision of possibilities must not be mistaken for assurances of a secure future. Despite Taylor's professed admiration for the religious and existential aspects of network culture, doubt pierces his text. Uncertainty must remain. Security means death, of that much we can be certain. One finds no such caveats in Antichrist's web of deceptions, LaHaye and Jenkins tell us. Whereas Taylor's thought retains an ironic message trapped between a warning and a welcome, Antichrist denies all such ambivalence.

More significantly, however, Antichrist seeks to make his Beast system more than a temporal solution—he attempts to elevate it beyond the constraints of space and time. He creates a new religion that combines the logic of the network culture with his own need for absolute trust and admiration. His "Beast religion" deifies his "Beast system" by proclaiming that we are all incarnations of the World Wide Web of information. Together we make up the spirit that undergirds Antichrist and supports his system. Thus, Antichrist requires religion as he seeks to bind the world together under his rule, since religion has historically played such a vital role in unifying cultures. After all, the term "religion" finds its probable origin in the Latin verb *religare,* which literally indicates a "binding back," but also carries the connotation of that which binds individuals back to something more powerful than themselves—a god. Antichrist may seem obsessed with economics and new technologies, but he cannily recognizes the importance of religion in American culture. Using his powers of omniscience and omnipresence gleaned from his mastery of technology, Antichrist builds a kingdom that enslaves his subjects. Citizens, however—with the notable exception of the Tribulation Force—do not protest these developments. They happily accept the conditions of their enslavement—so long as they are promised security and certainty in a risky world. After all, Antichrist works primarily through persuasion, not overt displays of power. His religion obtains plausibility by appealing to elements common to many world religions, only revealing its infernal design when it is already too late.

Accursed Be the Ties That Bind: The Enigma Babylon One-World Faith

Any description of the Beast system would be incomplete without a discussion of arguably its most important component: the global superchurch. Although prophecy writers impugn almost all aspects of the transition to network culture, they save their most damning indictments for the forthcoming One-World Church. Particulars have changed over the years, but the basic narrative remains: during the last days, an unholy union will assist Antichrist's ascent to power, consisting of Roman Catholics, liberal Protestants, New Agers, and just about any other nonevangelical religion with the exception of Orthodox Jews—the latter depicted as misguided but still worthy of a second-chance. LaHaye and Jenkins's attitude toward Jews reflects the carefully nuanced viewpoints of dispensational prophecy belief. Prophecy writers insist they are philo-Semitic, supporting the state of Israel at every opportunity. Yet their attitudes toward Judaism as a religion along with their attitudes toward individual practitioners reflect the latent, although occasionally more obvious, anti-Semitism found in the history of dispensational prophecy belief.

As historian Timothy Weber notes in his exploration of late nineteenth- and early twentieth-century evangelical attitudes toward American Jews, evangelicals do see Jews as "children of the covenant," but Jews nevertheless remain ideal objects of conversion.[50] Jews retain a privileged status but also merit special consideration for eternal punishment because of their proximity to Christianity. They have heard the message of Jesus repeatedly and will suffer for their obstinacy, prophecy texts like the *Left Behind* novels tell us. Only those who convert to conservative Protestantism will reap the promise of God's covenant.[51] Even so, the desire to bring the Gospel to Jews appears to stem mainly from a desire to advance God's apocalyptic timetable rather than from any altruistic motives. Jews remain important to prophecy writers to the extent they help fulfill prophecy. Unless a critical mass of Jews convert—at least 144,000—the prophecies cannot be fulfilled.

Muslims share a similar fate. While the authors consistently cast profound suspicion on Muslims throughout the series—they even retain ambivalence toward key members of the Tribulation Force such as Abdullah and Albie, both converted Muslims—the authors do seem to respect the intensity of Islamic belief, especially the resistance of Muslims to worshipping idols or false gods. The later novels, in fact, portray Muslims as respectable religionists, who remain doomed without Christ, but who nonetheless rank higher than most citizens of the Global Community. Coauthor Jerry Jenkins has even claimed in an interview that the widespread hostility directed against Islam after 9/11 caused him to reevaluate his own position. Jenkins writes, "Yes, although they [Muslims] will not be happy that we are still quite clear in showing that they can get to God only through Jesus. One of the strengths of the devout Muslim, however, is that he will resist an all-inclusive, one-world religion, as would many others, including Jews and believers in Christ."[52] Still, despite Jenkins's grudging respect, Muslims will meet the same fate as other unbelievers, according to the *Left Behind* novels.

Prophecy writers reserve a special dose of vitriol for Roman Catholics, whom they view as counterfeit Christians especially deserving of punishment due to their close, yet ultimately deceitful distance from the truth of Christ's message.[53] Historically, the Catholic Church has often played a diabolical role in prophecy narratives. One can trace such animosities back to the fourth century, as Paul S. Boyer explains:

> No Antichrist tradition has a more ancient lineage than that pointing to the Pope. As early as the 4th century, Hilary, bishop of Poitiers, taught that Antichrist would arise from within the Church.[54]

Historian Bernard McGinn notes that the animosity between temporal leaders and their church rivals took on a more sinister tone during the thirteenth century, when Pope Gregory IX identified the Holy Roman Emperor Frederick II as the Antichrist, inadvertently positioning "Antichrist" as a demonized representation of an especially troubling enemy.[55] Other mythmakers soon turned against the Pope and inaugurated the "Pope as Antichrist" legend, however. Although the Holy Roman Emperors accounted for some of this sentiment, McGinn notes that spiritualists within the Franciscan order probably fostered much of the medieval Pope as Antichrist speculation. The spiritualist Franciscans taught during the thirteenth century, following the writings of the prophet-monk, Joachim of Fiore, that a third age of the spirit was then dawning—challenging temporal hierarchies including the Papacy. Such teachings predictably incurred the wrath of the Vatican. Subsequent pseudo-Joachite writings (written to resemble writings of Joachim of Fiore but ultimately thought apocryphal) raised the specter that Pope Boniface II, among many others, might be either the Beast of Revelation or an immediate precursor.[56]

The Pope as Antichrist connection accelerated during the Reformation era, however, marking the careers of late-medieval clerical reformers, including John Wycliffe and Jan Hus.[57] The fulminations of the sixteenth-century German reformer Martin Luther against the Catholic Church, which he considered "Babylon," are perhaps best remembered, however.[58] Luther, although by all accounts neither an admirer of the book of Revelation nor a millennial thinker (Lutherans still do not officially support millennial beliefs) warmed to Revelation mainly because it provided him with rich imagery to deploy in his ongoing polemics against the Catholic Church.[59] Finally, anti-Catholicism has predictably extended into American apocalyptic thought, as Protestant leaders from the Puritan Cotton Mather to contemporary prophecy writers such as Hal Lindsey have implicated the Catholic Church as an organ of ultimate evil. Often associated with nativist extreme fringe movements such as the nineteenth-century Know-Nothings—an anti-immigrant political faction—and, more recently, the Ku Klux Klan, anti-Catholicism has also remained a persistent and troubling aspect of conservative Protestant thought throughout American religious history.[60]

Contemporary prophecy writers have not significantly adjusted this basic picture. Anti-Catholicism has remained a staple of evangelical prophecy literature. Such literature has often depicted the Pope as either the Antichrist himself,[61] or, more commonly, as his right-hand man, the False Prophet. Sometimes even a bishop can become the Beast, like Bishop Uriah Leonard in Carol Balizet's prophecy novel, *The Seven Last Years*. LaHaye and Jenkins steer a middle course, making Archbishop Peter Mathews their False Prophet pro tem in the early *Left Behind* novels. The authors have also taken a more moderate account of Catholicism, perhaps reflecting the closer cooperation between Roman Catholics and evangelicals in recent years, especially in political matters.[62] Nevertheless, LaHaye and Jenkins perpetuate many of the older suspicions. The authors make their judgments evident in their commentary to the *Left Behind* series. They write:

> The present pope is on record as believing in the Trinity and may indeed pray in the name of Jesus Christ. However, his infatuation with the vision of Fatima and his reverence for Mary (whom he credits with saving his life from an assassin's bullet) concerns some who fear he could be setting up the church and the religions of the world for the fulfillment of Revelation 17, where "Mystery Babylon, the mother of harlots" unifies all the religions of the world during the first half of the Tribulation.[63]

Despite the authors' more moderate tone, the reader intuits that LaHaye and Jenkins are among the "some who fear" the diabolical End-Times role of the Catholic Church. The authors do include their fictional Pope in the Rapture because he assents to the terms of the Augsburg Confession of 1530—essentially becoming a Protestant—but the *Left Behind* novels display consistent suspicion of and hostility toward the Catholic Church. Nevertheless, such tensions have lessened in recent years, in part, as noted above, due to closer political cooperation between the two groups. William C. Martin points to the closer alliances between Catholic pro-life groups and the more politically motivated wings of popular evangelicalism that have developed since the late 1970's, for example.[64] Jerry Falwell, Pat Robertson, and Tim LaHaye, among other prominent evangelical leaders, have reached out to conservative Catholics in an attempt to forge a "Moral Majority" for Falwell, and a "Christian Coalition" built from the grassroots by one-time Robertson understudy Ralph Reed.

Although among prophecy writers the Catholic Church may still represent the "harlot," which brings all of the world's religions together in the service of Antichrist, other religions and religious trends have not gone unnoticed. Ecumenism, a movement toward greater cooperation among twentieth-century mainline Protestants, has also come under indictment. Prophecy writers invariably lump the World and National Councils of Churches together with the United Nations. Their critique centers on the suspicion that mainline Protestant denominations, in attempting to bring the world's religions together for closer dialogue, have actually lost the distinctiveness that made them Christian. They have "put aside their differences," prophecy writers tell us, leaving their churches with nothing of particular significance, a denouement prophecy writers obviously seek to avoid within their own denominations.

Don Thompson's film *A Distant Thunder*—the successor to the evangelical blockbuster *A Thief in the Night*—parodies the fictional "World Church," for example, as an evangelizing organization hell-bent on forcing citizens to take the Mark of the Beast, which looks suspiciously like the emblem of the United Church of Christ (UCC).[65] The UCC, formed out of a 1957 merger between Congregationalists and the Evangelical and Reformed (E&R) denominations, finds itself the object of contempt not only for its commitment to ecumenism and progressive activism, but probably also for its slogan, "That they may all be one." The phrase comes from a New Testament verse, referring to all Christians as participating in the body of Christ, but prophecy writers have interpreted it in a more sinister light, especially given the UCC's continuing commitment to progressive political activism and interfaith dialogue. Moreover, the merger that formed the UCC was at the vanguard of many such unions and drew notoriety for its originality. Thus, the UCC, along with liberal and "mainline" Protestantism, in general, has also stirred the apocalyptic suspicions of prophecy writers.

The final category includes just about everyone else. LaHaye and Jenkins note that "Muslims, Buddhists, Hindus, pantheists, the Dalai Lama, and a host of others" reject Jesus Christ. But the mere existence of such varied forms of religious expression also tempts one to believe that "there are many ways to God," a notion the authors vehemently reject.[66] All of these religions, they claim, perpetuate a radical heresy with roots to the Tower of Babel. Whether "Hinduism, Buddhism, Taoism, Gaia worship, and a host of other cultic religions," all are subsumed under "Mystery Babylon," false religions that violate basic commandments, first among which is: "You shall not worship other gods! Make no graven images, nor worship them or serve them!"[67] All roads may lead to Roman Catholicism, it seems, but ancient Babylon is the final destination for the One-World Church.

Left Behind introduces Archbishop Peter Mathews, who becomes the head of the "Enigma Babylon One World Faith." Mathews, renamed Pontifex Maximus Peter II, becomes "the pope of all popes," and his see includes all organized religions that assent to Antichrist, not just the Catholic Church. LaHaye and Jenkins depict Mathews as a naïve and arrogant bumbler unaware of his larger role within God's eternal plan. Mathews's arrogance blinds him to his dangerous position, and he believes that the mass disappearances associated with the Rapture were actually part of God's plan to weed the misguided Protestant evangelicals from His true Church. Indeed, Mathews serves Carpathia's purposes without ascertaining his role as a tool of Satan. His organization provides spiritual legitimation for Carpathia's rule, before Carpathia ultimately replaces him, once his role of preparing the world for the Beast system loses its utility.

Mathews is also a comic figure, tragically ignorant but genuinely funny as depicted by LaHaye and Jenkins. In *Apollyon,* Carpathia offers safe passage to the spiritual leader of the believers, Dr. Tsion-Ben Judah, permitting Dr. Ben Judah to hold a rally for 50,000 of the faithful at Teddy Kollek stadium. Carpathia, however, decides to crash the party via helicopter. Accompanied by his right-hand man Leon Fortunato and Pontifex Maximus Peter II, Carpathia displays his magnanimity by offering the assemblage another opportunity to join his new world order. But first his prophets, Fortunato and finally Mathews, attempt to warm-up the crowd. The authors describe Mathews's colorful appearance with breathless delight:

> He wore a high, peaked cap with an infinity symbol on the front and a floor-length, iridescent yellow robe with a long train and billowy sleeves. His vestments were bedecked with huge, inlaid, brightly colored stones and appointed with tassels. . . . As if he had earned some sort of double doctorate from Black Light Discotheque University. . . . When Mathews turned around, he revealed astrological signs on the train of his robe.[68]

Mathews's subsequent attempts to win over the crowd by playing to their admiration of Dr. Ben-Judah bring only silence, however. Worse, he seems to have no clue why the group resists his Enigma Babylon One-World Faith. Mathews ends his brief appearance with a benediction that is anathema to evangelical religiosity, "I confer upon this gathering the blessings of the universal father and mother and animal deities who lovingly guide us on our path to true spirituality."[69]

Pontifex Maximus Peter II represents all that prophecy writers find troubling about contemporary American religion. Gone is the sense of dependence on a distinctly Protestant God, and one witnesses instead the rise of an ecumenism, centered in technological tricks, nature spirituality, and human self-development. God, in other words, becomes radically immanent, a disappearing object of religious faith and more a mystical, spiritual experience of divine self-affirmation.[70] LaHaye and Jenkins lump all of these themes together under the rubric "Mystery Babylon," the deceitful church of the last days. Although the Enigma Babylon faith offers peace and spiritual fulfillment, the authors view it as a deception of ultimate consequence.

Besides the obvious involvement of technologies in Antichrist's eclectic new religion, one also finds a related problem for contemporary evangelicals. Antichrist's religion calls into question the legitimacy of evangelical religious practices. Put simply, American evangelicalism—heir to centuries of Protestant doctrinal refinements—positions God at the center of its universe. Humans, while important, exist to worship a god who is wholly transcendent. Humans are not gods, nor do they have the potential to become gods. The order of the universe is plain and decidedly hierarchical. One can please God through proper beliefs (orthodoxy), and, to a much lesser extent, ritual (orthopraxy), but God retains the final decision on one's eternal fate. The Bible *reveals* the Truth to believers, who look to it as a final, objective measure against which to measure truth claims.

Historians of American religion point out another, antithetical strain of spiritual practice, however, what Catherine Albanese, among others, calls "natural religion." From philosopher Ralph Waldo Emerson to poet Walt Whitman and even Wiccan priestess Starhawk (Miriam Simos), Albanese notes that a significant number of Americans have been moved spiritually by an appreciation of the natural world rather than by adherence to traditional Protestant beliefs.[71] Historians Robert Ellwood and Robert Fuller also note this trend, pointing out that Americans since the 1960's, especially, have become increasingly attuned to truths derived from direct *experience* of the natural world, rather than the time-honored dictates of revealed, scripturally based religions.[72] Practitioners discover truth in rituals rather than in the dictates of churches or holy books. Ritual practices help humans relate to God, the Goddess, or the spiritual forces flowing through all creation in mystical, ecstatic moments when they potentially transcend their perceived limitations and experience God and the unity of all creation. For practitioners of the various and often informal strands of natural religion, God is not wholly other, but within all things, including humans. Often called "pantheism" but more accurately referred to as "panentheism," natural religions typically describe God as an energy or force that inhabits all things, but which may also extend beyond the visible world.

Ritual practice helps humans find the god force within, and religion becomes a matter of questing after truth and self-development. Everything and everyone remain in flux. To cite a publication by the aforementioned Starhawk, life is a "spiral dance," and humans must continue their quest to find their place in the universe pragmatically, using whatever works.[73] Natural religions stand in tension to conservative evangelicalism which holds that all critical truths must be found in the Bible and that the fate of the world has long since been settled in God's eternal plan. One must either accept or reject what God has decreed. For practitioners of natural religions, the matter is never quite so simple. Truth comes in many forms, and religions that claim exclusive truth appear crippling and wretchedly dogmatic.

Prophecy writers have noted such developments, of course. LaHaye and Jenkins condemn the mysticism inherent in much of American spirituality by citing it as a deadly deception that traces back to Genesis. The serpent in the Garden, after all, tempted Eve with the promise that she, too, could share the knowledge of God. Moreover, evangelical writer Constance Cumbey's scurrilous and highly influential publication, *The*

Hidden Dangers of the Rainbow, warns against menacing "New Age" spiritualities. Cumbey believes that the New Age movement and its practitioners are assisting Satan's attempts to prepare his infernal kingdom by contaminating the hearts and minds of those involved in such practices. Extra-Biblical knowledge—spiritual or otherwise—leads believers astray, according to Cumbey.[74]

Finally, and perhaps not surprisingly, Tim LaHaye believes that secular humanism lurks beneath all the pomp and pageantry of Antichrist's Beast religion and its infatuation with natural religion and human potential.[75] According to LaHaye, all roads leading away from conservative evangelical Protestantism lead to secular humanism, with "paganism" and New Age beliefs at the forefront. LaHaye's definition of secular humanism, as I discussed at greater length in chapter 2, is rather straightforward. He writes, "Simply defined, humanism is man's attempt to solve his problems independently of God."[76] LaHaye also provides a checklist of secular humanist beliefs (or *disbeliefs*) which include: "Disbelief in God, Belief in Evolution, Rejection of absolute morals, Deification of man as supreme, [and] Belief in the innate goodness of men to govern the world equitably."[77] Secular humanists, LaHaye continues, occupy political office at the highest levels of American government, and are especially active in international organizations such as the United Nations. Nevertheless, they represent a small cadre of activists hell-bent on bringing about a one-world government that will enable the ultimate dictator, Antichrist, to seize power. And they will make their ideologies enticing to the world by inverting Christian beliefs, encouraging the love of self and the worship of a global society without moral restraints. The chaos unleashed by humanist ideals, LaHaye believes, will make Antichrist's ascendancy much easier.

LaHaye, of course, encodes such anxieties throughout the *Left Behind* novels. If one examines LaHaye's concerns a little more carefully, however, one finds that his objections to natural religion and humanism, while important for their surface value, may also conceal a more fundamental struggle over questions of religious truth. That is, the struggles depicted in the *Left Behind* series reflect on one level the confrontations of contemporary prophecy believers and their reliance on proper belief (orthodoxy) against the immediate, mystical, and pragmatic strands of American natural spirituality (orthopraxy). Truth emerges from orthodoxy as a "take it or leave it" proposition, while practitioners of natural religions often derive truth from their own experience, keeping what works and discarding the rest. This type of epistemology threatens the more rigid orthodoxies of conservative evangelicals (even if their notions of truth do change subtly with the passage of time). Nevertheless, in the minds of La-Haye and Jenkins, the New Age and humanist movements shift the focus of truth away from an unchanging, transcendent God and onto mercurial humans and their experience of the created world.

LaHaye and Jenkins are not as different from their textual adversaries as they might lead us to believe, however. First, while it is well beyond the focus of the present study to explain the precise details, even orthodoxy as conceived by the authors has changed mightily over the past several centuries. Orthodox Calvinists, for example, sneer at dispensationalists at best, and consider them outright heretics at worst. The point here is that even what LaHaye and Jenkins consider God's eternal plan for the ages has changed—at least in the minds of its *human interpreters*—as much as the authors would have us believe otherwise. By shifting attention away from their own fragile epistemology and onto the more obviously pragmatic ones of their humanist counterparts, the authors may cover the holes in their own understandings, but they also run the risk of exposing themselves to precisely the same kinds of critique.

More important, as scholars Albanese, Ellwood, Fuller, Roof, and Robert Wuthnow, among many others have argued, Americans of a multitude of religious persuasions share a deeply rooted desire to explore and cultivate a sense of awe and mystery that transcends their everyday lives.[78] Prophecy believers, despite their attempts at critical distancing from what they consider idolatrous spiritualities, do not seem to differ significantly from their New Age and humanist counterparts on this score. The *Left Behind* novels offer their readers a universe of magic and intrigue not always apparent in modern life.

The Enigma Babylon One-World Faith, for example, promises to restore a sense of mystery and awe in a rationalizing world often devoid of magic and spiritual meaning. Antichrist accomplishes this by following a course plotted many times before by new religions—he develops what sociologist Peter L. Berger calls a "plausibility structure"—utilizing already extant, hence plausible beliefs to build a religion around.[79] In this case Antichrist selects compatible aspects of already extant religions and combines them with a thoroughly pragmatic understanding of the world, also using the apparent "magic" of new technologies as needed. This last element is not surprising, especially considering that most Americans believe, according to Schultze, that technology can deliver them from modernity's most pressing ills.[80] Indeed, the inherent inscrutability of the many recent technological developments has helped to further a sense of mystery and awe. Antichrist pragmatically uses the tools available to him to build his infernal kingdom upon a solid plausibility structure, incorporating more traditional religious symbols as necessary.

Moreover, the amorphous nature of the Beast religion is no doubt one reason why LaHaye and Jenkins initially refer to it as an "enigma." Simply put, duped believers are unable to see the evil that lurks behind their newfound spirituality; its true nature remains enigmatic to them. In some cases, especially with secular humanism, adherents are unable to recognize that it is a religion at all. But LaHaye, especially, goes to great lengths to demonstrate that religious ideas—albeit infernal ones—lurk behind humanism and the rest of the Beast religion. Antichrist's religion may present itself as an enigma at first, complete with mysteries and elaborate ritual practices, but LaHaye and Jenkins reveal that the Beast religion progressively directs believers away from the worship of God and toward the worship of their own human potential and technological accomplishments, and, ultimately, Antichrist himself.

That is, the advent of the information culture presents prophecy believers with their own subtle temptations. Prophecy believers are not immune from what they might, with greater reflection, consider idolatrous understandings of new technologies, as Quentin J. Schultze repeatedly points out. LaHaye and Jenkins criticize the growth of mystical, pragmatic, natural religions, yet their texts also bear these marks, even as they attempt to resist any religion that equates humanity with God. By using Antichrist's tools to evade and even defeat him, believers may incorporate his logic, including a *pragmatic, mystical* dependence on new technologies, using the latest gadgets to do what previous generations of prophecy writers reserved for the mysterious hand of God. After all, while Satan may need to keep up with the latest offerings of the Sharper Image catalog, God would seem to have little use for such bells and whistles.[81] Technology, after all, is a human product *par excellence,* one which the *Left Behind* novels inadvertently imply can help believers move closer to their goal of transcendence—a dangerous and risky proposition when one considers that even according to prophecy writers, technology and the fruits of this world belong to Satan himself.

Finally, to conclude the discussion of the Beast religion, I return to the symbol of the Beast himself, aka Antichrist. Evangelicals, unlike medieval polemicists, do not rely ostensibly on allegory. Antichrist will be a living, breathing person instantly recognizable to true believers. Nevertheless, LaHaye and Jenkins are much more concerned with what they consider problematic cultural changes than they are with one person. Antichrist represents, on one level, a particularly vile, power-mad villain, who promotes an agenda of rampant immorality and the total disregard for human rights. He is also, however, a symbol that allows the authors to transform confusing (or enigmatic) technological and cultural developments into an easily recognizable adversary that is everything believers seek to resist—an Antichrist. According to the authors, the Beast religion encourages humanity's worship of itself and its own problematic solutions to the world's problems, rather than relying on the power of God— in effect, deifying the network culture.

Conclusion: *Technologies of the Beast System*

The *Left Behind* novels alternate between deification and demonization of the network culture/Beast system and its technological infrastructure. According to Quentin J. Schultze, evangelicals exemplify the American fascination with the technological, what he labels, recalling the terminology of Leo Marx, "the technological sublime."[82] Leaving aside for the moment the enormous complexity of the term "sublime," one sees that Schultze reads it in its more popular sense as awesome, terrifying, and perhaps even beautiful, yet somehow *exploitable*. Schultze summarizes the evangelical version of the technological sublime as a belief that technology, while virtually all-powerful, is neither inherently good nor evil. Used by secular forces, technology becomes a potential tool of Antichrist, while conservative Protestants, especially televangelists, believe that technology can prove redemptive in their hands.[83]

Technology, Schultze suggests, becomes metaphysical for evangelicals regardless of their initial assessments of it. Control of the world will require technological mastery. Evangelicals view technologies as tools, albeit powerful ones, capable of facilitating either destruction or deliverance. So understood, the human use of technology attempts to dethrone God as humans build wired idols to their new, electronic deity.[84] Furthermore, Schultze compares prophecy fiction to mainstream science-fiction, noting that in both genres, "People are not omnipotent, but technologies are."[85] Noting the proliferation of technological themes within science-fiction, Schultze appears to read such texts as escape oriented, much like their evangelical counterparts. I think it fruitful to compare prophecy fiction to mainstream science-fiction, but I give both genres credit for a significance that extends beyond their ostensible treatment of a highly technologized future. Many such texts—often deeply humanist in perspective—tap into populist anxieties, discussing the survival of the human dimension and its uniqueness in a future (and present) world seemingly defined by inhuman and unresponsive technologies.[86] If anything, prophecy writers may prepare their readership to make the necessary, albeit risky, adaptations to the network culture. Such risk cannot be avoided. Nevertheless, LaHaye and Jenkins's polemical responses to other religions, along with their own dependence on technology in their novels, potentially complicates matters considerably.

Schultze's claim that televangelists view technology as neither inherently good nor evil seems difficult to refute. I suspect his insights also fit the *Left Behind* novels reasonably well, despite the additional complexity one finds in the texts. LaHaye and Jenkins would be wise to adopt a position vis-à-vis the technological that more closely fits Melvin Kranzberg's dictum that "*technology is neither good nor bad, nor is it neutral.*" Manuel Castells elaborates on Kranzberg's statement: "But its actual deployment in the realm of conscious social action, and the complex matrix of interaction between the technological forces unleashed by our species, and the species itself, are matters of inquiry rather than of fate."[87] The activist stance toward technology one finds in the *Left Behind* novels suggests that LaHaye and Jenkins understand its centrality in the emerging world, even if they often exaggerate its importance. Control of technology will prove vital to any community—especially a resistant one—that seeks the power to shape its values and identity. It is a risky game, to be sure. The novels often attribute functions to technology that it simply cannot accomplish. If believers fail to take the proper cautions, to weigh the risk against their giddy assessments of technology's potential, they, too, may find themselves, ironically, worshiping the Beast, transmitting its values rather than their own. Yet if LaHaye and Jenkins's hyperbolic yet paradoxical assessment of technology demonstrates anything, it proves just how connected they are to the fruits of modernity. Adapting the words of Mark C. Taylor slightly, "they cannot pull the plug."[88]

5

Marks of the Beast
The Struggle for Evangelical Identity

As the networks passing through us become more complex and the relations at every level of experience become more extensive and intensive, the speed of change accelerates until equilibrium disappears and turbulence becomes a more or less permanent condition. While occasioning confusion, uncertainty, and sometimes despair, this inescapable turbulence harbors creative possibilities for people and institutions able to adapt quickly, creatively, and effectively. Those who are too rigid to fit into rapidly changing worlds become obsolete or are driven beyond the edge of chaos to destruction.[1]
—Mark C. Taylor, "Screening Information"

Many conversion narratives bear witness to such dark nights of personal identity. At these moments of extreme exposure, the null response, far from declaring the question empty, returns to it and preserves it as a question. What cannot be effaced is the question itself: who am I?[2]   —Paul Ricoeur, "Narrative Identity"

The Dark Night of the Evangelical Soul

The *Left Behind* series, at its most basic level, addresses the question of what it means to be an evangelical. Whatever else LaHaye and Jenkins accomplish in their novels, they attempt, first and foremost, to reinforce evangelical identity against the subtly shifting threats of the modern age. The cosmic drama LaHaye and Jenkins depict indeed highlights numerous external threats. The most meaningful battles occur not for territories or world control, however, but center on the disposition of souls. Individuals, rather than structures, prove most meaningful to the authors.

The nineteenth-century revivalist Dwight L. Moody described humanity as a doomed vessel, with the evangelist attempting to save those floundering in the water. The metaphor remains apt for contemporary prophecy writers. LaHaye and Jenkins cite the numerous structural evils that oppress believers, but they ultimately appeal to the anxieties of a readership, struggling to make sense of their evangelical identity in the face of the emerging network culture. Nothing is as it appears to be, and only faith, the authors suggest, can deliver believers from the often crippling uncertainty in contemporary American culture that threatens to drown them.

Much of the uncertainty in the *Left Behind* novels stems from the sudden, mass disappearance of the righteous believers in the Rapture. LaHaye and Jenkins suggest, ironically, that the disappearances will trigger a turn to Christ among those left behind, but with all of the legitimate Christians removed, who or what will remain to certify the authenticity of the new converts? It is not surprising, then, that LaHaye and Jenkins, who situate the vast majority of their narrative within that unprecedented epoch of doubt and confusion known as the Tribulation, repeatedly return to such basic questions as, "who am I," and "what does it mean to be an evangelical?" In an age marked by uncertainty, the answer is by no means clear. Although the authors periodically offer assurances to their readers, they also undermine such offerings—wise perhaps, given Antichrist's dominance and propensity for deception. His Beast system—or network culture—challenges stable notions of selfhood.

Recalling terminology introduced in chapter 3, Mark C. Taylor defines contemporary selfhood as "nodular." The self, he argues, exists as a node among other nodes that together form a complicated network (culture) greater than the sum of its parts. Individual nodes, or selves, are not merely absorbed and enslaved by the network culture, however. They retain meaningful choices, even if such choices are circumscribed or even deceptive—screened—by the network culture. Indeed, selfhood for Taylor is a multimedia experience. Again displaying his propensity for puns, Taylor suggests here that in the network culture "who we are" is constantly *mediated* by multiple forces of which we may or may not be aware. Just as we lack unmediated knowledge of the external world, we also lack the ability to define our selves without the mediation of countless others. In other words, taking Taylor's multimedia metaphor a step further, our identity is constantly "screened" by people and cultural forces with which we interact. The self, moreover, both deploys screens and is *screened,* a condition which offers numerous possibilities. A screen,

Taylor notes, may be "something that serves to divide, conceal or protect." It might also be a "coarse sieve," "a system for appraising and selecting personnel," a "phosphorescent surface upon which the image is formed in a cathode-ray tube," or even "a forged banknote."[3] Put differently, we erect filters, or screens, between ourselves and our environments, screening who we are from who we are not. But others screen us, too, of course. The network culture and its imperatives, Taylor suggests, screens our possibilities as we struggle to find our place in the world.

The various ways Taylor uses "screen" may initially strike one as anything but precise. When examined more carefully, however, his notion of the nodular self as *screened* does find affinity with the ways LaHaye and Jenkins describe selfhood. First, the authors suggest that identity serves as a means to erect boundaries between what one is and what one is not. The saved must be clearly differentiated from the damned. The test of faith separates the wheat from the chaff, with those less committed carried away by the winds of indecision. Second, our lives have increasingly become dependent on the quality of information we receive—noted, most immediately, in images. Images become more important than whatever something might be in its essence, since the only data we have, in many cases, are mediated images and perceptions.

This gap between what exists and what we perceive requires a measure of trust. Philosophers have implied our dependence on mediated information since ancient times. But conservative evangelicals, relying on eighteenth-century philosophies of "common sense," that is, "what you see is what you get," have been late arrivals to the idea that our world is never quite as it seems.[4] What sociologist David Lyon calls "data-images," for example—virtual "persons" collected and shaped via credit reports, consumer preferences, and on-line browsing habits, among other factors—become our informational avatars in an increasingly anonymous culture, in which who we believe ourselves to be appears less significant than the data trail we leave behind.[5] Finally, images and virtual realities lend themselves to deception and fraud, since such technologies can involve the manipulation of appearances. Existence in the network culture thus requires discernment, a condition of which LaHaye and Jenkins are well aware. Those who act without God, the authors tell us, will inevitably fall prey to Satan, while those who place their trust in Christ will see through the schemes of history's most notorious confidence man.

The network culture calls into question the fundamentals of our personal and cultural identities. The problem is by no means isolated to prophecy believers, either, although they and other groups who perceive themselves marginalized by the network culture no doubt feel it most acutely. Identity has emerged as a fragile and contested category in contemporary life, and people increasingly attempt to define themselves by their consumption patterns, for example, the homes they build, the cars they buy, the clothes they wear, the wines they drink, or, in many cases, the spiritualities they profess. Religions, especially intense ones such as conservative evangelicalism, offer adherents a powerful sense of meaning and purpose in a world that offers people less and less of both. Prophecy belief, specifically, places believers within a symbolic universe that promises to end their existential doubt, both in this world and in the one to come. To this end, the *Left Behind* protagonists (and, presumably, readers) require some certification of their existential identities amid so much confusion. LaHaye and Jenkins, following the precedent established by their forebears in prophecy writing, deploy the symbol of visible marks to help provide believers with the existential assurance they seek. The quest for marks, then, represents a quixotic search for an assurance of one's identity as a believer, along with guarantees that others are who they profess to be.

Visible Marks

LaHaye and Jenkins attempt to overcome the doubt and confusion characteristic of network culture by introducing visible signs on the bodies of believers and nonbelievers alike, permanent marks which cannot be effaced. The protagonists have no foolproof way of knowing what lurks within others or even themselves. Marks allow them to identify themselves and separate friends from enemies. This seemingly superficial definition of identity—that one's selfhood can be encapsulated in a little mark on the right hand or forehead—is again remarkably consistent with Mark C. Taylor's definition of selfhood in the network culture. Taylor argues, discussing tattooing practices, that marks serve to screen who one is from whom one is not, identifying persons with specific groups. He writes, "When membership in a group is deemed vital to identity, it is not uncommon for the individual to be permanently marked. Among their functions, tattoos serve as inscriptions of sociocultural codes and structures on the body of the individual."[6] Tattoos mark individuals, not only with graphic designs, but also with the marks of the cultures they represent. Used by tribal groups, correctional institutions, and modern gangs, tattoos (marks) define whether one is inside or outside the group. For a subculture with such a close definition of internal identity, it is not surprising that LaHaye and Jenkins would turn to a similar form of indelible identification.[7]

Complementing Taylor's insights into tattooing practices, LaHaye and Jenkins project much that worries them about contemporary American culture into the unobtrusive Mark of the Beast. Although they later introduce a "Mark of Christ" for certified believers—a theme to which I will return shortly—they devote much of their attention to the Mark of the Beast. The Mark of the Beast is at once a Mark of new technologies, the global economy, religion, and even personal identity. A tiny microchip implanted into the skin, the Mark allows one to participate in commercial culture, certifies one as a believer in Antichrist's divinity, and contains everything anyone would need to know about the bearer. More than that, it represents Antichrist in all of his aspects. And it is permanently embedded in the bearer's skin—a part of their identity. Those who accept the Mark and participate in the ways of this world share Antichrist's fate. For the Mark grants the bearer life in a temporal sense, but once buried within the skin it sucks the eternal life away from its host. A parasite within the body, it offers sustenance for a brief time but ultimately betrays its host. Once one accepts the Mark, Antichrist ceases to be an external menace. The bearer incorporates evil within his or her own body where it oozes and burns forever.

One might be tempted to ask, then, if the Mark is so unequivocally evil, why prophecy writers express so much fear that people, perhaps even believers, might willingly accept it? Robert Fuller suggests that "Antichrist, it seems, almost invariably embodies those alluring traits and qualities that at a deeper level threaten to seduce even the 'true believer' into apostasy."[8] Slightly rephrasing Fuller's observation, the Mark indicates one's acceptance of Antichrist and all that he represents. As I noted in previous chapters, prophecy believers want the world on their terms. They do not necessarily turn their backs on it, at least not for long. The Mark tempts believers because it represents a stable source of meaning in an increasingly uncertain world. It offers, literally and metaphorically, a place in the world, including economic standing and an accepted social identity. It ends the tension many believers struggle with between the evangelical injunction to remain "in but not of the world," and a desire to participate in the benefits of American consumer culture.

The pressure to accept the Mark and the world it represents becomes intense, almost tortuous amid so much uncertainty. Yet it cannot be applied by force alone. LaHaye and Jenkins, despite their overarching concern with the power Antichrist wields during the Tribulation, suggest individuals can offer their most meaningful resistance at the personal level. One must still give one's assent to accept the Mark. The authors are adamant on this point. So how does one accept the Mark? Why would anyone take it willingly? One could describe the implantation of the Mark as a kind of torture. Global Community officials in the *Left Behind* novels threaten resisters with decapitation. Decapitation seems like more than just an attempt by the authors to fill their descriptions of the Tribulation with additional blood and gore, however. Without the Mark, one is "decapitated," wandering around headless without direction when so much about American culture is changing. The only way to make peace with the world, the novels suggest, is to accept the Mark and the sociocultural identity it proffers. Tempting as it is, the identity suggested by the Mark strikes prophecy writers as incompatible with core evangelical values, forcing believers to make a final, inalterable choice. Those who accept the Mark proclaim Antichrist and his culture as the one true God— the object of their spiritual quest. Taking the Mark constitutes an act of betrayal against both God and oneself, affirming that Antichrist and what he represents alone can offer deliverance.

The process of torture as understood by cultural theorists provides further insight into the struggles believers face when tempted by the Mark of the Beast. Torture, as Elaine Scarry describes it, does not serve—contrary to popular stereotypes—to extract information for its own sake. The torturer *claims* to seek information which only the subject can provide, but the process more closely resembles a cruel game in which the goal becomes the breaking down of the victim, not so much for information— perhaps of trifling value in any case—but for destroying his or her personhood. The torturer seeks, Scarry claims, to create a blank slate, to destroy the victim's old identity and force him or her to see the world as the torturer constructs it, and to accept a new notion of selfhood based on that construction. The "secret," or that which the torturer appears to seek so desperately, is little more than an elaborate ruse. The torturer may already know the secret. Nevertheless, the quest for it gives the torturer moral purpose. When the victim finally offers the desired information, it legitimizes the process. The torturer, after all, claims to seek only information, data which the subject stubbornly withholds. Yet torture does not so much extract information, as it *informs* the selfhood of its victim. Torture robs the individual not of information per se, but instead breaks down the individual's will to resist, along with destroying the tortured one's ability to inform his or her own identity.[9]

LaHaye and Jenkins provide a narrative example of Scarry's theory in *Armageddon* (#11), describing the torture of one of their key protagonists, Chloe Steele. Chloe, an ex-Stanford student and original member of the paramilitary evangelical resistance movement—the Tribulation Force—is captured by Global Community troops after she embarks upon an ill-advised scouting mission outside her San Diego safe house. Chloe, as a leading member of the evangelical resistance, is accorded celebrity status among her friends and enemies alike, and the troops immediately take her in for high-level questioning. This seems like a logical move. Not that Chloe knows that much about the Tribulation Force and its operations—at least anything that the Global Community does not already know. Rather, since Chloe began the series as a high-status, "trophy" convert to conservative evangelicalism, it makes perfect sense within the narrative that the Global Community would do anything to win her back. Chloe serves then as an archetype for a sophisticated, youthful demographic so important to contemporary evangelicalism. The "battle for the mind," as LaHaye calls it, centers largely upon those represented by Chloe—impressionable young people who must resist the "tortures" of the modern world if they are to remain Christians.

The authors' depiction of Chloe's torture resembles a cut-rate version of that found in "B" movies. Still, the chief interrogator, Jock Ashmore, knows the usual tricks. He attempts to extract information from Chloe using hunger, sleep deprivation, misinformation, truth serum injections, and even repeated plays of the Global Community anthem, "Hail Carpathia!"[10] Jock seeks the location of the San Diego safe house or so he claims. But he begins by asking Chloe a few personal questions, such as her name and the identity of her beloved toddler, Kenny. Jock, of course, already has such information. Sophisticated iris scans reveal Chloe's identity and affiliations. Jock simply wants Chloe to *confess* the information, thus betraying her old identity. Jock demands the location of the safe house, for example, but even incompetents like Jock know that the San Diego group will evacuate upon learning of Chloe's disappearance. The authors suggest Jock requires such information, but the narrative moves in a different direction. Jock ultimately wants Chloe to renounce her old affiliations and accept the Mark of the Beast—the identity offered by Antichrist. Chloe, however, buoyed by her privileged knowledge of End-Times events, Tribulation Force training, and a mysterious angelic visitor, successfully resists Jock.

The authors do a credible job of translating the amorphous anxieties of prophecy believers into the metaphoric language of torture. The threat posed by the emerging network culture is never quite as obvious as a torture narrative would suggest, however. Believers residing outside LaHaye and Jenkins's fantasy world are not as fortunate as Chloe. She faces her torturer directly, rather than struggling against an otherwise ill-defined and poorly understood concept. Readers of the *Left Behind* series face temptations from American consumer culture that never quite arrive at the same level of clarity and resolution that Chloe experiences. Nevertheless, the metaphor remains significant. The Mark represents an acceptance of the technological, economic, and social dimensions of the network culture. The acquiescence of believers to contemporary culture distracts them from spiritual, Christlike identities, turning them instead toward an incessant, market-oriented drive for consumption and creature comforts seemingly incompatible with evangelical piety.

LaHaye and Jenkins, like countless prophecy writers before them, highlight the significance of the Mark of the Beast because the symbol proves so powerful on a number of levels. As believers struggle to maintain their evangelical identity amid the perceived hostility of the network culture, the temptation to accept the certainty the Mark of the Beast offers becomes intense. Successful resistance requires the kind of high-maintenance, alternative worldview provided by evangelical prophecy belief. The authors reassure their readers of the reality of firm foundations, if believers remain faithful and discerning enough to find them. The faithful remnant, however, must avoid the constant, treacherous attempts of Antichrist and his associates to convince them otherwise. The remainder of this chapter tracks the efforts of LaHaye and Jenkins's protagonists to resist the Mark of the Beast without becoming a part of Antichrist's infernal system.

Dubious Marks

In the *Left Behind* narrative, Antichrist works with his associate, the False Prophet, to create a virtual kingdom rife with confusion. Such an at-mosphere helps foster conversion, as individuals question their existence as they have known it, and open themselves up to any possibility that offers an end to the potentially crippling anxiety and despair they experience. Religion scholars note that intense cultural anxiety and a general sense of groundlessness often accompany conversion experiences. What sociologist Peter L. Berger calls plausibility structures—beliefs and practices that lend coherence and meaning, hence, plausibility, to cultures and social structures—occasionally break down when individuals and communities face challenges to their most profound cultural assumptions.[11] Most people find subtle, constant means to adapt to changing conditions and retain the meaningfulness of their lives. Others such as prophecy writers, however, radically indict many of the changes associated with modernity, calling forth what amounts to a symbolically violent quest to restore order and meaning, encouraging anxious souls to seek out promises of eternal truth and firm, unchanging foundations.

Antichrist, LaHaye and Jenkins tell us, capitalizes on the doubt and confusion he fosters, destroying older worldviews and frightening citizens into acquiescing to his kingdom. God, however, the authors inform us, also benefits from the interval of crisis the Tribulation offers. The Tribulation will bring forth a great "soul harvest" numbering possibly over a billion persons, who, finally recognizing the signs of the times, will choose Christ as their savior. Thus, although Antichrist appears responsible for the doubt and confusion of the last days, in reality, he merely acts out his part in God's eternal plan of salvation. God, ultimately, uses the turmoil of the Tribulation to force individuals to choose sides once and for all in the cosmic battle between good and evil.

Few would choose Antichrist and the evil he represents if they could recognize it, LaHaye and Jenkins suggest, hence, Antichrist must dissemble and make himself look distinctly Christlike. Antichrist offers visible signs and wonders, while Christ waits the full seven-year period to make his Glorious Appearance at the end of the Tribulation. Antichrist has the upper hand, without question, since believers already missed their best chance to meet Christ with the Rapture. Nevertheless, hope remains, but the authors make it clear that salvation will not come easily for those left behind. Antichrist and his crew are a clever bunch, and they will co-opt even such traditional Christian categories as piety and miracles, as long as it serves their larger purposes. All in all, LaHaye and Jenkins imply that Antichrist's Beast religion will lend meaning to the unprecedented unrest of the Tribulation period, and his clerics will wear robes marked with numerous symbols of holiness. Underneath, however, an unwholesome surprise will await those who fail to use the Bible as their literal, inerrant guide through uncertain times.

The appearance of Pontifex Maximus Peter II—LaHaye and Jenkins's initial candidate for the position of the False Prophet—invokes a number of images which together in their dizzying array seem to indicate nothing of substance or foundation. His robe bears a representation of every major religion, yet effaces all of them by their juxtaposition in his "coat of many colors." Just as the authors present Mathews as a superficial character, the symbols that together compose his Enigma Babylon One-World Faith appear devoid of their cultural and historical contexts. They are shorn of depth and meaning in the all-encompassing drive toward unification. Mathews and his world church offer much to the faithful, yet direct them to nothing beyond *themselves*.[12]

Left Behind's Antichrist, Nicolae Carpathia, is not unaware of this, of course. After his assassination and subsequent resurrection, Antichrist, now possessed by Satan, realizes the Enigma Babylon One-World Faith, despite its unwholesome promise, cannot deliver what he needs most— the unquestioned love and obedience of the entire world. Mathews's church, because of its obvious emptiness, proves ultimately useless. The people, it seems, need a personal god, a visible, resurrected savior they can admire and worship. Carpathia explains the need for a reformation of his Beast religion:

> The Enigma Babylon One-World Faith failed because, despite its lofty goal of unifying the world's religions, it worshipped no god but itself. It was devoted to unity, yet that was never achieved. Its god was nebulous and impersonal. But with Leon Fortunato as the Most High Reverend Father of Carpathianism, the devout of the world finally have a personal god whose might and power and glory have been demonstrated in the raising *of himself,* from the dead.[13]

LaHaye and Jenkins also seem to recognize, however inadvertently, that a nebulous and impersonal indictment of the network culture will not work for *their* readership either. Evil may have become increasingly ill-defined and impersonal in recent years, leaving prophecy writers without well-defined adversaries like the Soviets, for example; but this does not stop the authors from giving the infernal Beast system a more coherent identity. Even if identity—all identity—seems dubious and fluid in the flows of the network culture, prophecy writers require that good and evil remain absolute, each with its proper name. As the dreams of firm foundations and fixed identities slip away with data and images moving at the speed of a flickering, optical digital light, individuals require a form of identification that promises to make their identities transparent to others—a mark.

Assigning the Mark of the Beast becomes Antichrist's first priority after his resurrection. Having found Pontifex Maximus Peter II self-serving and ineffective, he promotes longtime sycophant Leon Fortunato to the role of False Prophet. Reverend Fortunato must convince the world's citizens to accept the Mark of the Beast—to accept the identity that Antichrist has prepared for them. Fortunato, as Antichrist's image consultant and spin doctor, employs three means to convince those with little faith that Carpathia is the real thing. First, he orders the creation of an "image of the beast," a two-and-a half story bronze and iron statue of Carpathia, imbued with the power to speak. The statue commands worship with its fiery mouth and nostrils (fueled by burning Bibles), and punctuates its demands with an occasional belch of burning sulfur.[14] Later, after Carpathia's resurrection, the statue remains, along with its regional clones. Second, Fortunato augments his repertoire of deceit with ESPN-style instant replays of Carpathia's resurrection, intended to convince even the most skeptical of onlookers that—after further review—he is indeed their "risen lord." Third, he places "Loyalty Enforcement Facilitators," better known as guillotines, at each of the Mark application centers. Those who refuse the Mark are summarily executed as an example to others. Most citizens do not require such drastic enforcement measures and readily agree to take the Mark. After all, it provides them with a transparent affirmation of identity and a sense of place in the Global Community. Moreover, the Mark affirms their loyalty to a figure who promises to erase their uncertainty and restore order to an increasingly complicated world.

Antichrist forces the world to choose sides, hoping to eliminate ambiguity and separate, once and for all, the goats from the lambs. Even his dramatic efforts, however, cannot forestall the uncertainty that lingers beneath the appearances of his virtual kingdom. The Mark also signifies "the number of man." It represents on one level the "death of God" and the valorization of humans; but such humans also represent nothing at all, because the object of their faith and that to which their Marks would attest ultimately has neither form nor substance. False Prophet promises much, but when carefully examined, he delivers nothing. Lurking beneath his robe is a spiritual abyss, a haunting absence of any obvious foundation or purpose upon which to build one's identity. Perhaps the most unwholesome aspect of the Mark, then, is that it promises deliverance but, in the End, offers only an empty Gospel of lies and deception.

Prophecy writers nevertheless speculate as to what the Mark may resemble. Even though it ultimately delivers the believer unto nothingness, it must look like *something* in order to deceive so many. Prophecy writers, as we have seen, have become fascinated by information technologies. Thus, it is not surprising to find that the Mark, too, bears witness to technological processes. Specifically, prophecy writers imagine the Mark as either a bar code, or, more recently, an implanted, silicon "smart chip" that carries all of the important details of one's identity.[15] "No one may buy or sell without the Mark," as Revelation 13 puts it. But, as prophecy writer Peter Lalonde reminds his readers, the Mark is not only economic but also spiritual:

> When you consider that, according to the Scriptures, those who take the mark of the beast will be eternally damned, it becomes clear that the most important aspect of the mark is not economic but spiritual. . . . It is crucial to understand that the decision to take the mark of the beast involves some form of a pledge of allegiance to the antichrist, making it a spiritual decision that has only secondary economic benefits.[16]

LaHaye and Jenkins attribute to the Mark a number of functions. First, it permits the believer to participate in the Beast economy, using his or her implanted chip as a debit card, which helps to eliminate fraud and speed transactions. Second, the Mark gives its bearer a sense of place, specifying one of ten regional kingdoms for the bearer's homeland. Third, it conveys a permanent identity, taken in either the right hand or forehead, which cannot be effaced. It instantly announces to authorities one's identity and where one belongs, allowing Global Community officials to track citizens and make Antichrist's kingdom more secure. Finally, every Mark bears Carpathia's name, either as a numerical representation or the initials "NJC." Antichrist also displays a remarkable knowledge of consumer preferences, however, making provision for those who want a customized, vanity design. The ultimate content, however, remains identical.

But who is the Beast before whom one must bow and whose Mark one must bear? The Mark itself gives some indication. As a computer chip containing information, the Mark is a sign of technology, a product of the information culture. It is also, however, a Mark of identity, a symbol of agreement. Like the signs on False Prophet's robe, the Mark indicates continuity, despite aesthetic differences, a ceaseless flow of information that converts depth into surface, presence into absence, and foundations into doubt. It acts as a witness to the existential uncertainty characteristic of the network culture.[17] Trapped in interlocking webs of information, those bearing the Mark embrace an identity that appears solid and certain, but upon closer inspection "melts into the air," betraying its superficiality.

Lalonde's clarification of the Mark as spiritual proves significant, although as Mark C. Taylor suggests, economies, financial or otherwise, always have a spiritual component. All involve speculation or faith in an unknown that promises a return on one's confidence, what one might also term a *redemption*.[18] When one makes the correct choice, one's investment is rewarded. If, however, one speculates on the wrong commodity—a false god—a crash of spiritual proportions looms once the god is revealed as an empty idol. LaHaye and Jenkins's protagonists face such spiritual confidence men and must find God amid all the deception Antichrist and his unholy associates heap upon them.

Taylor describes the difficulties presented by such quests for certainty in his essay "Discrediting God." Working with Herman Melville's mid-nineteenth-century novel *The Confidence Man,* Taylor frames his reading of spiritual matters. To believe in God requires faith, but faith is gilded with uncertainty, since modernity with its scientific discoveries and Biblical criticism has stripped away the veil and revealed God as an abstraction lacking an unquestioned foundation. "Could God also be a confidence man?" Taylor asks. Although LaHaye and Jenkins would deny such uncertainty since God is always an absolute within their texts, the protagonists nevertheless face nagging doubts concerning the good-will of fellow believers; and, just as importantly, they learn that trust, or faith, carries the risk of betrayal and deception. God as such must remain fixed, but humans made in "the image of God" maintain the potential for deceit. With depth reduced to surface, and "reality" reduced to images—

or marks—in the continuous flows of information, nothing is ever quite as it seems, and even apparent certainty carries deception. Taylor describes the shift from an industrial economy to an information-based, network culture:

> As mechanical means of production and reproduction give way to electronic means of reproduction, ideality becomes reality in which everything is mediated as well as mediaized. When everything is always already mediaized, image becomes real and reality becomes imaginary.[19]

LaHaye and Jenkins's response to this persistent uncertainty produces more questions than answers. Protagonists might feel certain in their relationships to God, but how can they be assured of the same in other professed believers? The Mark, despite its promise to make good and evil visible to the faithful and damned alike, cannot eliminate doubt. Teenage computer prodigy Chang Wong, for example—the latest in a series of Tribulation Force operatives working within Antichrist's computer center at his palace in New Babylon—finds himself in a compromising situation. Although Chang has accepted Christ, his father remains one of Carpathia's staunchest supporters and desires above all for his son to become the first Global Community employee to receive the Mark of the Beast. The father prevails, dragging his son to the mark application facility. Chang does not want the Mark—the narrative makes this quite evident—but neither does he choose martyrdom, which the authors present as the only valid alternative for believers. Chang insists he has no choice, but the hundreds of martyrs the authors describe in gory detail later in *The Mark* (#8) indicate otherwise. He has chosen, if by default, a liminal, wild-card status.

Hours after receiving the Mark, Chang reveals his predicament to David Hassid, the Tribulation Force mole for whom he would ostensibly work inside the palace. Although Chang insists that he can now operate effectively "from the inside," David seems less than convinced. The narrative leads us to believe, too, that all will turn out all right. Yet David no doubt speaks for the nagging concerns of the authors who maintain profound uncertainty vis-à-vis Chang and what he calls his "bi-loyalty." David gives voice to these concerns:

> "I'm just wondering what's really inside you, Chang."
> "What do you mean?"

"Spiritually. Your sister is a tough prison guard. . . . But she glows with a spirituality, a humility. She has a real Christlike quality. . . . But what about you, Chang? Do you know who you are and who you're not? Do you understand the depth of your own depravity and realize that God saved you while you were dead in your sins?"[20]

Chang responds favorably, but David remains dubious.

Significantly, even believers have a mark. Compounding the dilemma, David notices that Chang bears *both* marks. The Mark of Christ lies alongside the more prominent Mark of the Beast. Although one can readily detect the Mark of the Beast, the Mark of Christ is more subtle, visible only through the eye of faith. The "mark of the believer," as the authors also call it, promises a sense of certainty and identity, assuring believers of their place in this world and the next. Dr. Charles, the Tribulation Force's physician, is the first to notice the mark. Examining Buck, Dr. Charles finds a curious patch on Buck's forehead that resembles a bruise:

"You *do* have a mark there," the doctor said. He pushed on it and around it. "No pain?"

"No."

"You know," Buck said, "you've got something on your forehead, too. Looks like a smudge."[21]

Dr. Charles and Buck find the marks inexplicable, but give them no further thought—"may have picked up some newsprint," Dr. Charles explains.[22] A short time later while Buck and Dr. Ben-Judah track Chloe, who is being held under guard at a Global Community hospital, they notice each other's marks. Incredulous, they each look in a mirror, only to find that they cannot see their own "shadow or bruise." One can only see the mark on the forehead of others, it seems, never oneself. Examining Dr. Ben-Judah's forehead, Buck finally begins to understand:

"Yes," Buck said. "Hey! This is like one of those puzzles that looks like a bunch of sticks until you sort of reverse it in your mind and see the background as the foreground and vice versa. That's a cross on your forehead."

Tsion seemed to stare desperately at Buck. Suddenly he said, "Yes! Cameron! We have the seal, visible to only other believers."[23]

LaHaye and Jenkins inform us that the Mark of Christ, in contrast to the Mark of the Beast, stands out as a relief, a subtle yet profound holographic image that projects depth and dimensionality—if one has the eyes to see beyond superficial distractions. While the Mark of the Beast projects one's identity with a flat efficiency, the Mark of Christ offers a more profound, dynamic image.[24] Moreover, because only believers can see the Mark, believers become less visible to Antichrist, making their identity a less risky proposition.

The idea of a "visible mark" for believers has long circulated within the evangelical subculture. LaHaye and Jenkins depart somewhat from other prophecy writers in their interpretation of the symbol, however. Prophecy writer Hal Lindsey, for example, limits the "visible mark" to the "144,000 Jewish 'bondservants' of God," who will use God's supernatural protection to spread the Gospel during the Tribulation period. But for Lindsey the "seal" also provides a guarantee of one's identity, as his market-oriented description suggests:

> The verb "to seal" means to make an imprint in wax with a signet ring. This was done in ancient business transactions of all kinds, and signified that whatever was thus sealed belonged to the one whose mark was on it. The idea of a *visible* mark of ownership and guarantee of protection is inherent in the word.[25]

Novelist Carol Balizet depicts Lindsey's scenario literally, as the 144,000 "sealed servants" receive the visible mark simultaneous with the Rapture of the Church.[26] LaHaye and Jenkins deploy the symbol more broadly, offering it as a guarantee for *all* Tribulation believers, and not just the 144,000 Jewish witnesses. At the same time as the authors extend the security of visible marks to all believers, however, they also undercut such assurances with the possibility of deception. Satan controls the Tribulation period, and uncertainty marks his rule. Even "visible marks," the authors suggest, do not eliminate the inevitability of risk.

David sees Chang's Mark, which would appear to validate Chang's authenticity as a believer. But David remains bewildered by the undecidability of Chang. The latter insists that his arrogance is "all just an act," but David detects a behavior that is not Christlike. David might be open to the idea of faking the Mark of the Beast—and the narrative depends on such openness to a great extent—but he cannot shake his doubt; and he suggests that fellow believers will have a difficult time with the concept, too. One can easily lose sight of the subtle Mark of Christ when one finds it juxtaposed with the more pronounced Mark of the Beast.[27]

Presumably Chang has been saved—he has the Mark of Christ—but he also bears the Mark of the Beast. Prophecy writers have typically frowned upon such ambivalence. Protagonists seeking to go "undercover" often lose their souls in the process, forgetting their identity in Christ and returning to their old, sinful natures. LaHaye and Jenkins, however, remain torn. In their commentary on the novels, they write:

> For the Bible is quite clear that a person *cannot* take the mark of the Beast accidentally. In fact, it will become the external sign of a *deliberate decision* to give one's *self* to the devil [emphasis added].[28]

The Bible may be "quite clear," but the authors retain significant doubt. On the one hand, they suggest that Chang's Mark does *not* serve "as an external sign of a deliberate decision to give one's self to the devil." Chang, after all, also bears the Mark of Christ. Yet how does one account for the sign? Which sign? Can we trust that the Mark of the Beast means what it indicates? "No one would fake the mark of the beast," David assures us. And since Chang presumably received his salvation and Christlike identity, it cannot be lost. But did he ever have it? Does the Mark of the Beast indicate damnation, as the authors' commentary indicates, or can one fake the Mark and go undercover inside Antichrist's network, bringing him down "from the inside," as the protagonists are fond of saying? The answer remains undecidable. The Marks, which promise to end existential doubt and bring forth certainty, just lead to greater confusion. Faith, it seems, must still be invested wisely. God may be able to "count every hair on one's head," but those left behind must continue to put their identities on the line.

Underscoring this point, one notes that the authors keep their readership in constant doubt. Deceit pervades the narrative as even trusted characters come under suspicion. For example, Amanda White—Rayford's second wife—displays all of the outward traits of a servant of God. She becomes a fixture in the New Hope Village Church; her testimony bears witness to a profound conversion experience; and, perhaps most important, she becomes a devoted evangelical wife. Doubts remain, however. Flying to join Rayford in New Babylon, her plane gets sucked into the Tigris River, a casualty of the Great Earthquake. At first Rayford does not know her fate. He fears she may be dead, of course, but he never doubts her ultimate fate until Dr. Ben-Judah, decoding some of the deceased Pastor Barnes's personal logs, discovers evidence that calls her identity into question.

Barnes received a number of e-mails from an unknown source, warning him of a mole inside the Tribulation Force. He attempted to issue a vague warning to his colleagues but did not give explicit details. Dr. Ben-Judah uncovers the late pastor's secret only after White's disappearance. The mysterious e-mails warn Barnes of "the root beer lady." Amanda White, it seems, is also A&W. But upon further investigation, Barnes discovers something far more sinister than the initials of a soft drink. Strong evidence indicates that White is actually the sister of Leon Fortunato, Carpathia's chief of staff and eventual False Prophet. Dr. Ben-Judah breaks the news to the group, and the anxiety lingers throughout the fourth novel, *Soul Harvest*. After receiving allegations concerning Amanda from Carpathia himself, Rayford finally dives into the Tigris to find the answer. He identifies her first by her salt and pepper hair, and finds her body still strapped to the seat. Worse, her corpse does not bear the Mark of Christ. Could it be true?

The authors attempt to end the uncertainty in the fifth volume, *Apollyon*. Although Amanda's recovered hard drive reveals extensive communications with Carpathia, Hattie Durham, in Tribulation Force custody, reveals that all of the files were planted. Hattie even sent the anonymous, incriminating e-mails to Pastor Barnes. When pressed for a better explanation of such an unlikely scenario as planting files, Hattie assures them that "Nicolae had experts trained in that."[29] Rayford accepts Hattie's explanation and his "faith in Amanda had been restored."[30] She did not yet have the Mark of Christ, or "the seal of God," because she had died before God dispensed his Marks. Hattie's explanation may satisfy Rayford, but the authors' quick dismissal leaves the reader with nagging doubts. Although recent technological developments have made the idea of remotely planting files on someone else's computer a bit more plausible, the authors cannot account for the Fortunato connection. The Tribulation Force may have regained their faith in Amanda, but the careful reader retains doubt.[31]

LaHaye and Jenkins, perhaps sensing the inadequacy of their explanations, undertake more explicit measures to sort out the confusion for their readers. Beginning with book seven, *Assassins*, the authors append a salvation scorecard to their preface, telling the reader who is saved and who is not. Curiously, as mentioned earlier, the updated scorecard for book eight, *The Mark,* includes an entry for "Albie B." Although he bears the Mark of Christ, LaHaye and Jenkins place the former Muslim into his own category: "professed believer." But why is he merely a "professed believer?" Why do the authors place doubt even within their certainty? The feeling lingers that a traitor lurks near the inner circle of the Tribulation Force. Having a visible mark, like Chang, is not enough to deflect suspicion from Albie. Perhaps the Mark of Christ does not proffer assurance, but instead delivers more uncertainty?

Mark C. Taylor, discussing the thought of philosopher Jacques Derrida, notes that Derrida insists upon certain marks within texts he calls *undecidables.* Undecidables cannot be reduced to a simple either/or solution. Put differently, they exist neither inside nor outside the structure they seek to oppose. Taylor remarks:

> If they were clearly outside the structure or system, undecidables would be incorporated within an oppositional structure and thus would be part of the system they are supposed to elude. . . . undecidables haunt all systems and structures as an exteriority, which is in some sense within even though it cannot be incorporated.[32]

Taylor's remarks remind one of the evangelical insistence on an "in, but not of" status vis-à-vis the world. Perhaps this is why the authors display obvious difficulty finding certainty, even when certification appears to come from God himself. To exist successfully within the Beast system, evangelicals must risk their identity. Such activity involves danger, but it may be the only way to interact with the network culture without becoming absorbed into it. Evangelicals, the authors' ambivalence suggests, cannot have certainty this side of eternity and must take "leaps of faith." Without such uncertainty and risk they are already a part of the system. Ambivalence and opacity to Antichrist and fellow believers may be their only tenable course of action.

Currencies of Faith

But the quest of believers to retain their evangelical identity remains a difficult and tenuous one, since the risk of deception never disappears. Consistent with the overarching theme of deception found throughout the series, the authors introduce another twist to the Mark of Christ in

Apollyon. They suggest that not even the subtle, virtually invisible Mark of Christ can eliminate the anxieties of those who can never identify the enemy with absolute precision. The authors deploy the Mark of Christ as a validation of the solid foundation one finds in obedience to Christ, yet Christ's mark can also be counterfeited.

Ernie, a mechanic at the airport where the deceased Tribulation Force pilot Ken Ritz housed his planes, pays close attention to the teachings of Dr. Ben-Judah, if only to take advantage of trusting, gullible believers. After Ernie makes a selfish claim on Ritz's buried gold bullion—displaying behavior that is definitely not Christlike—Rayford gets suspicious. He confronts the manipulative adolescent:

> No wonder Ernie's mark had appeared so prominent. He had refreshed it with whatever he had used to create it in the first place. . . . Ernie paled and tried to pull away, but Rayford grabbed the back of his neck and with his free hand pressed his thumb against Ernie's bogus mark. The smudge rubbed off.[33]

Rayford's inspection of Ernie's phony mark inaugurates a somewhat awkward practice among the Tribulation Force. From that point onward, the members make an elaborate show of examining the Marks of professed believers. Licking their thumb and placing it upon the subject's forehead, they determine if the Mark is any good.

The practice bears a resemblance to a crude method used by dubious characters in old Hollywood westerns to verify the purity of coins. Characters would conduct a "taste test" and bite into a coin to assess its softness and potential bullion content. Such cinematic images do have a basis in historical fact. Throughout history—at least within the Western world—precious metals such as silver and gold have served as "hard" currencies with a perceived, inherent value. But how could one recognize "the real thing?" Historically, one of the main purposes of governments has been to certify weights and measures, and by extension, the inherent value of money. A coin bearing the seal of Caesar, for example, could be trusted as "the real thing." What happened, however, as time effaced the coin's surface leaving a blank planchet? Worse yet, how could one gain assurance that the coin had not been "clipped," with shards of precious metal shaved off, or even debased with lesser metals by the mints themselves?

Such practices introduced inflation, since uncertainty ate away at coins' perceived value. During periods of inflation when people doubted the inherent worth of money, the prices of goods rose. The process became inevitably more abstract. For centuries, banks both public and private issued promissory notes on their stock of precious metals, promising full payment in gold or silver. Paper notes soon traded independently of their base of inherent value, however, and their worth varied based upon a bank's perceived ability to fulfill its promise of precious metal or *specie* payment. If noteholders lost faith in the bank's ability to repay, the notes quickly lost value. Panic might even trigger a "run on the bank," as people sought to recover something of tangible value in place of the worthless paper, occasionally leading to a financial collapse. Moreover, the risk of such panics increased, despite the presence of central banks to validate and stand behind the currency, since banks operated on a "fractional reserve," meaning that they issued much more paper than their store of precious metals could support if the public collectively lost trust.

As the twentieth century unfolded, however, paper currency increasingly took on connotations of hard currency or "cash." This proved a necessary development since the Crash of 1928 made the so-called gold standard an impractical basis upon which to build an economy. President Roosevelt, under penalty of law, recalled all gold privately held in 1933, and the United States drifted away from the gold standard.[34] President Nixon formally removed gold from the economic equation in 1971, and fixed rates of exchange fell away in 1973, with values allowed to "float" based on the perceived performance of a given economy, among other factors.[35] Currency was no longer then, as Taylor notes, "the sign of a stable 'transcendental signified,'" "bound to a secure referent." Instead, currency became "a floating signifier whose value is relative to other floating signifiers."[36] The modern financial economy, like the contemporary spiritual economy, lacks firm foundations. It is based instead upon the confidence of investors, or trust.

Ernie, among others, debases the currency of faith by rendering it dubious, by exposing it as a sign of God's promise that may indicate, as Taylor phrases it, "nothing at all." The Mark, just like any other abstract currency lacking inherent value, merely indicates the promise of redemption written on the believer's forehead. Like currency, such an identity can be counterfeited, and the Tribulation Force employs a number of counterfeit detection schemes. Ultimately, however, they must place their faith in God rather than in visible although potentially deceptive signs. Such faith carries significant risk, of course. As signs become doubtful any fool can manipulate them. Insistence on certainty in such an economy of faith makes one potentially vulnerable to spiritual hucksters peddling "cheap grace," leading one toward collapse and ruin. LaHaye and Jenkins imply, through the introduction of seemingly stable marks of identity and their subsequent debasements, that like dashed hopes in a fiscal economy, doubt in the spiritual economy leads believers to seek the "real thing," which comes only at great cost and sacrifice.

Left Behind protagonists nevertheless strive for marks of certainty amid the webs of deception that engulf them. They want to know who they are, and what backs or validates their identities as saved sons and daughters of God. Visible marks that others can see are never enough, if the other's mark never completely assures his or her identity. Believers constantly seek, again borrowing Taylor's terminology, a return to the gold or "God standard."[37] In fact, the quest for gold leads Rayford to the confrontation with Ernie in the first place. Trusting that both were believers, Ken Ritz entrusted Rayford and Ernie with the secrets of his buried treasure.

Ken, who to Rayford's surprise actually graduated from the London School of Economics, reveals to Rayford during his final, fateful journey to Israel his extensive plans to develop an international commodity cooperative for believers. But he also explains his rationale for hoarding gold:

> "So, Ken," Rayford said, "as an economics expert, do you still trust the banks?"
>
> "I didn't trust the banks *before* Carpathia came to power."
>
> "Where'd you stash your bullion then?"
>
> "Some bullion. Mostly coins. Who's got change for a brick of gold?"
>
> Rayford snorted. "Who's got change even for a gold piece? You'd have to buy out a store to keep from getting hundreds in change."
>
> "I hope it doesn't come to actually having to spend the gold as currency."[38]

Ken stored his gold deep beneath Palwaukee Airport. The Great Earthquake, however, shifted the ground and caused his treasure to fall even further, to the point that accessing it would require grave danger. Still, Ken never wanted to use the gold—that much is apparent to Rayford. He stored it as a security against the inflation rampant in the Beast economy. The one-world currency, dubbed "Nicks" in honor of Carpathia, would quickly lose their face value. Presumably, gold would provide a much better hedge against an uncertain future. Still, against his better judgment,

Ken risked his life to find his gold. Shaken by the Rapture and the subsequent earthquake, Ken thought the gold might ease his uncertainty, but when he found it, it did not deliver the security he sought. Gold, too, turned out to be an illusion, at least for Ken.

Rayford nevertheless attempts to find the hidden treasure upon his return, which precipitates a conflict with young Ernie and his fellow confidence-man, Bo. Ernie and Bo, learning of Ken's treasure, plotted to gain his trust before they secretly made off with the loot. Rayford foils the scheme, however, and unearths the gold, sharing Ken's wealth with a new character, Tyrola Delanty, the owner of the airport. "T," as he is known, turns out to be a believer, too, and knew about the buried treasure all along. "T," who prefers not to acknowledge his given name, "Mark," offers Rayford free use of the airport and planes in exchange for the gold. Rayford also entrusts "T"—or Mark—with organizing the transportation schemes for Ken's international commodity cooperative.

T comes to function in the narrative as a prophetic figure, rebuking Rayford when he falls short of the Mark. Notably, Rayford tries to force God's hand in book six, *Assassins,* asking, no *begging,* that God make him the instrument of Antichrist's foretold assassination. None of the other characters has sufficient moral authority—not even Dr. Ben-Judah—to upbraid Rayford, except the mysterious T. Rayford must first find the ever-meddling Hattie Durham, however, who has once again deserted the Tribulation Force. Bo, it seems, arranged to smuggle her out of the country for a tidy sum. Hattie will also do anything to get to Israel and kill Carpathia. Rayford confronts Bo and offers him a substantial payoff in exchange for Hattie's whereabouts. T witnesses the scene as a figure of unquestioned moral standing, yet he casts his eyes downward during the transaction, as if sensing Rayford's less than noble ambitions. Rayford notices his reluctance and decides that T may be in league with Bo. After all, he has witnessed betrayal before. Rayford confronts T:

> "What do you call it, T? You guys working together against me, behind my back, or what?"
>
> T shook his head sadly. "Yeah, Ray. I'm in concert with a kid two sandwiches short of a picnic so I can turn the tables on my Christian brother."[39]

T takes his turn, remarking to Rayford that he is "beginning to wonder who you are."[40]

T does not lose trust in Rayford, however. Instead, he indicts him for his paranoia and excessive use of deceit in the transaction with Bo. Believers must remain not only on guard, but they must also keep the enemy in focus and maintain their vigilance against where they would never expect to find the spirit of Antichrist—within *themselves*. T continues:

> He's the enemy, sure, but he's not one of those we treat like scum to make sure they don't find out who we really are. He already knows who we are, bro. We don't buy and sell guys like Bo, Rayford. We don't play them, lie to them, cheat them, steal from them, blackmail them. We love them. We plead with them. . . . What you did sure didn't feel loving and Christian to me. . . . You were as bad as he was.[41]

T, although not challenging Rayford's status as a saved believer, nevertheless accuses Rayford of not acting Christlike. Worse, Rayford forgets the ultimate mission of the Tribulation Force—to be evangelicals and spread the Gospel to the unsaved. By focusing on his quest to capture Hattie and murder Carpathia, Rayford loses sight of what matters most.

Put differently, Rayford's impatience with God and his lack of trust in his comrades also cheapens the currency of faith. The cash he foists upon Bo is debased, T tells him, figuratively speaking. Rayford has placed too much value in abstract measures that lack inherent value. T matters, as do the other members of the Tribulation Force. Rayford, however, threatens to destroy all they have accomplished through his paradoxical quest for certainty—to take matters into his own hands that rightfully belong under God's judgment—along with his increasing suspicion of those in whom he ought to place his trust.

A precarious balance exists between remaining vigilant against deceivers and confidence men, and becoming so suspicious that one cannot see the forest for the treason. Mark C. Taylor's discussion of Melville's *The Confidence Man* presents a similar challenge. A riverboat barber, so mistrustful of counterfeiters, places a sign bearing the words "No Trust" outside his shop. Faith, however, along with the deeds of the Tribulation Force, require trust. LaHaye and Jenkins expose a rift between existing as evangelicals in defiance of the Beast system, and the specter of incorporation—becoming "as bad as they are," as T (Mark) puts it.[42] One must maintain a tension with the system, the authors gently suggest, as too little tension dulls one's awareness of existential dangers, while too much threatens to make one into that which one ostensibly resists.

As Taylor notes, if one resists the system too vigorously one becomes a part of it, institutionalized as "opposition."[43] The question becomes which Marks the Tribulation Force, and by default LaHaye and Jenkins's readership, will bear? The texts whisper—even if the authors' official voice insists otherwise—that the choice may not be a simple either/or. The Mark may be ambiguous like Chang's, trapping the believer in a "dark night of the soul." Rather than ending abruptly, the quest for the Mark may be ongoing, a tension that cannot be lifted by an inflated currency of faith. Evangelical survival within the Tribulation, or the network culture, may depend on an appropriate level of tension and adaptation. The quest for God presents great opportunities as well as insidious dangers. Grace that comes too easily may be nothing more than fool's gold or a false god. Examining the Marks with anything other than the eye of faith may prove problematic, too. The only certainty during the Tribulation is that grace, like anything else of value, will not come cheaply.

Conclusion

> Rather than a parasite that feeds on the body of mass or the mass of the body, surface consumes bodily mass, thereby rendering substance superficial. Far from insign-ificant clothing for essential structures, surfaces actually constitute the masses they appear to adorn.[44]
> —Mark C. Taylor, "De-signing"

Mark C. Taylor devotes a significant amount of discussion in his 1997 text, *Hiding,* to the question of marks. According to Taylor, the emergence of network culture has eroded firm foundations, whether one speaks of understandings of selfhood, culture, or even God. There are no hard and fast guarantees. Marks in the *Left Behind* novels promise to reveal beyond question the identity of oneself and others, but they often prove deceptive. LaHaye and Jenkins, sensing the cultural anxieties of their readership, take the logical step of granting their protagonists hard and fast signs that indicate their identity and ease their tensions. Marks, however, prove deceptive in the network culture. Nothing is ever as it seems.

The authors seem vaguely aware of this, offering their protagonists a sense of certainty, then taking it back, filling them with additional uncertainty. No doubt this adds intrigue to the plot, but I suspect something else may be at work. The kind of End LaHaye and Jenkins imagine in the earlier novels—at least through book eight, *The Mark*—resembles what literary theorist Stephen O'Leary calls the *comic* apocalypse. As I wrote in chapter 2, this does not mean the Apocalypse is necessarily funny. It indicates rather that the results are somewhat open ended and "require the denial of all claims to absolute knowledge," as O'Leary puts it.[45] Individual believers display greater dynamism and enjoy more extensive existential possibilities than those who embrace the closed and determined versions characteristic of tragic apocalypses.[46] LaHaye and Jenkins's characters resemble—as long as they accept the open-ended possibilities and ambiguities inherent to their cultural situation—real people with real problems.

Finally, Taylor's quote points up the central problem of marks, especially when one reads them as foolproof signs of identity: rather than merely indicating what an individual or culture stands for deep inside, marks come to *constitute* the person in the minds of others, and perhaps even themselves. The *Left Behind* narrative through *The Mark* retains a fleeting knowledge of this. Those who accept the Mark of the Beast clearly become evil, their identities literally tattooed on their hands or foreheads—permanently. They can be nothing other than what the Mark indicates. Significantly, even the Mark of Christ seems to offer a foolproof sense of personal and cultural identity. If one bears the Mark of Christ, one must be Christlike. But the authors resist such an easy identification, introducing deception and uncertainty throughout the novels, especially in the figure of the teenaged airplane mechanic and con-artist, Ernie. Ernie fakes the Mark of Christ. He applies a temporary tattoo of sorts that allows him to pass as a Christian among gullible believers. Taylor warns against precisely this phenomenon, noting that the problem of meaning in the network culture is not its absence, but its proliferation. Simply put, when firm, unquestioned foundations collapse, signs and marks multiply, increasing the possibility of deception. Those who assume a direct correspondence between a particular mark and a given identity may prove tragically mistaken. Despite their resistance to totalizing the marks, however, LaHaye and Jenkins cannot maintain such an ambiguous stance long. Their readership craves answers, and the authors ultimately offer them. After *The Mark*, the series takes a tragic turn.

6

Beast, Inc.

Evangelical Resistance and the Internalization of Evil

That is the tragedy of where we find ourselves.[1]
—Character Steve Plank in *The Remnant*

The Lakers and the Kings moved out of the Great Western Forum
in Los Angeles in 1999, but the walls are still crowded with midair
photos of Kareem Abdul-Jabbar and Shaq ads for American Express. The old concession stands are still in place, and so are the
locker rooms and weight machines and showers. What's new is the
owner. Last year the Forum was purchased by Faithful Central
Bible Church.[2]   —"13,000 Fans of God," the *New York Times*

By mythologizing these threats—by naming the Antichrist—they
seek to push back the threat of chaos, restore order, and secure
their sense of agency and well-being. The historical record seems to
indicate, however, that apocalyptic name-calling has rarely functioned in ways that lead to a productive engagement with life.[3]
—Robert C. Fuller, *Naming the Antichrist*

Irony marks the study of evangelical prophecy fiction. Prophecy writings
do not describe a simple, monolithic community united in resistance to a
fallen world. The picture is decidedly more complicated. A closer inspection reveals a subculture rife with tensions and disagreements on the best
way to tackle the ills of the modern age. Specifically, how do prophecy believers resist modernity without becoming too much a part of it? And
how do they critically engage the world without losing their particular
identities? Prophecy-believing evangelicals, in contrast to the popular

stereotypes of fundamentalists, have not withdrawn from the world. They wish to save it from its own sins, but how? What are the consequences of their attempts to redeem the world? The *Left Behind* novels, on one level, depict not so much the battle for the souls of nonbelievers but for the souls of prophecy believers themselves.

The kind of this-worldly engagement one finds in the *Left Behind* series, along with what seems like a parallel drive toward otherworldliness, strikes one as paradoxical. The texts strive to maintain the evangelical identity of prophecy believers by following a time-honored formula of remaining "in but not of the world," but the question remains whether their acts of resistance disrupt this fragile, liminal balance. LaHaye and Jenkins obviously struggle with a desire to help Christ bring in the millennium through direct action while still respecting traditional, dispensational injunctions against interfering with events which only God can actualize. On the one side, the texts recognize that prophecy believers, whatever their objections to the world, appear in no hurry to leave it behind. After all, the *Left Behind* series takes quite a long time and a lot of pages to bring forth the End. Believers can do much of their own volition to alter the world before the End arrives. On the other side, the novels advocate a fatalism that expresses despair over the state of the modern world. Believers, according to this latter view, would appear to be just "along for the ride." Yet the picture, as always, is significantly more complicated.

As much as the novels promote the former, engaged perspective, the latter, nonfatalistic stance becomes much more evident as the series progresses. Prophecy-believing evangelicals want the fruits of this world, yet they want to enjoy them on their own terms in a world ruled by Jesus himself. Moreover, believers can act in the world, but they can do nothing of prophetic significance, unless their actions accord with God's eternal plan. The *Left Behind* protagonists attempt to engage the world—at least such aspects of the world as modern technology and material consumption—but remain haunted by the fatalistic assumptions endemic to the previous generation of prophecy novels. As a result, protagonists, and, by extension, their real-world counterparts, risk getting trapped in self-fulfilling prophecies, attributing to God (or Satan) the consequences of their own actions and denying their moral responsibility, potentially endangering critical aspects of their evangelical identity.

The fatalistic attitudes found in the final volumes of the *Left Behind* series, again, do not necessarily signal otherworldliness or a drive toward escape. Rather, they point to a desperate desire for this-worldly change, change which believers can aid, but which only God—or leaders able to discern His will—can initiate. Historian Wouter J. Hanegraaff, extending the insights found in Arthur O. Lovejoy's *The Great Chain of Being*, challenges the simple dichotomy between "other-worldly" and "this-worldly" orientations. Modifying Lovejoy's terminology, Hanegraaff defines what he calls strong and weak forms of this-worldliness:

> Implicit in Lovejoy's description of this-worldliness is a distinction between a focus on our world of experience *as such,* or on a better "this-world" to come which is modeled on the present world, but better. I propose to refer to the first variety as "strong this-worldliness" and to the other as "weak this-worldliness." Within this weak variety, again, the better "this-world" may be envisaged either as located on this earth (which amounts to some form of millenarianism) or in another reality beyond death.[4]

Although Hanegraaff focuses on weak this-worldliness within New Age beliefs, one can find resonances of weak this-worldliness within the apocalyptic worldview of LaHaye and Jenkins. The authors repeatedly insist on otherworldly solutions to the present cultural crisis they perceive, yet such otherworldliness defies contemporary trends, in which prophecy believers increasingly position themselves as consumers and political activists. Prophecy-believing evangelicals retain a stake in this world. They want their SUVs, Christian bookstores, and "moral" public policies, too. They have accommodated so much to the world already that the persistent appeals in the *Left Behind* novels to escape it ring hollow. *Left Behind* protagonists have, in effect, "bought into it,"[5] and seek beneath their fatalistic and desperate rhetoric a profound transformation of *this* world, a transformation made on the basis of prophetic rather than purely political imperatives. They are called to actualize God's will, not their own, making openness, compromise, and tolerance of other views much less likely—especially if their readers adopt such views.[6]

In sum, I refer the reader back to chapter 2, in which I introduced three political orientations characteristic of prophecy writings. The first and most obvious involves a rejection of the world and its politics, encouraging believers to withdraw and passively await Christ's return during the last days. One finds this stance—an outgrowth of mid-twentieth-century Protestant fundamentalism—reflected in many of the prophecy novels that preceded the *Left Behind* series. LaHaye and Jenkins, however, like authors Larry Burkett and Frank Peretti before them, add a second possibility, one that corresponds closely to the political resurgence of the so-called New Christian Right during the 1970's and 1980's. Such authors have developed creative means of circumventing the fatalistic limitations of prophecy belief, encouraging their readers to remake the world before Christ's return.

But as I suggested in chapter 2, the characteristics of dispensational prophecy belief ultimately put forth a third possibility: a despair that is neither otherworldly nor withdrawn. Instead, prophecy believers despair of their abilities to bring about any large-scale differences of their own volition, all the while following the dictates of a seemingly inexorable apocalyptic framework. *Left Behind* protagonists no longer encounter the world dynamically and accommodate to it, but become instead mere actors on the apocalyptic stage. They lose their dynamic, individual characters, becoming temporary players of eternal roles, ironically condemning themselves to follow slavishly their own interpretations of ancient texts.[7] Despair in this case does not indicate the first possibility—that of turning away from the world. Nor does it reflect the potential openness of the second possibility, one which, while certainly driven by a belief that adherents are following God's will, allows a measure of compromise—at least in theory—since such matters are not inherently preordained (it is, after all, a politics of the "pre-tribulation tribulation"). Rather, the third possibility of politically engaged despair one finds in the *Left Behind* novels commands evangelicals to remake the world, buttressed by the strength and certainty of a fixed heavenly mandate.

Moving into the Forum

The unprecedented success of the *Left Behind* series and related Christian publishing ventures has dovetailed with a boom in evangelical megachurches.[8] An "evangelicalism of scale" appears to be supplanting smaller Bible churches in rapidly growing suburbs.[9] God, it seems, as the *New York Times* writer suggests in the epigraph, must now compete with a pantheon of sports celebrities for the enthusiastic affection of pom-pom wielding supporters. Evangelical congregations have enjoyed tremendous success in recent years, with membership spilling out of traditional church edifices and into arenas and onto cable and satellite television—the so-called electronic church.[10] *Left Behind,* for example, features large stadium rallies in which Dr. Tsion Ben-Judah, along with Moses and Elijah, entertain crowds with gospel preaching and an occasional penchant for turning water into blood. The crowds even know when to boo and hiss the adversary. When Global Community Potentate Nicolae Carpathia, Pontifex Maximus Peter II, and Supreme Commander Leon Fortunato crash a rally at Teddy Kollek stadium in Israel, they quickly find that Dr. Ben-Judah has a home-field advantage.[11] But what is lost in such mass evangelicalism? Beneath the din of enthusiasm and the simplified visions of good versus evil, might the crowds have more in common with Carpathia than they care to admit?

Faithful Central Bible Church is not unique in its acquisition of a basketball arena. A few months earlier, Lakewood Church in Houston, known locally as "The Oasis of Love," purchased the 16,500-seat Compaq Center, the erstwhile home of the Houston Rockets basketball franchise.[12] It is not an unusual move for the dynamic Lakewood Church, a congregation shepherded for so long by the late pastor and religious broadcaster Dr. John Osteen. The enthusiastic style of worship fostered by Lakewood—complete with pom-poms—would appear to fit nicely within a stadium complex. With the construction of sports arenas accelerating nationwide, it does not seem surprising that burgeoning evangelical congregations are filling the voids created by the empty buildings.

One cannot escape the irony presented by such developments, however. Evangelical churches are no strangers to End-Times belief. In fact, one could attribute much of their growth to the sense of security they lend to those shaken by uncertain times. LaHaye and Jenkins would probably be bigger stars within the walls of the Forum now than Shaquille O'Neal. The authors, after all, have become the superstars of dispensational theology. Like most prophecy writers, however, they consistently warn of the "New Roman Empire." Their Antichrist, Nicolae Carpathia, hails from Romania but has Italian roots. His kingdom, the "ten-horned beast" of Daniel 7:7–8, embodies the resurrection of a Roman Empire synonymous with worldliness and the bloody martyrdom of Christians—often thrown to the lions—in the *Forum.*

Conservative evangelicals, despite the frequent attempts at self-marginalization found in their prophecy writings, now face an even more deadly adversary. Their success has allowed them to enter the Forum, and they have engaged the world as never before. This has placed evangelicalism in a tenuous position. Standing on the faultline between overaccommodation and obscurantist irrelevance, contemporary evangelicalism must constantly straddle the rift, aiming for the middle course that spreads the Gospel while retaining its particular significance. Their chief adversary in this endeavor, ironically, may not arrive from outside but may come as a by-product of their own success. The Beast, in a sense, may become incorporated.

Despite the tension and uncertainty one finds in many of the *Left Behind* novels—conditions that call forth faith and powers of discernment among the protagonists—one detects within the novels' trajectory a drive toward a sense of certainty and security rendered problematic by the network culture. LaHaye and Jenkins, it seems, are not content to rely on faith alone, but offer readers a sense of certainty as magic, miracles, angelic visitations, and direct messages from God pervade the final volumes. The characters are transported into a Biblical universe, in which their options are suddenly predetermined and their moral responsibility diminishes. Those who have accepted Christ *cannot* act against him, while those who have accepted the Mark of the Beast cannot act Christlike. Even the undecided remnant, having waited too long, may have their hearts "hardened" by God, their moral responsibility removed by their indecision. Moreover, the authors' tone becomes increasingly strident and resolute, and their protagonists no longer have any reservations about killing the "enemy." "This is war," we are told. But the authors, unfortunately, do not address the problem of friendly fire.

Evangelical identity, which hovers between mistrust and faith in the previous novels, becomes fixed in the ninth, tenth, and eleventh volumes: *Desecration*, *The Remnant*, and *Armageddon*. The difficulty, of course, is that barring miraculous intervention such inflexible identity appears doomed to fail in the emerging network culture. Historically, evangelicalism has survived in large measure due to its dynamism and adaptability, as illustrated by Rayford's resolution to his crisis of faith both in God and his fellow Tribulation Force members in *Apollyon*. Rayford must rely on faith and the tools of discernment God grants him. As long as one lives in the Tribulation, or the world dominated by Antichrist, deception remains a distinct possibility. Antichrist, too, can conjure "signs and wonders." Only the believer endowed with faith can know the difference.

What makes the *Left Behind* series so fruitful for issues of identity, however, is that the authors present several countercurrents. Although their texts suggest a simplistic reduction of the complexity characteristic of modernity, they drop plenty of clues for their readers that ambiguity remains. The *Left Behind* novels, like many works of science-fiction—especially of the apocalyptic variety—do not necessarily present a factual accounting of the way things *are*. Rather, the novels imagine possibilities for the future of evangelicalism. The evangelicalism presented by the authors when discussing Rayford's reliance on faith is one possibility, just as the absolute moral certainty and insistence on visible signs one finds in the latter novels is another. Which current will triumph and for which evangelicals remains uncertain. The authors, however, express in their narrative the fruits of such possibilities.

I begin first with a closer look at the resistance of the Tribulation Force and their attempts to disrupt Antichrist's machinations. If uncertainty and deception characterize the Tribulation, believers, the authors suggest—if they hope to resist Antichrist—must adopt tactics similar to those deployed by Antichrist. Second, I further discuss evangelical counternetworks—LaHaye and Jenkins's answer to the network culture. Chloe Steele, for example—following the plans of the deceased pilot and part-time economist Ken Ritz—builds an international commodity co-op network that links believers from across the world excluded by the Beast economy. Finally, I reassess the central question of this chapter: Do prophecy believers, despite their apparent success and insistence on an "in but not of" stance vis-à-vis the mainstream culture, become co-opted into the mainstream, not by external coercion but through their own tactics of resistance?

Evangelical Parasites: Infiltrating and Disrupting Antichrist's Networks

LaHaye and Jenkins's protagonists do not sit idly while Antichrist executes his nefarious schemes. Although evangelical prophecy fiction as a genre has tended to produce a crippling form of fatalism that renders characters—and possibly readers—without any meaningful plan of resistance, the *Left Behind* novels feature characters who actively participate in the events of the End-Times. Despite the immutable nature of the dispensationalist End-Times scenario, LaHaye and Jenkins—reflecting political currents in contemporary evangelicalism—have found ways to justify enhanced political activity in their narratives. The protagonists may know how it will all end, but they do not know the fate of individuals; and, true to their evangelical heritage, the authors at times seem more concerned with the individual details than with the overarching, largely predetermined historical outlines. As I discussed in chapter 2, however, the evangelical concern with fostering a favorable environment for evangelism often justifies more activist interventions.

In the *Left Behind* series, the core group of those formerly lukewarm turned fervent Christians remaining after the Rapture quickly gather together to form an organization called the Tribulation Force. The name points up not only the significance of the times, but it also indicates that these believers, unlike their predecessors in earlier prophecy novels, will fight to the End. As I detailed in the introduction and chapter 3, the Tribulation Force consists of an ensemble cast that nevertheless retains a few constants. The founding members include Rayford Steele, an airline captain; his daughter Chloe, a Stanford student; Chloe's future husband Buck Williams, an Ivy League graduate and celebrity journalist; and the penitent youth pastor of a suburban Chicago Bible church, Bruce Barnes. Although Antichrist assassinates Pastor Barnes, Dr. Tsion Ben-Judah, a converted Orthodox rabbi, replaces him and proves an even more troublesome adversary to all things evil. The Tribulation Force also has a medic and computer technician always on call. Finally, a constantly changing support staff, including pilots and smugglers, assists them in all of their activities.

The Tribulation Force begins as a small prayer group within the New Hope Village Church in Mt. Prospect, Illinois. Uncertain about their futures but anxious to disrupt Carpathia's plan for world domination and mass deception, they decide to interrupt and infiltrate Antichrist's developing networks. Serendipitously, Rayford becomes Carpathia's pilot and eavesdrops on his business meetings with a hidden listening device. Buck, as a star journalist, accepts Carpathia's call to publish his major news organ, *The Global Community Weekly.* Thus, hidden within Antichrist's inner circle, the Tribulation Force gathers data and develops tactics of disruption. One can summarize their major modes of operation within three categories that partially overlap each other: co-optation, infiltration, and deception.

They are, in a sense, parasites.[13] Antichrist is not the only one who can infiltrate the enemy. Believers can also invade his territory and use his technological dependence against him. The ability of believers to act depends on Antichrist first providing them with the necessary data—

through acts of self-betrayal. Believers are not strong enough to confront Carpathia directly, but must move within *his* space, purloin *his* data to interrupt *his* schemes. They draw their sustenance from Antichrist's carelessness. But despite such advantages, the Tribulation Force must nonetheless act with caution—they play on Antichrist's home-turf, after all. Evangelical resisters must use what theorist Michel de Certeau calls *tactics*—limited maneuvers—rather than large-scale campaigns built around *strategies*.

Michel de Certeau refers to *the tactic* as a means of operation, necessarily limited, and available to the disempowered. He writes, "It operates in isolated actions, blow by blow. It takes advantage of 'opportunities' and depends on them, being without any base where it could stockpile its winnings, build up its own position, and plan raids. What it wins it cannot keep."[14] Practitioners of the tactic must continually struggle to influence their environs, a process that remains tenuous since the powerful utilize *strategies*—long-term, large-scale operations which *do* have a base. The powerful, once they discover the parasites in their midst, move quickly to eliminate the underground operatives and reverse their actions. Acting as a parasite is a dangerous, risky business.

Tactics, however, become especially valuable because they involve what Certeau calls *poaching*—stealing strategic resources and disrupting communications and network infrastructures. The tactician does not possess sufficient power to plan and execute long-term campaigns, but may know where the powerful are most vulnerable. Recalling the descriptions of network culture from chapter 3, one can see that successful tacticians try to find and disrupt strategic nodes, known as hubs. By attacking hubs they can interfere, at least temporarily, with the strategies of the powerful. The tactics of the Tribulation Force, in fact, although introduced in the novels several years before the al-Qaeda attacks on the World Trade Center and the Pentagon on 9/11, bear disturbing albeit superficial resemblances to those of the infamous terrorist network. Such resemblances do, however, become a bit stronger as the Tribulation Force gradually shifts its emphasis from one of piety and passive resistance to aggressive, often militant survivalism late in the series.

The Tribulation Force begins with an emphasis on piety and passive resistance, consistent with the limitations imposed on such ventures by dispensational theology. They travel the world bringing the *Truth* to scattered enclaves of receptive listeners at great risk to themselves. At home, they build underground shelters completely self-sufficient and invisible to

Antichrist. Indeed, they do not seem like much of a "force" at all and instead resemble a prayer group bent on little more than survival. For example, in the second novel, *Tribulation Force,* even when presented with the opportunity to assist American Patriot militias, assembling to attack Antichrist, they remain passive and resigned. After all, attacking the Antichrist, according to dispensationalism, will invariably fail this side of Christ's return at Armageddon. Yet the militia sequence in *Tribulation Force* foreshadows the changes the Tribulation Force undergoes as the novels progress. Buck Williams, owing to his privileged position as an elite journalist, learns that the president plans to mobilize the militia to oppose Antichrist. Buck knows the coup will fail, but secretly sympathizes with its larger goals:

> Buck's one act of resistance to Carpathia was to ignore the rumors about Fitzhugh plotting with the militia to oppose the Global Community by force. Buck was all for it and had secretly studied the feasibility of an anti-Global Community Web site on the Internet.[15]

Buck later learns in a private audience with President Fitzhugh that the U.S. militia, joined by England and Egypt, will soon attack Antichrist's UN headquarters "before it is too late."[16] Buck listens quietly, knowing that Fitzhugh's actions will fail and play into the hands of Antichrist.

The Tribulation Force, however, fails to heed Buck's early insight, and gradually develops into much more than a band of pious albeit mischievous missionaries and scripturally supported Internet entrepreneurs. They even come to assume the role of the militia groups, in fact, except fighting for God, not country. Buck's response to Fitzhugh in the novel *Tribulation Force* corresponds closely to dispensational belief. By contrast, the rise of the Tribulation Force as an effective guerrilla group disrupting Antichrist's global empire does not appear consistent with such belief. This development poses just as much risk to what prophecy-believing evangelicals seek to protect—their identity, namely—as it does to the forces of Antichrist during the Tribulation. The transition from passive to active resistance ultimately threatens the protagonists' existence as evangelicals. They may even play into the hands of Antichrist, as surely as the militias Buck once observed.

The Tribulation Force—already moving beyond its pious origins—must constantly move between safe-houses, since Antichrist operates a superior surveillance network. Yet the same tools Antichrist deploys to tighten his grip on the world also make him vulnerable to the parasites gnawing at his flank. Like the first consumers who took advantage of the principles behind ARPANET and used ordinary telephone lines for e-mails and sundry data transmission, the Tribulation Force utilizes the tools available to them to infiltrate Carpathia's technological networks. Tribulation Force operatives initially lament such technological developments; but, despite their initial misgivings, it does not take long for Tribulation Force members to infiltrate Carpathia's "always-on" network, deploying a legion of operatives wielding state-of-the-art laptop computers, secure cellular phones, and even, through the help of insiders within Carpathia's computer network, fraudulent identities certified by the Global Community's own computer databases.

They are, essentially, parasites, but not simply in the commonly understood sense, as that which draws sustenance out of a host organism without providing anything in return. On the first count, they do not live within their hosts, except in a symbolic sense. Theorist Michel Serres writes, "Men, whom I call parasites, are never, as far as we know, inside another animal. Except the great beast, the 666, the Leviathan."[17] Operating within the Beast system, the Tribulation Force targets not the strongholds of the Global Community, but the networks that link it together. They accomplish what Serres defines as the primary characteristic of the parasite: the creation of disruptive *noise*.

First and foremost, the parasite interrupts the system. It produces noise, or static, that cannot be readily assimilated into meaningful information.[18] If seamless networks of communication sustain Antichrist, the Tribulation Force must interrupt the flows of information before they are effaced by them. Hence, they do not operate directly on the Global Community, but instead gnaw parasitically on its technological infrastructure. They are so well integrated into the same infrastructure, in fact, that when Leon Fortunato, Antichrist's False Prophet and right-hand man, orders David Hassid to shut down the Tribulation Force's network, Hassid calmly and without deception responds, "We're all served by the same system. . . . It's the reason we've never been able to shut down the Judah-ites' Internet transmissions."[19]

Besides co-opting and contaminating data flows, however, the Tribulation Force also infiltrates the hierarchy of the Global Community. In the later novels, they always have agents on the inside, especially in Antichrist's computer operations. These secret agents, whether computer genius David Hassid or his young protégé Chang Wong, or even the erstwhile publishing executive turned undercover operative Steve Plank, must maintain a duplicitous status using, ultimately, any available means of deception. For Chang, this involves the seemingly forbidden step of taking the Mark of the Beast. The authors seem ambivalent about this development, as I discussed in chapter 5, despite Chang's usefulness. Nevertheless, Chang exemplifies what Mark C. Taylor calls the *paralogic* or the key to parasitic success. To carry out the proper tactics without becoming incorporated within the system it seeks to resist, the parasite must maintain *undecidability,* a tenuous, ambiguous identity "in but not of" the system. Significantly, prophecy writers often consider believers "in but not of" the world. Taylor quotes J. Hillis Miller:

> Para is a double antithetical prefix signifying at once proximity and distance, similarity and difference, interiority and exteriority, something inside a domestic economy and at the same time without it. . . . A thing in "para," moreover, is not only simultaneously on both sides of the boundary line between inside and out. It is also the boundary itself, the screen, which is a permeable membrane connecting inside and outside. It confuses them with one another, allowing the outside in, making the inside out, dividing them and joining them. It also forms an ambiguous transition between one and the other.[20]

If readers remain suspicious of Chang's dubious position within both the Tribulation Force and the Global Community—bearing *both* marks of loyalty—it is because he occupies an undecidable, "parasitic" position. He is not fully within either organization.[21] His wild-card status, however, offers the Tribulation Force valuable insight into the inner workings of the Enemy. But his thorough knowledge of the believers' operations also means that any slipup on his part, any inadvertent betrayal, could doom them. Risk and uncertainty, however, may prove unavoidable in the Beast system. As Taylor writes describing the network culture, "Uncertainty, in other words, is not a result of ignorance or the partiality of human knowledge but is characteristic of the world itself.[22]

The members of the Tribulation Force, like Antichrist, feed on such uncertainty, at least initially. They are nothing if not disguised globetrotters, jetting around the world at a moment's notice to frustrate Antichrist's schemes with their fake IDs and reinvented images. Whenever they require a new identity, Tribulation Force operatives turn to the socially awkward but uniquely talented Gustav Zuckermandel, Jr., a "middle-twenties longhair covered with tattoos," who "had made his living tattooing, pinstriping cars and trucks, and airbrushing monster cars and muscle cars onto T-shirts."[23] Since his conversion, however, the "all-black wearing, flabby forger" uses his talents for deception for presumably more edifying purposes. Buck Williams's encounter with "Zeke Jr." exemplifies the transactions:

> "Hey, Buck," Z said flatly, putting his stuff away and slowly rising. "What can I do ya for?"
> "Need a new identity."[24]

Z digs through his files for a suitable ID, once utilized by a deceased Global Community employee, and gives Buck a new name and the papers to go with it. Zeke can also dye hair, install oral appliances, and perform almost any procedure short of major surgery to confound identity.[25] Although Chang may represent the only figure who fulfills the role of parasite as Serres, Taylor, and Hillis define it, his comrades also straddle the line, especially given the cloud of doubt the authors maintain over many of them throughout the series. Deception—not only among characters but also between authors and readers—marks the *Left Behind* novels, as evangelical identity remains uncertain, at least for a season.

The parasite, however, has an even more profound function to which the authors do not call attention, even if their texts bear its marks. Networks, like cultures, as Taylor among others points out, can be understood as "self-organizing systems." To survive, networks—whether composed of evangelicals or of the hordes of Antichrist—must develop the ability to transform "noise" into meaningful information and use the new data to achieve higher, more productive levels of complexity. Evangelical noise may interrupt Antichrist's system, at least temporarily, but the system may also adapt and incorporate the noise for its own purposes. Serres describes such adaptation with an ambiguous pronoun that could be imaginatively read in this context as referring to Carpathia himself, "Thus he has a constant relation with the interruptions; they are familiar to him; he knows how to tame them; he is acclimated to them. He is vaccinated by the parasites."[26] Parasitic activity, in other words, may have unintended effects for the Tribulation Force. Even though LaHaye and Jenkins depict Antichrist and his Global Community agents as incompetent fools, Antichrist may yet achieve his objectives not through his own actions, at least directly, but through those of the Tribulation Force. The parasite, it must be added, can also switch roles with the "host." If the parasite fails to maintain a dynamic, undecidable position, it may co-opt the Beast without ever recognizing it.

Beast Co-opted: The Rise of Evangelical Counternetworks

Antichrist's pronouncement that all global citizens must either accept his Mark of loyalty or face execution forces believers to develop underground, cooperative networks. The clandestine networks allow believers, otherwise excluded from the Beast economy, to obtain survival supplies from other believers. The idea of a co-op system first appears in book six, *Apollyon,* when Tribulation Force pilot and London School of Economics graduate Ken Ritz articulates his vision of an underground economy. Working with journals left behind by the late Tribulation Force computer expert Donny Moore,[27] who perished in the Great Earthquake, Ritz seeks a way to link the isolated underground safe-houses proposed by Donny, along with the cell churches envisioned by Pastor Barnes, into a fully-functioning, interactive network. Ritz, moreover, articulates a strategy to connect the operations of the Tribulation Force with the emerging cooperative network, potentially creating a network to challenge Carpathia's Beast system. As Ritz puts it to Rayford, describing the intense spirit of cooperation required to pull off such a coup, "'it seems to me we're going to be pretty much a commune from now on.'"[28]

Ken's proposed cooperative network, in addition to including an extensive communications and transportation infrastructure, also includes farming, "a sea-harvesting operation, even private-banking."[29] All in all, Ken presents quite an ambitious plan for an allegedly struggling and highly marginalized underground movement. He also suggests that a small portion of the proceeds will enable the Tribulation Force to carry out its disruptive missions. Ken dies on the subsequent mission to Israel, and Rayford takes his journals and entrusts them, along with the creation of the co-op network, to Chloe.

Literary theorist Amy Johnson Frykholm remarks in her work on the *Left Behind* novels that after Chloe assumes control of the cooperative network, "Ken's appeal to the 'commune' of the New Testament Christians is left behind. . . . Clearly the Christian cooperative will not be about providing for the needs of the world's Christians, but will be an imitation of capitalism down to the very details."[30] Frykholm's assertion that the cooperative network represents a clone of capitalism overlooks the nuances found in the novels and greatly oversimplifies what distinguishes the cooperatives from capitalism—both historically and in the *Left Behind* novels. The cooperative network Chloe develops does not sell items, but rather barters them in trade. It is a highly organized network of *producers* who exchange what they have for what they need, without necessarily resorting to an objective measure of value such as cash to settle their debts.

While the world outside the novels suggests that evangelicals have indeed embraced global capitalism wholeheartedly, fictional devices such as the introduction of populist co-ops betray uneasiness on the part of LaHaye and Jenkins concerning the commercial turn within contemporary evangelicalism. Their vision of believers' co-ops reads as much like fantasy as the more obviously supernatural elements of their novels, given the extent to which evangelicals are already implicated in the sordid world of consumer culture and material possession.[31] The Tribulation Force, through the introduction of the co-op networks, attempt to liberate believers from the bonds of consumption, returning them to a time when yeoman farmers and craftworkers traded what they produced for what they needed, with little excess wealth produced that might lead believers into the den of luxury and vice and away from religious commitments. In this sense, contra Frykholm, global capitalism *is* the problem for the Tribulation Force. LaHaye and Jenkins concoct a fantasy world in which ordinary people—remarkably homogeneous in wealth, culture, and belief—seize control of their destinies from an overwhelmingly powerful yet strangely vulnerable enemy. Their fantasy could describe how many evangelicals view the early-mid-nineteenth century, when the so-called Protestant Kingdom dominated an American culture not yet sullied by Darwinism, the influence of German Biblical criticism, waves of immigration, or the upheavals associated with the Industrial Revolution.

As I discussed in chapter 2, LaHaye and Jenkins's dystopian utopia also bears, in fact, a close resemblance to the audacious although ultimately unsuccessful Farmer's Alliance network that overran Texas and dotted much of the American South in the 1880's. Locked into debt peonage by price-gouging suppliers, many farmers worked together to improve market conditions for their produce, while negotiating better terms from suppliers of raw materials.[32] As historians Michael Kazin and Lawrence Goodwyn note, much of the moral force behind Populist movements like the Farmer's Alliance derived from nineteenth-century evangelicalism.[33] LaHaye and Jenkins may look to their forebears for a strategy to help evangelicals preserve their identity during the Tribulation when grace—analogously to the products of nineteenth-century agricultural suppliers—will not be cheap. LaHaye and Jenkins's populist unrest is not strictly material or economic, of course, but emerges from a religious imperative.

Frykholm is nevertheless perceptive to suspect that the co-ops harbor troubling contradictions. The authors' co-op narrative may not recapitulate global capitalism, but it does point to an unsettling political tendency that has developed among conservative evangelicals during recent decades. As sociologist Christian Smith asserts, the primary goal of evangelical political engagement, emanating as it does from religious concerns, may not be to reconstruct an idyllic Christian kingdom. What evangelicals want, Smith claims, is the freedom to pursue their faith and preserve their evangelical identities.[34] Nevertheless, the slippage of LaHaye and Jenkins's narrative into overt political struggle—and, one could argue, a type of domination—suggests the ambivalence of the authors toward such traditional American political values as pragmatism and compromise. LaHaye and Jenkins may be developing a language that allows them to justify aggressive political activity in the name of protecting their own freedom to exist as evangelicals.

The authors' political turn, however, if actualized in policy, might also undermine their own status as evangelicals—and by extension, that of their readers—if believers insist on informing political activity and evangelical identity through apocalyptic understandings. The danger always looms that those who deploy such strategies may lose sight of their precarious existential position and attempt to change the culture on a forcible basis, endangering both their own identities and the identities of others. Believers, rather than maintaining an "in but not of" stance vis-à-vis the world, may instead incorporate its basic assumptions while remaining under the impression that they are resisting it, with their peril masked by a deceptive sense of security. They may, in other words, build the perfect Beast, even as they purport to resist it.

It does not take long for Chloe to implement Ritz's vision of the global cooperative network. Across the world, small cell-churches and local co-op branches provide community centers for the protection and sustenance of believers. Such centers also serve as recruiting stations, providing a constantly renewed supply of pilots, planes, weapons, and other resources for the Tribulation Force. The Tribulation Force, in fact, becomes synonymous with the co-ops, operating as the military arm of the cooperative network. The spiritual, and by default, political wing of the movement resides first in the various safe-houses, before Dr. Tsion Ben-Judah and his staff relocate to the protective caves of Petra. Ultimately, the economic, political, and military wings of the evangelical network merge, however, and Dr. Ben-Judah—acting as the symbol of the unified evangelical network—dies in book eleven, *Armageddon,* fighting the forces of Antichrist in the streets of Jerusalem.[35]

As the believers' alternative network develops and prospers in book ten, *The Remnant,* its success allows the Tribulation Force to decentralize—to become, in effect, distributed nodes within the evangelical network. The Global Community discovers their headquarters and safehouse at the Strong Building in Chicago and obliterates it with tactical nuclear weapons. The Tribulation Force, however, has already recognized their vulnerability and has distributed themselves to critical locations (nodes) across the world. As renowned botanist and Tribulation Force elder Chaim Rosenzweig remarks to Rayford, "perhaps the safe house of the future will be in a thousand places, not just one."[36] Dr. Ben-Judah, for example, shepherds his flock from his base in Petra—complete with highspeed Internet—while Chloe, Rayford, and Buck relocate to San Diego. As the evangelical cooperative network decentralizes, it intensifies its power and, ironically, presents an arguably more effective outfit than Carpathia's own Global Community network.[37]

Up to this point LaHaye and Jenkins's protagonists display a remarkable savvy for dealing with Antichrist's network culture. They beat him, in effect, at his own deadly game, cleverly utilizing his resources to fuel their resistance. Yet success brings an odd problematic: LaHaye and Jenkins's tacticians violate Michel de Certeau's injunction against tacticians becoming strategists. The success of the Tribulation Force encourages its members to jettison many of the tactics that made them successful in an effort to solidify their holdings—which, according to Certeau, a tactician cannot do—and embark once again upon the quest for firm foundations.

The narrative in book eleven, *Armageddon,* features the protagonists giving up their scattered safe-houses and fleeing to the safety of the ancient Jordanian city of Petra. There, believers receive divine protection, along with plenty of fresh water and twice daily portions of delicious manna. The erstwhile parasites consolidate their winnings and take up a base of operations, complete with a sophisticated computer center that rivals and eventually overmatches Antichrist's facilities at his palace in

New Babylon. Although the authors continually remind the readers that the protagonists must take such actions to flee the prominence of Antichrist all around them, their insistence on the powerlessness of believers vis-à-vis Antichrist rings increasingly hollow.

The evangelical insistence on a secure base of operations in this world also presents an additional, more profound difficulty. In his account of *the parasite,* Michel Serres notes that the roles of *parasite* and *host* are by no means static. When the parasite becomes too engorged and self-satisfied, *too secure,* it becomes subject to a peculiar reversal. The host may become the parasite. More significantly, the erstwhile host's mode of operation may prove insidious—difficult to detect. Serres writes that "the host counter-parasites his guests, not by taking away his food from them (first meaning) but by making noise (second meaning)."[38] LaHaye and Jenkins's Antichrist cannot cut the supply lines of the Tribulation Force, nor can he effectively disrupt their communications and transportation infrastructures. He cannot do to the Tribulation Force quite what they do to him, interrupting their communications and related infrastructure. But he can take subtler measures.

Noise, in Serres's usage, also indicates raw information that seems meaningless until one learns how to decode it properly. Antichrist, like the Tribulation Force, thrives as a noisemaker. Both sides try to throw a monkey wrench into the operations of the other. But Antichrist might have the upper hand. After all, noise is his specialty, especially the use of noise to foster doubt and uncertainty. As the Tribulation Force becomes too engorged and secure (and especially self-satisfied with their technological prowess), they make themselves vulnerable by increasingly seeking certainty in a world that cannot, even by their own admissions, provide it. They play right into Antichrist's hands by unreflectively adopting his tools and tactics to advance their own goals. Might then LaHaye and Jenkins's Antichrist, although depicted as a power-mad bumbler, not be "crazy like a fox?" Perhaps, perhaps not. The relative aptitude of Antichrist matters less at this stage than the responses of the Tribulation Force to his actions. Put differently, does Antichrist have to prevail overtly to achieve his aims? The texts explicitly answer "yes" to this question, although the authors' own description of Antichrist and the Tribulation period—as we saw in chapter 1—suggests "no." The Tribulation Force incorporates many aspects of Antichrist's strategy in its attempts to resist him, with damaging results.

Onward Christian Soldiers, Marching into a Trap?

The authors insist in the tenth novel, *The Remnant,* that the Beast system remains an overwhelming threat. Indeed, dispensational prophecy literature as a genre claims that the world belongs to Antichrist before Christ's Glorious Appearing at the end of the Tribulation. Believers cannot safeguard themselves or the world in any large-scale manner, since conditions will get much worse before they improve. The Tribulation, which LaHaye and Jenkins inadvertently depict as a rollicking adventure, becomes even less threatening in *The Remnant.* Judgments continue, of course. Nonbelievers are cursed by water turned to blood, with a sizzling heat wave followed by days of total darkness awaiting those who manage to persevere. Believers, however, enjoy a measure of divine protection. Blood turns to water upon contact with believers, intense heat becomes tolerable, and God grants special "night-vision" to his faithful, allowing them to pierce the darkness.[39] If the Global Community remains powerful or intimidating, the authors do not depict it as such.

The plagues and judgments allow the Tribulation Force and representatives of their cooperative network to travel without fear of harassment. This permits them to extend their reach even as Antichrist's own Beast system, crippled by God's judgments, gradually disintegrates. It becomes increasingly difficult for the Tribulation Force to claim a marginalized status. Those who oppose the Tribulation Force are killed, often by God. But believers also know how to defend themselves. George, a Tribulation Force commando and pilot, brutally kills his female captor, leading Antichrist himself to remark, "My kind of man. Why cannot he be on our side?"[40] Mrs. Pappas, a leader of a Greek underground co-op, sends her Tribulation Force guests off with more than a prayer, "Mrs. P held up a hand. 'There is nothing wrong with working while someone is praying. Someone put extra ammunition clips in a bag while I pray.'"[41] "Praise the Lord and Pass the Ammunition," as the World War II novelty song goes.

Equally problematic is the juxtaposition of divine mercy and devastating judgments. The primary purpose of the Tribulation, we are told, is to separate the wheat from the chaff. But the offer of salvation, it seems, expires quickly, and no exchanges or returns are allowed. Moreover, it excludes all of those who do not subscribe to a particular variant of conservative evangelical Protestantism. Even their spiritual spokesperson, Dr. Ben-Judah, expresses uncertainty over the deterministic turn in the late

Tribulation. "Does this sound exclusivistic?" he begins, before responding that while "the will of God is that all men be saved," the time to decide may have already passed. He deflects his crisis of conscience, finally, by appealing to a rigid, absolute moral standard.

He appeals to the undecided to make their decisions, one way or the other, but also admits that God may have already "hardened their hearts," in effect making the decision for them. When a group of undecided spiritual seekers question Dr. Ben-Judah's leadership, they find out the hard way that dissent in the ranks has immediate consequences:

> As soon as he [Dr. Ben-Judah] finished speaking, the ground under hundreds of rebels opened and swallowed them. They went down into the pit, screaming and wailing as the earth closed upon them, and they perished from among the congregation.[42]

Such an attitude indicates that "one is either with us or against us." Absolute beliefs drown the voices of ambiguity, nuance, and uncertainty. But such absolutism may also have negative consequences for believers. Boundaries—or screens—as I have noted, are important to the survival of evangelical identity. When the boundaries become too tightly drawn, however, the results can be crippling to personal and collective identity, especially when the community makes fatalistic assumptions. Paradoxically, the insistence on a personal decision—an act of free will to choose or reject Christ so critical to contemporary American evangelicalism—encounters the immovable force of a salvation drama written two thousand years ago. In the End, does one really have a choice? The dispensational apocalypse, it seems, waits for no one. Identities, once seen as fluid and dynamic, hence able to adapt to the network culture, become irredeemably fixed.

As the evangelical co-op network becomes more powerful, it also becomes increasingly secure. The existential doubt that drives faith and compels Rayford to question his own assumptions about God and his comrades, for example, disappears, buried beneath a flood of magical interventions, miracles, and divine visitations. The archangel Michael, for example, demonstrates to Mac, a Tribulation Force helicopter pilot, how to transform blood into potable water. At the same time, three angelic figures, known as Christopher, Nahum, and Caleb, make personal appearances to believers and the undecided alike, making trust, or faith, much less of an issue.[43] Moreover, an air of arbitrariness surrounds the

"decisions" of the undecided remnant. For example, a group of undecideds choose to leave Petra and go church-shopping, meeting the spiritual
representative of the Global Community in the desert adjacent to Petra.
The spiritual seekers are killed, however, regardless of whether or not
they take the Mark of the Beast, by a horde of venomous snakes.[44] Later,
Rayford and a comrade, operating in South America, encounter a similar
flood of humanity, this time traveling to see the three angels. But like
those who wandered forth from Petra, they do not seem to know why
they ought to trust the mysterious men. One traveler remarks to Rayford
that "it is as if we have no choice, sir."[45]

The evangelical imperative to present the Christian message to others
collides with the deterministic character forced upon evangelical identity
by the fixed parameters of dispensational prophecy belief. The Tribulation Force, it seems, *knows* God. His representatives help them navigate
planes and helicopters, avoid missiles, and even give them warning messages when they improperly load co-op planes.[46] The necessity of trust
during uncertain times gets washed away by continuous waves of miraculous banality. Faith, as a result, becomes a far less risky venture. What
is more, when one is "sealed" either for or against Christ, moral responsibility appears to evaporate. Believers cannot disobey, and those bearing
the Mark of the Beast, as much as they might desire otherwise, can only
follow the directives of Satan.

Significantly, even Chang, the undecided wild-card working as a parasite within Carpathia's New Babylon headquarters, flees late in the series—like the rest of his comrades—to the caves of Petra. There, Dr. Ben-
Judah and his elders pray that God remove the Mark of the Beast from
Chang's forehead. Against all dispensational injunctions, the Mark of the
Beast miraculously disappears, and Chang once again becomes the exception that proves the rule.[47] Chang, however, loses more than the Mark
of the Beast. He also forfeits his liminal, undecidable position, signaling,
ultimately, that the need for faith in an uncertain world diminishes as miracles and the importance of visible signs multiply.

Another problem, of course, is that Antichrist can also perform signs
and wonders. The Most Reverend High Father of Carpathianism, Leon
Fortunato, sends out false messiahs to tempt the undecided away from
Christ.[48] After all, his "messiahs" can perform all sorts of magic tricks to
convince the onlookers of their direct connection to the deity. The authors
suggest that such ruses may bear fruit, since Antichrist is the "god of this
world" and can offer signs galore to the gullible. Believers, wary of the

emptiness of such signs in the network culture, rely instead on faith and their knowledge of the Scriptures. The proliferation of miracles, however, undercuts the centrality of these assumptions. How can believers choose between two potential deceptions? The authors suggest late in the series, significantly, that they do not choose at all. Perhaps they never could. The Tribulation Force, renowned for the aviation skills of its members, ironically put its moral responsibility on autopilot. The authors' internal struggle between orthodox Calvinism with its tenet of double predestination and the free-will approach of later, Enlightenment-influenced evangelicalism reasserts itself, with Calvinism gaining the upper hand.[49]

The authors' insistence on the rigidity of the Marks proves especially significant. Whereas LaHaye and Jenkins send decidedly mixed signals concerning the value of visible signs in book eight, *The Mark,* they attempt to deflect all such doubt in *The Remnant,* reifying the Marks into absolute and irreversible indicators of identity (with the temporary exception of Chang, of course). But even such fixed and foolproof external signs cannot efface the complexity of the protagonists' human struggles. Rayford remarks that "many undecideds and even some who had taken the mark of the Antichrist risk their lives by downloading Buck's magazine from the Tribulation Force site."[50] Buck's cyberzine bears the suggestive name of *The Truth.* But for those who have taken the Mark of the Beast, knowing the truth will not set them free, as hard as they might seek it.

The authors illustrate this most poignantly in the martyrdom of one of their undercover operatives, Steve Plank. Plank began the series as Buck's editor at the *Global Weekly* and later became Carpathia's spokesperson, before accepting Christ and going undercover for the Tribulation Force disguised as a Global Community officer named Pinkerton Stephens. Stationed in Colorado, Stephens (Plank) effectively hides his true identity from his coworkers—at least for most of the series. Once Stephens's junior officer discovers he has not taken the Mark, however, the younger officer suggests that Stephens rectify the situation at once. Plank (Stephens) lost most of his face in the Great Earthquake early in the Tribulation and now wears a plastic mask to shield his gruesome visage. Chang suggests to Plank that he follow a similar course to the one he deployed, essentially faking the Mark or taking it by omission. After all, Chang reasons, no one could bear to look beneath the plastic mask. Plank, however, views such an act as a cowardly denial of Christ. The only alternative to accepting the Mark of the Beast, he knows, is to remove the mask and reveal himself as a believer, ensuring a swift martyrdom. He chooses to die as a witness for his faith rather than deceive anyone as to his true identity.[51] He does, however, finally reveal his identity as a believer to his junior officer, Vasily Medvedev. To Plank's surprise, the Russian responds to his testimony, and acknowledges that Plank has found the truth. But it is too late for Medvedev. He has already taken the Mark of the Beast. Although he reads Dr. Ben-Judah's sermons, Buck's cyberzine *The Truth,* and affirms the witness of Steve Plank, he cannot accept Christ, despite his desire to do so. The final scene that unfolds between the two obvious friends presents the pathos—and lurking uncertainty—of LaHaye and Jenkins's deterministic view of Bible prophecy:

> "Vasily, I only regret that when you came to me it was already too late for you. You had taken the mark, and proudly."
> "I'm not so proud of it anymore."
> "That is the tragedy of where we find ourselves."
> "I know."
> "You do?"
> "You think I do not sneak a look occasionally at the Ben-Judah Web site? I know my decision is irreversible."[52]

But he no longer has a choice. After Plank falls victim to the guillotine, Medvedev commits suicide.[53]

The scene presents the reader with a pair of tragic ironies. First, the martyrdom of Stephens (Plank), designed to witness bravely for Christ, fails to save his close friend, Medvedev, even when the latter displays a willingness to accept the Gospel message. Second, and more significantly, Plank, disguised as Stephens, plays his role too well. He never witnesses to Medvedev. He is too busy copycatting Antichrist's deceptive techniques to remove his mask and show his true face. And when he finally reveals himself—when he finally takes a leap of faith and risks his temporal safety for the eternal salvation of another—he fails. LaHaye and Jenkins's turn toward certainty and visible signs in *The Remnant,* ironically, does not reinforce evangelical identity, but instead appears to *efface* it as the example of Plank demonstrates.

Recall again O'Leary's distinction between the comic and tragic apocalypses. The comic apocalypse—which features greater open-endedness and a reluctance to make absolute truth claims—disappears in the latter novels along with the humanity of the protagonists. As O'Leary suggests, "The role of the interpreter in tragic apocalypticism is reduced to the breaking of the divine code. For argument in the comic frame, by contrast, authority is necessarily more mutable and can be refashioned to fit human needs."[54] The apocalyptic rhetoric in the latter novels turns decidedly tragic, however, and no longer "fits the human needs" of the *Left Behind* protagonists. Significantly, even Rayford, the steadfast leader of the Tribulation Force, questions the senselessness of the tragic apocalypse in book eleven, *Armageddon,* finding many suffering souls he wishes he could help, but cannot. The authors describe Rayford's anguish:

> Rayford knew the prophecy—that people would reject God enough times that God would harden their hearts and they wouldn't be able to choose him even if they wanted to. But knowing it didn't mean Rayford understood it. And it certainly didn't mean he had to like it. He couldn't make it compute with the God he knew, the loving and merciful one who seemed to look for ways to welcome everyone into heaven, not keep them out.[55]

Rayford cannot reconcile the developments of prophecy with what he knows of God and his own identity as an evangelical. Ultimately, the tragic apocalypse overpowers the humanity of Rayford and the rest of the Tribulation Force.

The Omega Code, an evangelical prophecy film contemporary with the *Left Behind* series (1999), also highlights the difficulties of the tragic apocalypse, offering cinematic insight into a problem that haunts the *Left Behind* novels.[56] In an awkward moment, the Antichrist-elect turns to his would-be false prophet and wonders aloud whether or not he himself might be the Beast of which Revelation speaks. "What if," he asks, "we perform our roles perfectly, are we then damned for it?" The Antichrist-figure, philanthropist Stone Alexander, appears greatly distressed by the fatalistic turn of events, almost as if stifled by the paralytic apocalyptic scenario in which he finds himself. His false prophet figure, however, displaying decidedly less conscience, reminds Alexander that he need only "trust the code." As long as he follows the codes—the prophecies—his dreams, most of them seemingly benevolent, will come to pass. This awkward moment of uncertainty ends with Alexander receiving the requisite fatal head wound from his impatient false prophet. Alexander's moment of uncertainty, during which he perceives his tragic circumstances, ends fittingly with an act of violence. The prophet, or the prophecies, as it were, destroys the humanity of the prospective Antichrist, reducing him to an evil automaton or nothing more than a "divine code-breaker," as O'Leary would put it.[57]

The Omega Code presents the issue in a nutshell. The problem of uncertainty is eliminated once and for all, but at the price of the protagonists' humanity. The film asks—albeit briefly—what it means to be an evangelical as well as a human being. Most nonevangelicals not well versed in prophecy belief would find the answer bewildering. To be evangelical, it seems, means surrendering vital components of one's humanity in order to find existential security. But this is inconsistent with the recent trajectory of American evangelical attitudes concerning human volition— notions prevalent since the mid-nineteenth century (if not longer)—and also with what prophecy writers ostensibly teach about the ability of individuals to freely choose for or against the Gospel of Christ. An evangelical, logically enough, is one who must share the Gospel message out of sheer excitement; he or she must *evangelize*. Plank's existence as an evangelical, as well as the saving faith of the other members of the Tribulation Force, seems threatened by LaHaye and Jenkins's insistence on miracles and visible signs. Who needs faith if one is already a first-hand witness, and who needs to witness if individual paths have in some sense already been determined? By evading *undecidability* and *uncertainty*, and by constructing a powerful network that relies on *strategies* rather than *tactics* through the assured protection of guardian angels, members of the Tribulation Force, despite (or because of) their resistance, do what Antichrist cannot accomplish directly: they undermine their existence as evangelicals.

Michel Serres points out that not only is the host/parasite pair subject to reversal, but he also adds that they are both dependant upon a *third*. This third is the ultimate parasite: noise.[58] Successful adaptation to the emerging network culture requires dynamism, an identity that while retaining its uniqueness, also manages to transform the potentially disruptive noise characteristic of networks into meaningful information. Adaptation requires that individuals and groups retain flexibility and openness so they can make sense of the uncertainty—or noise—in their lives. This requires that one face the challenges and ambiguities of contemporary existence. One may not always know the answers, but when "uncertainty characterizes the world itself,"[59] trust (or faith in the evangelical sense) allows the individual to rise above the gaps and fissures in one's knowledge. LaHaye and Jenkins do appear implicitly aware of this, but such knowledge becomes faint when the texts insist upon the violent recovery of security.

Conclusion: Paying the Price of Success?

The recent resurgence of conservative American evangelicalism, whether in real-life or as depicted in the *Left Behind* novels, has allowed believers to enter the Forum—so to speak—and their networks and institutions, whether megachurches, television ministries, relief agencies, political action committees, or even publishing houses, now rival those of their secular opponents. Prophecy believers, however, stand on the precipice of overaccommodation, incorporating many of the values of the secular (Beast) culture they ostensibly resist. Their dilemma stems not so much from excessive otherworldliness—neglecting the here and now for a promise of "pie in the sky, by and by"—but from what historian Wouter Hanegraaff terms "weak this-worldliness," a tepid recognition of the importance of this-worldly existence with a desire to remake it in a form more amenable to conservative evangelicalism.

The otherworldly language of miraculous deliverance one finds in the *Left Behind* novels emerges in part, I suspect, from an impulse among evangelical leaders such as LaHaye and Jenkins to reclaim a sense of marginalization, to get back the spiritual edge lost as evangelicals reentered the public arena and achieved a measure of worldly success. The authors turn to a theme of violent resistance late in the series as part of a nostalgic longing for a simpler world with well-known enemies and an ample sense of personal and cultural meaning. The *Left Behind* series depicts protagonists who want it all: the trappings of material success and nice suburban churches with an ample intensity of belief. They want the best of both worlds, in other words—this one and the next—yet the balance that believers seek, that is, an "in but not of the world" existence, remains precarious. Ironically, prophecy believers may lose their evangelical identity in their frenzied, occasionally paranoid efforts to save it from their own temporal success.

The evidence I present in this chapter suggests that evangelicals who deploy dispensational prophecy belief will be unable to escape the Beast—barring a miracle—regardless of their actions. The matter, of course, is never quite so simple. Using the interpretive framework offered by Mark C. Taylor and literary theorist Stephen O'Leary, one finds a pair of complementary schemas for understanding the dilemmas in which prophecy believers find themselves. The quest for Marks and a failsafe sense of identity and existential security gets stymied by the mysterious "T" in *The Mark*, but the drive toward certainty and a crippling rigidification of evangelical identity continually reemerges until the texts no longer seem to resist it. At this point the comic nature of the apocalypse surrenders to the tragic sense, one in which determinism supplants open-endedness, and blind obedience replaces the hope for successful adaptation to an increasingly complicated world. Although the authors valorize faith and its necessity in a culture with no guarantees, their reliance on supernatural solutions undercuts faith, creating just another oppressive network—another Beast.

By embracing the tragic frame, the *Left Behind* protagonists inadvertently do to themselves what Antichrist cannot, surrendering vital components of their evangelical identity—along with their humanity—in their often violent attempts to resist evil. They hurl themselves into a desperate, predetermined world of moral irresponsibility, in which their identities are fixed by unreflective readings of ancient prophecies. Despite the occasional protests of figures like T, the narrative seems to incorporate the designs of Antichrist without the authors ever recognizing it. Such lack of awareness—and not so much the predetermined script—seems most tragic.

It is not all that remarkable, however, to suggest that evangelical prophecy literature promotes despair and fatalism. Scholars have argued this throughout the twentieth century. What *is* remarkable is that post–Cold War variants such as the *Left Behind* novels stop to consider the dilemma from *within* the context of evangelical discourse. The texts begin by offering empowerment, and even promote a kind of accommodation to the world. But as the protagonists insist on rigid distinctions between themselves and others, the novels take a familiar, desperate turn. As the texts themselves remind us, however, any visible sign can be deceptive during the Tribulation. Nothing is ever as it seems. Even within the most tragic of predetermined fates, such as that of Lt. Medvedev in *The Remnant,* a remarkably human voice remains that suggests the protagonists have become aware of the ambiguity, even troubled by the easy determinacy that surrounds them. Trusting the prophecies and their ability to dissolve ambiguity—along with a concomitant loss in human freedom—leads not to internal security, the *Left Behind* novels whisper, but rather *infernal* security. Granted, such voices quickly disappear in the texts, just as many of the undecided find themselves swallowed up by the ground in *The Remnant*. But their voices (screams, really) *are* heard, metaphorically speaking. Even within the most deterministic and predictable sections of the novels, one finds something quite remarkable: not everyone agrees with the proceedings and outcomes of the tragic apocalypse.

Nevertheless, LaHaye and Jenkins's ultimate attempt to surgically separate contemporary evangelicalism from the Western intellectual tradition, especially what they refer to as "secular humanism," tragically results—at least in the narrative universe of the *Left Behind* novels—in the diminishment of the evangelicalism they seek to defend and purify. For contemporary evangelicalism features a notion of identity influenced as much by an Enlightenment emphasis upon human choice and moral responsibility as by ancient Biblical writings.[60] In addition, faith, the need to witness, and moral responsibility all emerge as vital aspects of evangelical identity in the novels. All are valorized at some point in the *Left Behind* series, and all are, ultimately, threatened by rampant fear, insecurity, and a quest for scapegoats and easy answers. The *Left Behind* series presents scholars, however, not only with predetermined policy statements on matters of culture and politics, but it also exposes many profound existential uncertainties lurking within evangelical prophecy circles.

LaHaye and Jenkins begin their novels by eschewing despair as typically found in prophecy fiction—what one might call fatalistic, overt otherworldliness—and adopt instead a position of weak this-worldliness. They desperately attempt to balance the needs of Enlightenment-influenced evangelicalism and their own intimate connections with modernity on the one hand, with a deeply rooted urge to reject Enlightenment "humanism" on the other. Ultimately—owing to the inexorable nature of dispensational prophecy belief—they must turn, like orthodox Calvinists, toward a vision of an uncompromisingly all-powerful God. Humans, it would seem, become quite puny as the apocalypse unfolds. Put differently, the authors are forced by the imperatives of prophecy belief to return to a position of fatalism and despair. However, fatalism in this new reading attempts to remake the world according to divine fiat—and in so doing, buries any awareness that humans, and not God, remain the primary actors. The characters continue to act against Antichrist, except the roles they play are already prescripted—they cannot, in and of themselves, make any difference—or so they believe. Prophecy belief, which began as a quest for signs of God's will, becomes—in the final analysis—an idol which usurps the position of God, trapping prophecy believers beneath a mass of their own fatalistic assumptions.

In sum, the *Left Behind* series suggests that evangelicals—especially prophecy believers—stand on the brink of apocalyptic change, at least in the way both evangelical culture and individual believers approach the world. Granted, the belief that one's own generation will witness the events of the last days extends to antiquity. The question, however, is not so much the empirical validity of prophecy writers' claims, but rather how they conceptualize their present and future existence as evangelicals. The *Left Behind* novels exhibit two notable possibilities. On the one side, the protagonists respond to contemporary uncertainties by adapting to them, however reluctantly, with greater openness and self-reflection. On the other side, one finds a recurring temptation to harden identity and draw sharp distinctions between good and evil. *Left Behind* leans much closer to the tragic, fatalistic understanding, although not without lingering doubts. The future of evangelical identity may depend upon which option believers more closely favor. The price of embracing change and uncertainty is a high one, but the cost of oversimplifying the complexity of their cultural situation may prove higher still.

Prophecy literature may also encourage believers to bury their insecurities about the contemporary world beneath a drive toward certainty and a quest for rigid distinctions between "us" and "them." Such moves may backfire in a world in which evil can move in clandestine networks, and friends are not always easy to separate from enemies. The predominant, tragic use of apocalyptic language in the *Left Behind* novels may influence prophecy believers to chase shadows unreflectively rather than face the demons within. As the quotation from Robert Fuller suggests in the epigraph, attempts to preserve cultural identity by demonizing others—or *marking* them—do not appear helpful. If—especially after 9/11—those Americans influenced by prophecy belief continue to pursue the evil in their midst without sufficient reflection and soul-searching, they may ultimately build the very Beast they seek to resist.

Epilogue

American public life, on the other hand, offers the opportunity for the marginalized to develop market appeal and come closer to the center. It often displays a facile tolerance, a tendency to absorb, approve, and domesticate traditions and movements on previously established, safe cultural terms. Sometimes Americans kill their rebels and prophets, but a more likely fate for them is to be assimilated, tamed, and even converted, somehow, into commercial profit.[1]
—Joel A. Carpenter, *Revive Us Again*

Such an absolute separation between good and evil in the cosmic drama directs the plot to the ultimate dialectic of victimage. The sacrifice of the perfect victim, the Lamb, dialectically enables the transformation of victimage into power with the defeat and slaughter of the beast. When such a dramatic pattern is applied to the social world, the consequences can indeed be tragic. Absolute truth inspires absolute commitments; the valorization of martyrdom leads, by the Iron Law of history, toward war and sacrifice.[2]
—Stephen D. O'Leary, "Arguing the Apocalypse"

Ironic Escapes

Reading the quotations in the epigraph, one is immediately struck by the contrasting possibilities they describe. On the one hand, Joel Carpenter suggests that even the most radical prophet runs the risk of becoming tamed and commercialized by the American marketplace (as one can witness by the tremendous commercial appeal of the *Left Behind* novels and their spin-off products). On the other hand, Stephen D. O'Leary points out the tragic consequences of prophecy believers who take their own prophetic interpretations too seriously. The *Left Behind* series prominently features both possibilities. Moreover, the authors rarely depict either option in its purest form, although the latter novels come closest to valorizing the more tragic possibilities. Rather, LaHaye and Jenkins imagine a continuum of outcomes in their novels, attempting to navigate a fragile balance between an overaccommodation to the world that leaves prophecy-believing evangelicals culturally irrelevant, and a violent, destructive quest to wrest spiritual meaning from what they perceive as an increasingly depraved and meaningless world. What is most striking in each scenario, however, is the absolute failure to achieve what the narratives ostensibly seek: escape from the mundane world of rapid cultural change. Deliverance in the *Left Behind* narrative does not indicate escape, ultimately, but becomes instead a tense, ongoing process of negotiation with the forces of modernity.

Years pass, both in the "real-time" of publishing and in the narrative world of the *Left Behind* novels, and escape always seems promised but never quite delivered. The novels constantly defer the apocalypse. Yes, we know it has to end sometime; even the authors, their agents and publicists, and the publisher know as much. Yet the escape promised by the *Left Behind* narrative ultimately proves ironic because outside of the first few pages with the Rapture and the last few with the Glorious Appearing and return of Christ, life on earth continues, just much more chaotically—hence worse and more complicated—than before. Thus, as tempting as it would be to describe the *Left Behind* series as a flight of fancy away from the mundane world, the novels prevent this, depicting characters who must remain and struggle against the forces of evil. Not unlike late-twentieth-century science-fiction productions such as the cyberpunk of William Gibson or the film noir of Patrick McGoohan's short-lived 1960's serial, *The Prisoner,* the novels tantalize with escape but instead prepare their readers for an adjustment phase that will not be easy. Hence, I have chosen to treat the novels—despite their unmistakably escapist sentiments—as "adjustment narratives" rather than "escape narratives." Perhaps, in the world outside of LaHaye and Jenkins's narrative universe, the long-promised airlift to heavenly bliss will finally come or perhaps it will not. On this count, only God knows. Regardless, in the meantime believers must make the best of what they have here on earth, and the novels suggest numerous ways to do this.

The accommodationist tendency is much stronger in the earlier volumes of the series. The reason for this is not difficult to discern—protagonists know that the promised End still lies distant in the future, veiled by the sufferings that await them as the most horrible phases of the

Tribulation approach. Protagonists must find the means to stay alive in a world increasingly hostile to their particularistic beliefs, building alternative structures that promise to protect believers against the onslaughts of Antichrist and his dreaded Beast system. In this sense, the novels seem to mirror life. Contemporary prophecy believers have had to build their own alternative structures in order to adapt to a network culture that threatens to render their beliefs obscurantist and ultimately obsolete. The *Left Behind* novels reflect both how believers have already begun to adapt to the network culture, along with offering them additional survival tactics. The novels inform believers that no matter how bad the signs of the times may appear, God remains in control. As long as believers place their faith in God and in each other, they will pass through the tribulations of the network culture. In this sense, apocalyptic literature produces an adaptive rather than a dangerously reactive response.

As the End approaches within the *Left Behind* cosmos, however, and believers pass through the Tribulation, the prophecies themselves assume paramount importance. Instead of serving the adaptation of God's elect to the cultural mainstream, the prophecies become an End in themselves, so to speak. The *Left Behind* protagonists—and, by extension, the authors—come to reify prophecy, taking it too seriously and raising it to the status of an inerrant idol that instead of indicating the possibility that God will soon restart the apocalyptic clock of the last days, inadvertently usurps God's position. Understood thusly, prophecy belief becomes tragic, as O'Leary dubs it, severely restricting the human possibilities of its adherents, along with the opportunities for contemporary evangelicals to adapt to the emerging network culture. It also places, ironically, severe limitations on an allegedly all-powerful and dynamic God, since God, presumably, must also follow the strictures of ancient prophecies as interpreted by His humble servants. The prophecies become, in other words, omnipotent, omniscient, and omnipresent to believers, assuming the cardinal attributes of God, while relegating God to a subordinate role—everything prophecy believers accuse the Beast and his unwholesome associates of accomplishing. The *Left Behind* protagonists succumb not to an external menace, but rather one of their own creation.

It is as if the authors get trapped inside their own narrative universe, mistaking the messenger for the prophetic message. The earlier novels address the contemporary world quite closely. In the later novels, however, one finds a disconnect between the narrative world of *Left Behind* and the "real" world of the network culture. In such a scenario, prophecy believers lose, rather than gain, their promised deliverance. The authors ultimately create the very Beast they fulminate against, a Beast speaking great, prophetic things that dominates believers' actions and identities rather than allowing them to accommodate themselves to a rapidly changing world. Moreover, during times of crisis, such a drive toward security and easy answers may also spill over into the American mainstream, causing Americans to reify the idol of security as an end in itself. The main difficulties, however—as I hope this section makes abundantly clear—lurk for prophecy believers themselves.

Thus, I ultimately focus not so much on any influence the novels may have on the values of the American mainstream—although I have periodically suggested in this text that such consequences may indeed be forthcoming. Instead, I analyze questions of personal and collective identity among prophecy-believing evangelicals. Their ambitions may be self-defeating in more than one sense. Although the cultural pessimism, anxiety, and despair that emerges late in the novels may impact American society as a whole, especially during times of crisis when such sentiments are ill-afforded, I argue that the main impact will be on evangelicals themselves.

At their core, the *Left Behind* novels address questions of personal and collective identity. On a personal level, LaHaye and Jenkins inform readers what they must do to avoid being left behind. On the collective level, the novels try to negotiate the narrow straits of modernity, attempting to assimilate the most useful aspects of the network culture without surrendering critical aspects of what it means to be an evangelical. Prophecy belief, in moderation, can help evangelicals maintain a productive tension that helps them ride the crest of modernity without getting pulled under. Granted, one finds a drive to turn away from the world and construct protective enclaves with the blessed and the damned identified—at least metaphorically—by marks. But one also finds—especially early—a tendency to read the apocalyptic script as an invitation to become more engaged with modernity, accepting ambiguity and uncertainty with the strength of faith. The matter is not a simple one.

The Political Question

At least some of the ambivalence one finds in the novels reflects the recent return of conservative evangelicalism to the political arena. Many of the big-name evangelical activists such as Tim LaHaye and Jerry Falwell, for example, proclaim dispensationalism as their eschatology. Yet dispensational theology would not seem to permit extended political involvement. Only by arguing that political activity enhances their ability to protect evangelical identity and win souls during the last days can dispensationalists begin to work through the contradictions inherent in their positions. The imperatives of dispensational belief would appear to make large-scale political activism distasteful or even dangerous for evangelical identity—functioning more as a social safety valve for dangerous discontent than as an active engine of change, whether for progressive or reactionary ends.

The earliest novels illustrate LaHaye and Jenkins's reluctance to take large-scale action, even in matters to which they are sympathetic. For example—as we saw in the last chapter—in the second novel, *Tribulation Force*, Buck declines to participate in the resistance of the American militia/patriot movement uprising against Antichrist, although he secretly sympathizes with them. Buck knows, according to the dictates of dispensational prophecy belief, that such efforts of overt resistance will fail during the Tribulation. But as I also pointed out, the Tribulation Force subtly shifts its modes of operation throughout the novels and becomes, in effect, the same kind of paramilitary force Buck initially rejected. Such a development, of course, is not consistent with Tim LaHaye's own version of dispensational theology. The protagonists, moreover, despite their extensive knowledge of dispensational theology fed by Dr. Ben-Judah, appear completely unaware of their strategic shifts.

This observation helps illustrate an analogous example: the increasingly close relationship one finds in the *Left Behind* novels between the ideals of dispensationalism and those of its less politically inhibited cousin, Christian Reconstructionism, although it is important not to confuse Reconstructionism with militia movements.[3] Reconstructionists, sometimes known as dominion theologians, rather, have a marked desire to change or "reconstruct" American culture and are not hampered by the constraints of dispensational belief, as Reconstructionists hold to a post-millennial eschatology. It is not a question of whether politically active prophecy believers will shed such doctrines as the Rapture and the Tribulation, the longer the End delays. Their theology will likely remain distinctive from that of Reconstructionists in this regard. But what may instead happen—as the *Left Behind* novels suggest—is that a politics of despair may emerge among prophecy believers, a politics that, rather than promoting an engagement with structural ills, may only make matters that much worse by disguising the question of political agency.

Basically, the injunctions against political activity exist because prophecy believers think they can only do so much before God returns and does everything Himself. But LaHaye and Jenkins subtly transform their dynamic protagonists throughout the *Left Behind* novels into actors for God's eternal plan, role-players who take on wider political involvements precisely because they believe they *are* actualizing God's End-Times plan, rather than simply bending its rules but otherwise respecting its limitations. Thus, although prophecy belief may still act as a restraint on large-scale political activity among prophecy believers, the tethering rope may become weaker the longer the End tarries. The *Left Behind* novels suggest that dispensational prophecy believers may be embarking on a slippery slope toward the more unrestrained, reactionary positions of their Christian Reconstructionist cousins, albeit for very different reasons.

Prophecy Believers and the Network Culture

Protagonists in the *Left Behind* novels do indeed take action. They struggle against Antichrist and the rise of his infernal Beast system—an interlocking series of networks that unite the world's governments, economies, and religions under the rule of Antichrist. A number of social scientists have observed a similar phenomenon, albeit without attributing to it such sinister overtones. Theorists Manuel Castells and Mark C. Taylor, for example, have discussed the rise of the network society and the network culture, respectively, emphasizing the increasingly interconnected nature of contemporary life. The network culture breaks down barriers, both physical and epistemological, that have long separated cultures and calls into question—through the rapid exchange of information made possible by new communications technologies—rigid understandings of the world and firm, unquestioned foundations.

Such developments have threatened prophecy believers, who insist upon the necessity of firm foundations, with Jesus representing "the real thing" that gives their life temporal and ultimate meaning. *Left Behind* protagonists fight back against the network culture/Beast system by building their own networks of resistance, a move that, ironically, only heightens their dependence on the network culture. It also demonstrates—despite their insistence on escape—that their fates lay in *this* world much more than in the next, at least as articulated in the novels. Prophecy believers are already too closely implicated in modernity for escape to be anything more than a comforting thought.

Left Behind and the Question of Technology

The relationship of the *Left Behind* novels to the question of technology is also an important and ambiguous one. LaHaye and Jenkins—far from technophobes—are obviously fascinated by the power of new technologies, especially new communications technologies. Unlike many of their predecessors in prophecy fiction, LaHaye and Jenkins attribute positive roles to technology. Technology, for example, allows the Tribulation Force to mount its resistance to Antichrist. Evangelical paramilitary commandoes rocket across the world at a moment's notice to interrupt Antichrist's webs of communication. Yet the authors also recognize that the same networks that support their disruptive activities also make Antichrist's rapid rise to prominence possible. For the authors, technology is a double-edged sword. Too often, however, the authors suggest that the solution lies in who controls technology, ignoring the inherent qualities of technological tools.

This leads to a naivety among the *Left Behind* protagonists, as they assume that they can purloin Antichrist's tools without suffering any consequences. But this is definitely not the case. As Melvin Kranzberg and Manuel Castells remind us, technology may be neither inherently good nor bad, "but it is not neutral."[4] Whereas previous generations of prophecy writers tended to demonize technology, LaHaye and Jenkins, if anything, deify it, ironically coming perilously close to worshiping the Beast they seek to resist. Once again, the *Left Behind* protagonists—and, by extension, the authors and contemporary prophecy believers—are too tightly implicated in modernity to remain unaffected by the ironic consequences of their entanglements. Although the Tribulation Force believes they are fighting Antichrist using his tools, for example, they are tragically unaware that they are already inside the Beast, coparticipants in his infernal system. This tragic lack of awareness points to what I consider the central tension of the *Left Behind* novels.

The Central Tension: The Temptation of Marks

The central challenge presented by the *Left Behind* novels takes one back to a formative moment in the history of American evangelicalism. Meeting in a St. Louis hotel in 1942, a group of moderate fundamentalists sought to overcome the bitterness, divisiveness, and occasional hostilities that characterized conservative American Protestantism, proposing instead an enthusiastic, positive, and most important, culturally engaged religious movement. The twentieth-century evangelical movement—or, as it has sometimes been referred to—the neoevangelical movement, emerged from a larger convention held the following year in Chicago. The National Association of Evangelicals (NAE) had been born.[5] From the beginning the NAE had to navigate a perilous course between progressive/modernist groups like the Federal Council of Churches (FCC), and the various fundamentalist splinter groups, including Carl McIntire's American Council of Christian Churches (ACCC). McIntire, a New Jersey Presbyterian whose career was tarnished by numerous, acrimonious schisms, harangued the NAE into a more conservative position, and in 1944, the NAE banned members from participating in the progressive Federal Council of Churches.[6] Despite McIntire's challenges from the right flank, however, the NAE represented an honest effort to open up to American culture, maintaining the essence of American evangelicalism without separating from the mainstream. The members of the NAE sought, in other words, to provide what Christian Smith calls an "engaged orthodoxy," a socially relevant form of evangelicalism that still held to the fundamentals of the faith without smothering it beneath waves of defensiveness.[7]

Sociologist Christian Smith, overlaying the historical findings of Joel Carpenter with his own survey data on contemporary evangelicalism, argues that evangelicalism, far from being buffeted into obscurity by the forces of modernity, has actually thrived under the challenge. The establishment of the NAE in 1942–43 makes a wonderful example because erstwhile fundamentalists found the means to suspend many of their more contentious arguments without putting aside their differences—and their particularities. As a result, the movement prospered and inspired related efforts at bringing together cross-sections of American evangelicalism, most notably the Youth for Christ organization. Youth for Christ, featuring a young Billy Graham as one of its leading speakers and rising stars, brought evangelicalism to war-time American youth by imitating the slick marketing and entertainment strategies of the mainstream.[8] Evangelicals found, at least for a time, a balance between retaining their particular identities, and engaging the world with a greater measure of openness. The balance, however, has remained a tenuous one. Nevertheless, Smith argues that evangelicalism has somehow managed to navigate the narrow straits of its often paradoxical existence. He summarizes his findings:

> The American evangelical movement, by contrast, has been relatively successful because it has managed to formulate and sustain a religious strategy that maintains high tension with and high integration into mainstream American society simultaneously. . . . This provokes a situation of sustained dissonance, if not outright conflict, between evangelical believers and the nonevangelical world with which they—with tension—engage. And this fosters religious vitality.[9]

Smith presents a model of American evangelicalism that suggests a self-regulating mechanism. That is, evangelicalism seems to adjust to the American mainstream and produce just the right amount of tension and distance required to thrive. Smith does have a point. This is why I described prophecy belief in the Introduction as a "cultural thermostat," as prophecy belief seems helpful in providing evangelicals with the appropriate level of tension. When believers get too close to the mainstream, for example, prophecy belief helps them create tension—sometimes artfully—between themselves and the surrounding culture. By contrast, the cultural thermostat also encourages prophecy believers to cool off when their apocalyptic expectations lead to overheated, exaggerated conflicts with the mainstream.

We witnessed this in chapter 5, for example, as the mysterious "T" upbraids Rayford for his lack of faith in God and in his Tribulation Force comrades. The authors even cast doubt upon the value of visible marks, and the protagonists must live with their nagging uncertainties. The narrative throughout much of the *Left Behind* series almost resembles the kind of engaged orthodoxy Carpenter and Smith find among mid- and late-twentieth-century evangelicals, respectively. LaHaye and Jenkins's protagonists—at least until book eight, *The Mark*—remain engaged in and at least somewhat open to the world, while simultaneously maintaining critical aspects of their evangelical identity. They oscillate between an all-too-cozy acceptance of the mainstream, and a dangerous, hostile rejection of the outside world.

The *Left Behind* novels also present a darker, more reactionary vision for the future of American evangelicalism, however. The ghost of Carl McIntire haunts the later novels, as the protagonists rigidly cling to the value of visible marks as foolproof means of identification, and they surrender many of their most important evangelical traits in an ironic attempt to safeguard the "fundamentals of the faith." As we saw in chapter 6, the delicate tensions the authors maintain throughout much of the series falls away as their anxious protagonists insist upon absolute certainty in a world that simply cannot give it. Prophecy belief, rather than functioning as a cultural thermostat designed to provide an adequate level of cultural tension, runs amok, literally becoming an End in itself rather than a comforting narrative to the faithful. As protagonists struggle to remain correct to the prophecies, it is as if they surrender their humanity to a literal reading of ancient texts, losing the dynamism that made twentieth-century evangelicalism so successful. In what the French existentialist Jean-Paul Sartre might call an act of "bad faith," the protagonists act on behalf of the prophecies without recognizing the human choices they invariably exercise.

In conclusion, the main danger the novels point up is a resurgent fundamentalism that inadvertently appropriates the most problematic traits of its opponents in a defensive effort at self-preservation. The danger, then, lies—on one level—between the poles of evangelicalism and fundamentalism. Evangelicalism displays a measure of cultural openness with the flexibility required to adjust to the emerging network culture. Fundamentalism, by contrast—at least as historically understood—has attempted to preserve the faith by withdrawing and eliminating all contact with the world or as much as reasonably possible. The resurgent fundamentalism one finds in the *Left Behind* novels differs in a significant way from its early to mid-twentieth-century predecessors, however. While it, too, hardens the boundaries between "us" and "them" so tightly that adjustment to contemporary culture seems unlikely, it also engages the world in a slippage that places it perilously close to the activist positions of its more radical Christian Reconstructionist cousins. In sum, the fundamentalism one finds depicted in the later novels is not a disengaged one, but rather one which despairs of human possibilities for growth and change, while deploying an aggressive form of political rhetoric designed to bring forth the commands of God through naive obedience to contemporary and controversial *interpretations* of ancient prophecies.

The Final Analysis

Despite such suggestive and dire possibilities, however, it is important to remember what the novels can and cannot tell us. They cannot tell us, for example, precisely how evangelical readers will respond, nor can we make the facile connection between the pronouncements of Tim LaHaye and Jerry Jenkins—fictional or otherwise—and concrete policy decisions within everyday evangelicalism or indeed national policy. Indeed, Christian Smith refers to such an assumption as "the representative elite fallacy," in which rank-and-file evangelicals are assumed to follow without deviation the suggestions of their self-appointed spokespersons.[10] This no doubt happens to a certain extent. Yet readers have their own ways of appropriating the texts, making ultimate outcomes all the more difficult to predict.

Nevertheless, we cannot ignore the possibilities the novels do suggest. Whatever else they may represent, they are not simply innocuous fiction. I argue that the *Left Behind* novels indicate that prophecy believers may be reevaluating their strategies of relating to the contemporary world. The novels bear witness to an ongoing debate among believers—not necessarily to a compulsory call to arms led by their presumed generals Tim LaHaye and Jerry Jenkins—but to a debate with genuine repercussions. On the one side, believers may read the prophecy language of the novels as an invitation to embrace at least some of the ambiguity of their contemporary lives as evangelicals in a world increasingly hostile to such particularistic notions of identity. On the other side, the *Left Behind* novels may encourage readers to adopt a fatalistic stance that damages their evangelical identity more than it helps it, along with raising alarm among the American cultural mainstream.

One can find both tendencies in the novels. The tone and trajectory of the novels suggest that LaHaye and Jenkins promote a more rigid, fatalistic, and fundamentalist stance. Indeed, if readers adopt a similar attitude of rampant anxiety and despair, prophecies of the Beast and all of its machinations may prove self-fulfilling. Nevertheless, we would do well to remember that the *Left Behind* novels resemble on one level what the nineteenth-century Danish existentialist Kierkegaard deemed "imaginative constructions." The novels present possibilities to their readership, which is not required to follow the path the series indicates. Put differently, LaHaye and Jenkins, as prominent evangelical leaders, wield significant rhetorical power, influence which LaHaye has effectively deployed in the past, as I noted in chapter 2. Nevertheless, we must not underestimate the creativity of evangelical readers, who will appropriate the novels in their own ways.[11] Thus, no matter what LaHaye and Jenkins or their novels ultimately advocate, the readers will, in the End, write their own conclusions.

Notes

NOTES TO THE PREFACE

1. See James Davison Hunter, *Evangelicalism: The Coming Generation* (New York: Oxford University Press, 1987); and Christian Smith, *Christian America? What Evangelicals Really Want* (Berkeley: University of California Press, 2000), 16. Sociologist James Davison Hunter, borrowing from the work of Donald Barrett, estimated in 1980 the percentage of conservative Protestants—the group most amenable to my definition—at 22 percent of the United States' population. Twenty years later, sociologist Christian Smith put the percentage of conservative Protestants at 29 percent. These two figures provide a decent range for estimating the number of potential prophecy believers in the United States and are certainly more reliable than media polls that routinely put as many as 50 percent of Americans into the category of prophecy believers. Nevertheless, the precise number is difficult to determine.

2. Quentin J. Schultze, "Keeping the Faith: American Evangelicals and the Media," in *American Evangelicals and the Mass Media,* edited by Quentin J. Schultze (Grand Rapids, Mich.: Zondervan, 1990), 24–25.

3. George Marsden, ed., *Evangelicalism and Modern America* (Grand Rapids, Mich.: Eerdman's, 1984), x.

4. Paul S. Boyer, *When Time Shall Be No More: Prophecy Belief in Modern American Culture* (Cambridge, Mass.: Harvard University Press, 1992), 304–311.

NOTES TO THE INTRODUCTION

1. Tim LaHaye and Jerry Jenkins, *Are We Living in the End Times? Current Events Foretold in Scripture and What They Mean* (Nashville, Tenn.: Tyndale House, 1999), x.

2. Mark C. Taylor, *The Moment of Complexity: Emerging Network Culture* (Chicago: University of Chicago Press, 2002), 3.

3. The *Left Behind* series includes twelve novels, although a prequel and sequel to the series may also follow. Tim LaHaye and Jerry B. Jenkins, *Left Behind: A Novel of the Earth's Last Days* (Wheaton, Ill.: Tyndale House, 1995);

Tribulation Force: The Continuing Drama of Those Left Behind, 1996; *Nicolae: The Rise of Antichrist,* 1997; *Soul Harvest: The World Takes Sides,* 1998; *Apollyon: The Destroyer is Released,* 1999; *Assassins: Assignment: Jerusalem, Target: Antichrist,* 1999b; *The Indwelling: The Beast Takes Possession,* 2000; *The Mark: The Beast Rules the World,* 2000b; *Desecration: Antichrist Takes the Throne,* 2001; *The Remnant: On the Brink of Armageddon,* 2002; *Armageddon: The Cosmic Battle of the Ages,* 2003; and *Glorious Appearing: The End of Days,* 2004.

4. I derive my understanding of network culture especially from Manuel Castells, *The Rise of the Network Society* (Malden, Mass.: Blackwell, 2000); and Taylor, *The Moment of Complexity.*

5. See also Paul S. Boyer, *When Time Shall Be No More*; Robert C. Fuller, *Naming the Antichrist: The History of an American Obsession* (New York: Oxford University Press, 1995); and Bernard McGinn, *Antichrist: Two Thousand Years of the Human Fascination with Evil* (New York: HarperCollins, 1994). A number of scholars have tracked the periodic Christian tendency to locate the evil in their midst. Boyer and Fuller specifically discuss contemporary American examples. McGinn takes a more historical approach, devoting much of his attention to the medieval Church.

6. Boyer, *When Time Shall Be No More,* 254. Joel A. Carpenter, *Revive Us Again: The Reawakening of American Fundamentalism* (New York: Oxford University Press, 1997), 234–236.

7. Carpenter, *Revive Us Again,* 235–236.

8. Personal communication with Robert C. Fuller. On another note, I must admit at least the possibility that some readers appropriate the *Left Behind* novels for entertainment purposes only, rejecting the theological imperatives presented by the books. For the most part, however, I suspect that readers rarely enjoy the books for the sole sake of the writing quality or cliffhanger plots as better alternatives exist among secular authors on both counts.

9. For sociological analysis of contemporary evangelicalism, see Mark A. Shibley, *Resurgent Evangelicalism in the United States: Mapping Cultural Change since 1970* (Columbia, S.C.: University of South Carolina Press, 1996); and Christian Smith, *American Evangelicalism: Embattled and Thriving* (Chicago: University of Chicago Press, 1998). The findings of Shibley and Smith, despite crucial differences, do not support the notion that evangelicals are a desperate lot seeking their eternal reward and little more.

10. Smith, *American Evangelicalism,* 150.

11. Rodney Stark, "How New Religions Succeed: A Theoretical Model," in *The Future of New Religious Movements,* edited by David G. Bromley and Philip E. Hammond (Atlanta, Ga.: Mercer University Press, 1987), 15–16. Sociologist Rodney Stark's notion of "medium tension" is helpful in this regard. Stark writes, commenting on the success or failure of a new religion, that "the

movement must maintain a substantial sense of difference and considerable tension if it is to prosper. Without significant differences from the conventional faith(s) a movement lacks a basis for successful conversion. Thus, it must maintain a delicate balance between conformity and deviance."

12. For my adaptation of cultural tension to prophecy belief I owe much to Christian Smith's more general work on the evangelical subculture vis-à-vis the American mainstream in *American Evangelicalism,* as well as the literary theory of Stephen D. O'Leary. See Stephen D. O'Leary, *Arguing the Apocalypse: A Theory of Millennial Rhetoric* (New York: Oxford University Press, 1994).

13. Smith, *American Evangelicalism,* 148–151. Smith points to the example of the United Church of Christ (UCC), citing a 1985 study of UCC members in which many could not identify any meaningful or distinguishing characteristics of the denomination. In fairness, the UCC clearly identifies itself as a "peace church" and aligns itself with issues of social justice. Such stances may not fully resonate among pewsitters, however. On the question of why conservative churches have grown during the twentieth century, despite (or because of) requiring greater sacrifice by their members, see Dean Kelley, *Why Conservative Churches are Growing* (New York: Harper & Row, 1972). Smith argues, contra Kelley, that high demands are only a *sign* of church dynamism and not necessarily the reasons conservative churches have grown while many in the mainline have dwindled.

14. Prophecy novels did occasionally appear prior to 1970, notably including *Raptured* by Ernest Angley, published in 1950. Still, 1970 represents an important historical breakpoint for a number of reasons that this text will make clear, including the sudden increase in volume and sophistication of the publications.

15. Hal Lindsey with C. C. Carlson, *The Late Great Planet Earth* (Grand Rapids, Mich.: Zondervan, 1970).

16. *Dispensationalism*—an apocalyptic worldview that gained popularity among American evangelicals during the latter part of the nineteenth and especially early twentieth centuries. Synthesized by an Irish-Anglican dissenter named John Nelson Darby in the mid-nineteenth century, dispensationalism divides history into seven distinct ages or dispensations. Each dispensation corresponds to a covenant between God and humans, and ends when the latter fail to meet the terms of the covenant and merit judgment. The present dispensation— *The Church Age*—began with the destruction of the Second Temple in Jerusalem in 70 C.E. and will continue until *Antichrist* signs a treaty, allowing the Jews to rebuild the Temple and resume sacrifices. This doomed peace accord will usher in seven years of unprecedented suffering and woe known as the *Tribulation,* when humankind gets its last chance at salvation under the most trying of circumstances.

17. Carol Balizet, *The Seven Last Years* (Lincoln, Va.: Chosen Books, 1978), 9.

18. Kirban, *666* (Chattanooga, Tenn.: AMG Publishers, 1998).

19. Ibid., 210.

20. Ibid., 206.

21. *666* has also benefited retroactively from the *Left Behind* phenomenon, however, and was reissued in 1998 by AMG Publishers as part of a renewed surge of interest in prophecy fiction.

22. Ken Wade, *The Orion Conspiracy* (Nampa, Idaho: Pacific Press, 1993). Wade probably refers to the Carpenters' song, "Calling Occupants of Interplanetary Craft," which proclaimed itself the anthem of "World Contact Day," an event which never took place.

23. Bob Larson, *Abaddon* (Nashville, Tenn.: Thomas Nelson, 1993). Bob Larson, an evangelical radio host and self-styled expert on the occult, operates a highly controversial ministry focused on exorcism: the practice of identifying and chasing out demons thought responsible for everything from depression and suicidal thoughts to rebellious behavior. Larson operates a training program for hopeful exorcists called, "Do What Jesus Did." See also Bob Larson's website, http://www.boblarson.org. Last accessed July 19, 2003.

24. Gary M. Cohen, *The Horsemen Are Coming* (Chicago: Moody Press, 1974), 75.

25. Randall Balmer, *Mine Eyes Have Seen the Glory: A Journey Into the Evangelical Subculture* (New York: Oxford University Press, 1992), 62.

26. *A Thief in the Night*, directed by Donald W. Thompson (Des Moines, Iowa: Mark IV Pictures, reissued 1995); *A Distant Thunder* (Des Moines, Iowa: Mark IV Pictures, reissued 1995); *Image of the Beast* (Des Moines, Iowa: Mark IV Pictures, reissued 1995); *The Prodigal Planet* (Des Moines, Iowa: Mark IV Pictures, reissued 1995).

27. Dan Betzer, *Beast: A Novel of the Future World Dictator* (Lafayette, La.: Prescott Press, 1985).

28. Ibid., 10.

29. Frank Peretti, *This Present Darkness* (Westchester, Ill.: Crossway Books, 1986); *Piercing the Darkness* (Westchester, Ill.: Crossway Books, 1989).

30. Frank Peretti, *Prophet* (Wheaton, Ill.: Crossway, 1992); *The Oath* (Dallas, Tex.: Word, 1995). *The Visitation* (Nashville, Tenn.: Word, 1999).

31. Pat Robertson, *The End of the Age: A Novel* (Dallas, Tex.: Word, 1996).

32. Hal Lindsey, *Blood Moon* (Palos Verdes, Calif.: Western Front, 1996).

33. Larry Burkett, *The Illuminati* (Nashville, Tenn.: Thomas Nelson, 1991).

34. Ibid., 305.

35. Steve Rabey, "No Longer Left Behind," *Christianity Today*, April 22, 2002. Available on-line at http://www.christianitytoday.com/ct/2002/005/1.26 .html.

36. LaHaye's titles, most of which I detail later in the text, notably include his three-volume work on human temperaments, *Transforming Your Temperament*

(New York: Inspirational Press, 1991). For a nominal fee LaHaye will analyze one's temperament—based on a questionnaire—and the results include a personalized printout listing one's strengths and weaknesses. LaHaye claims an accuracy rate of 92 percent.

37. Rabey, "No Longer Left Behind."

38. Ibid. *Christianity Today* writer Steve Rabey also notes that although the *Left Behind* franchise began as one novel, agent Rick Christian quickly negotiated a trilogy that then became a twelve-volume series. Recently, however, Jerry Jenkins has confirmed in interviews that he anticipates both a prequel and a sequel, bringing the total number of volumes to fourteen. The End, it seems, may be delayed as long as the series remains commercially successful.

39. Ibid.

40. Gayle White, "Countdown to the End Times: The World's Demise Gets Lots of Ink—and Debate," *Atlanta Journal-Constitution,* May 17, 2003.

41. *The Rapture*—based on a reading of 1 *Thessalonians* 4:17 that Christ will return and "meet believers in the air," the Rapture signals the end of the Church Age, although an indefinite period may remain between the Rapture and the beginning of the Tribulation, initiated by the peace treaty between Antichrist and Israel.

Antichrist—a figure who arises during the Tribulation to lure people away from Christ, using deception to confuse potential believers, along with miracles to make himself appear more "Christlike." Dispensationalists view Antichrist as a literal figure, although many early Church Fathers, including Augustine, spiritualized "Antichrist," interpreting it as an allegorical symbol for attitudes and behaviors that did not correspond to Church teachings.

Tribulation—the signing of a peace treaty between Antichrist and Israel ushers in a seven-year period known as the *Tribulation,* a time of suffering which offers humankind a last chance at salvation, while conditions continue to worsen. Plagues and purges by both God and Antichrist reduce the population to a tiny remnant before Christ returns to establish his millennial kingdom after destroying his enemies at the Battle of *Armageddon.* Prophecy writers often divide the Tribulation into two distinct periods of equal length: the lesser *Tribulation,* and the *Great Tribulation,* during which Satan "indwells" or possesses Antichrist, literally ruling the world for period of three and a half years.

42. LaHaye and Jenkins, *Are We Living in the End Times?*

43. John F. Baker, "LaHaye's Big Deal at Bantam," *Publisher's Weekly,* February 18, 2002. LaHaye's first volume of the new Random House deal appeared in October 2003—cowritten with novelist Gregory Dinallo—titled *Babylon Rising* (New York: Doubleday, 2003).

44. See http://www.christianwritersguild.com. Last accessed May 29, 2002.

45. Jerry Jenkins, *Soon: The Beginning of the End* (Nashville, Tenn.: Tyndale House, 2003).

46. Michael R. Smith, "Author LaHaye Sues *Left Behind* Film Producers," *Christianity Today.* http://www.christianitytoday.com/ct/2001/006/14.20.html. Last accessed May 29, 2002. *Left Behind: The Movie* did do quite well in video sales, however, selling over three million copies. The producers, Peter and Paul Lalonde, also followed up *Left Behind: The Movie* with a sequel, *Tribulation Force,* released in 2002. *Tribulation Force,* which reunited most of the original cast of *Left Behind: The Movie,* this time unabashedly avoided theatres, again selling large quantities of DVDs and videocassettes in a direct-to-video strategy.

47. *The Omega Code,* written and produced by Paul and Matthew Crouch (Santa Ana, Calif.: TBN Films, 1999).

48. Smith, "Author LaHaye Sues *Left Behind* Film Producers."

49. LaHaye and Jenkins, *Tribulation Force,* 338. The authors also add *The Family Radio Network* to the list, rounding out Carpathia's multimedia empire.

50. The name Viv Ivins is a subtle reference to Ms. Ivins's unwholesome connections, as the first six characters of her name are the Roman numerals VI VI VI, or 666.

51. *False Prophet*—a shadowy figure, probably ecclesiastical (often the Pope or a high official in the Roman Catholic Church), who emerges during the Tribulation to direct praise toward Antichrist, without attempting to draw attention to himself.

52. http://www.leftbehind.com. Last accessed August 13, 2002.

53. Tim LaHaye, it must be noted, is also an avid pilot, which might help explain the authors' obsession with aviation themes.

54. Joel A. Carpenter, *Revive Us Again.*

55. I thank Robert C. Fuller for urging me to make this point more explicit.

56. Again, I thank Robert C. Fuller for reminding me of this point.

57. Fuller, *Naming the Antichrist,* 13. In a similar vein, Fuller writes that "by projecting Americans' doubts and uncertainties onto a demonic 'other,' the act of naming the Antichrist protects their personal and collective sensibilities from the frailties of human existence."

58. Boyer, *When Time Shall Be No More,* 288.

59. Ibid., 290.

60. Ibid., 289.

61. Ibid., 304–311. For the purposes of my study, evangelical prophecy literature indeed expresses—in a mythological style—a loosely organized, populist protest against the perceived loss of cultural identity and selfhood in contemporary culture.

62. Ibid., 17. Christopher Hill quoted in Boyer.

63. See Nathan D. Wilson, *Right Behind: A Parody of Last Days Goofiness* (Moscow, Idaho: Canon Press, 2001). Wilson's parody of *Left Behind,* although genuinely funny and insightful at times, ultimately proves banal and rather offensive.

64. Sales of the ninth installment, *Desecration*—published in late October 2001—sold more copies in its first week than any previous novel in the series. Moreover, *Desecration*—despite its late start—was nevertheless named the best-selling fiction title of 2001 by *Publisher's Weekly*, offering an additional indication of its runaway popularity.

65. Mark C. Taylor, "Awe and Anxiety." See http://www.press.uchicago.edu/News/911taylor.html. Last accessed May 24, 2002.

66. The notion of "cultural tools" comes from the work of sociologist William Sewell, paraphrased in Michael O. Emerson and Christian Smith, *Divided by Faith: Evangelical Religion and the Problem of Race in America* (New York: Oxford University Press, 2000), 76.

67. Nancy Gibbs, "Apocalypse Now," *Time Magazine*. http://www.time.com/time/covers/1101020701/story.html. Last accessed June 23, 2002.

68. Boyer, *When Time Shall Be No More*, 15. Many sociologists and historians of evangelicalism also make this observation, noting that evangelicalism is not so much a separate, easily quantifiable denomination, as it is a loose network that crosses denominational lines easily.

69. George Marsden, ed., *Evangelicalism and Modern America*, x.

70. Nathan O. Hatch, *The Democratization of American Christianity* (New Haven, Conn.: Yale University Press, 1989), 212.

71. See David Goetz, "Suburban Spirituality." http://www.christianitytoday.com/ct/2003/007/1.30.html. Last accessed June 23, 2003. Goetz provides an articulate and insightful reading of the spiritual challenges of the suburbs from an evangelical perspective. See also Boyer, *When Time Shall Be No More*, 13–15. Boyer cites his own observations, but also adds the survey data of sociologist James Davison Hunter, who notes that evangelicals, while "somewhat lower," increasingly share a status similar to most middle-income Americans, with similar levels of education. See also Christian Smith, *American Evangelicalism*, 76–82. Smith and his associates call almost all of Hunter's assumptions into question. They find that evangelicals are by no means lower in education, income, and similar measures, but may actually have a higher status than those who identify as "mainline Christian," "liberal Christian," or "nonreligious."

See also Mark A. Shibley, *Resurgent Evangelicalism in the United States*, 83–110. Sociologist Mark Shibley provides data even more startling than those of Hunter. Shibley tracks a phenomenon within evangelicalism that he dubs "new-style evangelicalism." New-Style evangelicals share theological common ground with the older generation of evangelicals but embrace the popular culture of shopping malls and rock music. New-style evangelicals, Shibley believes, constitute the major force for growth within evangelicalism and are redefining its contours. Older stereotypes concerning income and levels of education may retain some slight predictive value, but Shibley finds that those gaps are closing.

The *Left Behind* novels, I argue, appeal to Shibley's new-style evangelicals, with their awareness of pop culture trends and a generally suburban and not-so-southern middle-class orientation.

See also Joel A. Carpenter, "Contemporary Evangelicalism and Mammon," in *More Money, More Ministry: Money and Evangelicals in Recent North American History*, edited by Larry Eskridge and Mark A. Noll (Grand Rapids, Mich.: Eerdman's, 2000), 399–405; and Christian Smith, *American Evangelicalism*. Carpenter and Smith both refer to the liminal position contemporary evangelicals have increasingly come to inhabit. No longer quite so separate from the mainstream—contrary to still rampant stereotypes—evangelicals seek to inhabit a rather tricky "in but not of" position vis-à-vis "the world," attempting to retain their distinctiveness while adapting to cultural changes.

72. See especially Robert C. Fuller, *Spiritual but Not Religious: Understanding Unchurched America* (New York: Oxford University Press, 2002); Wade Clark Roof, *Spiritual Marketplace: Baby Boomers and the Remaking of American Religion* (Princeton, N.J.: Princeton University Press, 1999); and Robert Wuthnow, *After Heaven: Spirituality in America since the 1950s* (Berkeley: University of California Press, 1998).

73. Smith, *American Evangelicalism*. Smith argues that, contrary to the findings of fellow sociologist James Davison Hunter, conflict and tension with modernity may actually help evangelicalism thrive. Even when conflict is not present, evangelicals may seek it out, Smith suggests.

74. R. Laurence Moore, *Selling God: American Religion in the Marketplace of Culture* (New York: Oxford University Press, 1984), 251–255.

75. Paul Ricoeur, *On Paul Ricoeur: Narrative and Interpretation*, translated and edited by David Wood (New York: Routledge, 1991), 21–25.

76. O'Leary, *Arguing the Apocalypse*, 220.

NOTES TO CHAPTER I

1. LaHaye and Jenkins, *Are We Living in the End Times?* 8–19.

2. LaHaye and Jenkins, *Nicolae*, 1.

3. Timothy C. F. Stunt, *From Awakening to Succession: Radical Evangelicals in Switzerland and Britain (1815–1835)* (Edinburgh: T&T Clark, 2000), 164.

4. Ibid., 165–166.

5. Ibid., 168–170.

6. Boyer, *When Time Shall Be No More*, 86–87. Boyer briefly discusses the importance of Irving and Drummond to Darby's thought. See also Arthur W. Wainwright, *The Mysterious Apocalypse* (Nashville, Tenn.: Abingdon Press, 1993), 81–87.

7. Ernest R. Sandeen, *The Roots of Fundamentalism: British and American Millenarianism, 1900–1930* (Chicago: University of Chicago Press, 1970),

62–69. As Sandeen puts it, "The true church, the bride of Christ . . . could only exist as a spiritual fellowship."

8. Ibid., 18–22.

9. Wainwright, *The Mysterious Apocalypse*, 83. Boyer, *When Time Shall Be No More*, 88.

10. Ibid., 83. Ibid., 87.

11. Cyrus I. Scofield, ed. *The Scofield Reference Bible: King James Version* (New York: Oxford University Press, 1945), 1269. All Biblical citations in this text are taken from this edition. Cyrus Scofield, the American editor who contributed quite a bit to dispensationalism himself, also adds in his famous verse commentary that "not church saints only, but all bodies of the saved, *of whatever dispensation* [emphasis added], are included in the first resurrection, as here described, but it is peculiarly the 'blessed hope' of the Church." This would indicate, among other things, that those who had obeyed the covenant of their particular dispensation would also be "caught up," including, presumably, ancient Hebrews who had fulfilled the terms of their covenant—in theory at least.

12. Wainwright, *The Mysterious Apocalypse*, 83. Stunt, *From Awakening to Succession*, 221–237. Stunt, in a chapter titled "Scottish Parallels," notes similar developments in radical Scottish Evangelicalism, and mentions Margaret Macdonald, the oft-noted Scottish prophetess, who Boyer suggests may have inspired Darby's views on the Rapture. See Boyer, *When Time Shall Be No More*, 248. It seems that Stunt's suggestion of a parallel may be more likely, however, as similar eschatological ideas emerging from apparently common sources shuttled back and forth across the Irish Sea during the 1820's and 1830's.

13. Marsden, *Fundamentalism and American Culture* (New York: Oxford University Press, 1980), 59. Marsden credits Darby's American successor Cyrus I. Scofield with the codification of this "common sense" hermeneutic within conservative evangelicalism. Scofield described his views in *Rightly Dividing the Word of Truth,* a title that has become an evangelical cliché for proper Biblical interpretation.

14. Those intimately familiar with contemporary evangelicalism will recognize the contempt many believers hold for the late-nineteenth, early twentieth-century occult figure and spiritual provocateur Aleister Crowley (1875–1947). Crowley, who called himself the "Beast" and the "666," was obviously quite familiar with prophecy belief, having grown up in a milieu of Plymouth Brethren believers. Thus, Crowley, who many contemporary evangelicals view as a representative of Satan on par with the late head of the Church of Satan, Anton LaVey (1930–1997), has managed to irritate prophecy believers both during his lifetime and well after it.

15. Stunt, *From Awakening to Succession*, 287–295. See also Sidney E. Ahlstrom, *A Religious History of the American People* (New Haven, Conn.: Yale University Press, 1972), 808–809. See also Boyer, *When Time Shall Be No More*,

87. Stunt and Ahlstrom disagree on the dating of Darby's break with the Anglican Church and his involvement with the Plymouth Brethren. Boyer avoids giving precise dates altogether—perhaps wisely. When giving dates here I have followed Stunt, since he is a specialist in this particular area.

16. Ahlstrom, *A Religious History of the American People,* 808.

17. Boyer, *When Time Shall Be No More,* 88. See also Marjorie Reeves and Warwick Gould, *Joachim of Fiore and the Myth of the Eternal Evangel in the Nineteenth Century* (New York: Oxford University Press, 1987).

18. Reeves and Gould, 1–8.

19. Ibid., 8.

20. Herbert Grundmann, *Studien über Joachim von Floris* (Leipzig, Germany: G.B. Teubner, 1927), 56–66.

21. Ibid.

22. Ibid., 57. My translation from the original German.

23. Eugen Weber, *Apocalypses: Prophecies, Cults, and Millennial Beliefs through the Ages* (Cambridge, Mass.: Harvard University Press, 1999), 15.

24. See Edgar Whisenant, *Eighty-Eight Reasons Why the Rapture Will Be in 1988* (Nashville, Tenn.: World Bible Society, 1988). Prophecy writer Edgar Whisenant did not attempt to calculate the exact hour, but instead gave a range of possible dates corresponding to the Jewish High Holy Days (JHHD) in September of 1988. When his prophecy failed, he admitted a "miscalculation," and moved the event back to 1989, corresponding with another best-selling publication. The popular evangelical radio host Harold Camping made a similar error, using the JHHD as a range in 1994. Even veterans like Hal Lindsey and Pat Robertson expected the Rapture to occur sometime during the 1980's, based upon the reestablishment of Israel in 1948 and the purported length of one Biblical generation, 40 years. Lindsey, in fact, originally thought the Rapture would occur no later than 1988.

25. Ahlstrom, *A Religious History of the American People,* 809–810

26. Ibid., 810. I am indebted to Ahlstrom for his cogent, if necessarily brief, summary of the dispensations.

27. See Albert Schweitzer, *The Quest of the Historical Jesus,* translated by W. Montgomery, J. R. Coates, Susan Cupitt, and John Bowden (Minneapolis: Fortress Press, 2001).

28. Scofield, *The Scofield Reference Bible,* 1034. Scofield writes concerning the question of "this generation" in his famous Bible margin notes, "That the word is used in this sense is sure because none of 'these things,' i.e. the worldwide preaching of the kingdom, the great tribulation, the return of the Lord in visible glory, and the regathering of the elect, occurred at the destruction of Jerusalem by Titus in A.D. 70. The promise is, therefore, that the generation—nation, or family of Israel—will be preserved unto 'these things'; a promise wonderfully fulfilled to this day."

29. Boyer, *When Time Shall Be No More*, 87–88.

30. Scofield, *The Scofield Reference Bible*, 915.

31. Ibid., 914.

32. Sandeen, *The Roots of Fundamentalism*, 59–80. Sandeen offers a much more extensive treatment of Darby's mostly cool reception in the United States and the later spread of his dispensational teachings. A great part of Darby's difficulties lay in his insistence that believers separate from their churches, following his own example with the Anglican Church, something not many Americans were apparently willing to do.

33. Moody's immediate predecessor in urban revivalism, Charles Grandison Finney, also used a similar metaphor.

34. Marsden, *Understanding Fundamentalism and Evangelicalism* (Grand Rapids, Mich.: Eerdman's, 1991), 40.

35. Weber, *Apocalypses*, 26.

36. Ibid., 28.

37. Boyer, *When Time Shall Be No More*, 91–92.

38. Ibid., 92.

39. Ibid., 97.

40. Ibid., 98.

41. Moore, *Selling God*, 253.

42. Boyer, *When Time Shall Be No More*, 98.

43. See Carpenter, *Revive Us Again*, 16–22.

44. Lindsey, *The Late Great Planet Earth*.

45. Clarence Larkin, *Dispensational Truth, or, God's Plan and Purpose in the Ages* (Philadelphia: Clarence Larkin, 1918). Larkin's prophecy charts can still be found in many evangelical prophecy manuals, and even appear in an evangelical film, *Image of the Beast*. I thank David A. Adcock for loaning me his rare, first-edition copy of *Dispensational Truth*. In case of the Rapture, David, it's mine!

46. Lindsey, *The Late Great Planet Earth*, 118. Lindsey writes that "God's plan for the world until the Prince of Peace returns is not an international one-world government, but nationalism. This is the one way the world can keep from falling under a dictator who could virtually destroy mankind."

47. Ibid., 130–132.

48. Ibid., 116–134.

49. Tim LaHaye, *The Hidden Censors* (Old Tappan, N.J.: Revell, 1984), 64.

50. LaHaye and Jenkins, *Left Behind*, 252.

51. Lindsey, *The Late Great Planet Earth*, 132.

52. Ibid.

53. Ibid., 113.

54. Ibid., 112–113.

55. See Timothy P. Weber, *Living in the Shadow of the Second Coming: American Premillennialism, 1875–1925* (New York: Oxford University Press,

1979). Historian Timothy Weber provides an authoritative account of prophecy believers' ambivalent attitudes toward Jews during the early years of dispensationalism.

56. Lindsey, *The Late Great Planet Earth,* 53–54.

57. Boyer, *When Time Shall Be No More,* 88. One can forgive Boyer and others for this oversight, since many prophecy believers make a similar assumption, although most Dispensational commentators, including Tim LaHaye, emphasize that the Rapture in and of itself has no prophetic significance. That is, it does not trigger other events and may, in fact, be followed by a lag-time of several years before the Tribulation begins.

58. Small portions of this section, significantly revised and updated, have been adapted from a conference paper presented to the *1999 Annual Meeting of the American Academy of Religion* in Boston, and a subsequent paper presented to the *2nd Crossroads in Cultural Studies Conference* in Summer 2000 in Birmingham, England.

59. Tim LaHaye and Jerry B. Jenkins, *Have You Been Left Behind?* VHS Videocassette (Wheaton, Ill.: Tyndale House, 1999). This is LaHaye and Jenkins's version, featuring a fictional Reverend Billings explaining to viewers why they have been left behind and what they must do to receive salvation during the Tribulation.

60. A number of prophecy writers follow a "Markan priority," however, viewing Mark as the first of the Gospels. Mark shares many themes with later Gospels such as Matthew, including the Olivet Discourse, which also appears in Mark 13.

61. Robert Bragg, *Babylon Is Fallen* (New York: Vantage Press, 1977).

62. LaHaye and Jenkins, *Are We Living in the End Times?* 27.

63. Ibid., 34–36.

64. Ibid.

65. Ibid., 38.

66. Ibid., 42–43. The authors take the metaphor of the labor pains from Matthew 24:8 and the "beginning of sorrows," cross-referenced by such prophetic figures as Isaiah, Jeremiah, Hosea, and Micah.

67. Ibid., 84–87.

68. Ibid., 88–89. The "lignostone" legend is not new, having made the rounds within prophecy circles since at least the 1970's, although the origin remains unclear.

69. Ibid., 107–112. See also Mary Stewart Relfe, *When Your Money Fails: The 666 System Is Here* (Montgomery, Ala.: Ministries, Inc., 1981).

70. Ibid., 116.

71. LaHaye and Jenkins, *Tribulation Force,* 55.

72. LaHaye and Jenkins, *Are We Living in the End Times?* 157.

73. Tim LaHaye, *The Beginning of the End* (Wheaton, Ill.: Tyndale House,

1991), 56–60. Because the Temple in Jerusalem must be rebuilt before the Tribulation can begin, prophecy writers look for any sign that this may be happening. Their quest has given rise to another legend. Allegedly, during the 1960's American Jews purchased a large quantity of Indiana limestone—a variety supposedly similar to that found in Jerusalem—giving rise to speculation that the limestone would be used for rebuilding the Temple. LaHaye, after several fruitless inquiries, appears to have given up on this legend.

74. LaHaye and Jenkins, *Are We Living in the End Times?* 145. Originally written in *Left Behind*.

75. Tim LaHaye, *Revelation Unveiled* (Grand Rapids, Mich.: Zondervan, 1999), 143.

76. Ibid., 144–147.

77. Ibid., 163–172.

78. Revelation 9:4. LaHaye and Jenkins, *Apollyon*, 314–317.

79. LaHaye and Jenkins, *Apollyon*, 317.

80. LaHaye, *Revelation Unveiled*, 175–177.

81. LaHaye and Jenkins, *Assassins*, 132.

82. LaHaye, *Revelation Unveiled*, 255–256.

83. Ibid., 258–259.

84. Jack van Impe, *11:59 and Counting!* (Royal Oak, Mich.: Jack van Impe Ministries, 1983), 106.

85. Chuck Smith, *The Final Curtain* (Costa Mesa, Calif.: Word for Today, 1984), 7.

86. John Wesley White, *The Coming World Dictator* (Minneapolis: Bethany Fellowship, 1981), 27.

87. LaHaye and Jenkins, *Are We Living in the End Times?* 169.

88. Ibid., 170.

89. Ibid., 172.

90. Ibid., 176–177.

91. Arthur Bloomfield, *How to Recognize the Antichrist* (Minneapolis: Bethany Fellowship, 1975), 31.

92. Bragg, *Babylon Is Fallen*, 32.

93. Ibid., 32–33.

94. Bloomfield, *How to Recognize the Antichrist*, 31.

95. Carl Johnson, *Prophecy Made Plain for Times Like These* (Chicago: Moody Press, 1972), 77.

96. Kirban, *666*, 22–23.

97. Leon Wood, *The Bible and Future Events* (Grand Rapids, Mich.: Zondervan, 1973), 112.

98. Kirban, *666*, 23. Prophecy writers often assume that those living during the Tribulation will be greatly impressed by miracles. Living as we do in an age of technologically generated "miracles," and perhaps even jaded by advances in

science, this seems like a highly dubious assumption, one much more suited for the first rather than the twenty-first century.

99. The number, presumably, is 666.

100. Relfe, *When Your Money Fails*, 38–47, 117.

101. LaHaye and Jenkins, *Are We Living in the End Times?* 201.

102. Ibid., 203–204.

103. Ibid., 196.

104. Ibid., 197.

105. Ibid., 198.

NOTES TO CHAPTER 2

1. Tim LaHaye, *You Are Engaged in the Battle for the Mind: A Subtle Warfare* (Old Tappan, N.J.: Revell, 1980), 46. The reader will note throughout this chapter that although I discuss some empirical examples of the politics of prophecy belief, my primary aim is not to describe the "New Christian Right" and track its specific political moves. Rather, I explain *why* prophecy believers have become politically involved in recent years, along with the potential consequences of such involvement, especially as evidenced in the *Left Behind* novels and the nonfiction writings of Tim LaHaye.

2. Moore, *Selling God*, 250.

3. See Robert Dreyfuss, "Reverend Doomsday: According to Tim LaHaye, the End Is Now," *Rolling Stone*, January 28, 2004. Dreyfuss's article is the latest to call attention to the mysterious Council for National Policy (CNP), mysterious only because Tim LaHaye does not refer to it—at least often—in any public capacity. The CNP plays a similar role to the now defunct Moral Majority, in which LaHaye also assumed a prominent role, screening candidates acceptable to the Christian Right. Along these lines, President George W. Bush allegedly met with the CNP in 1999 to seek their blessings, and apparently satisfied any evangelical concerns regarding his candidacy. Dreyfuss, however, ultimately asks what direct impact LaHaye and the CNP may have on American politics, suggesting that Tim LaHaye wields enormous power. While this is no doubt true and squares with my thesis in this chapter, LaHaye's mode of operation, like that of most wielders of power, is more insidious. Put differently and contra Dreyfuss, it does not matter beyond questions of trivia whether President Bush has actually read *Left Behind* or any of its sequels. What matters is that Tim LaHaye is in a unique position to provide theological justification for many otherwise secular policy determinations—a far more problematic development. Finally, according to my reading of Tim LaHaye's published writings, the End is not now. Indeed, the term "apocalypse" refers to major change, not annihilation. Tim LaHaye may be seeking to usher in a new order, so to speak, but as I point out throughout this book, he is not a prophet of the End

of all things, just the End of a political and cultural climate disagreeable to conservative Protestants.

4. LaHaye, *The Battle for the Mind,* 26.

5. Ibid., 34.

6. Ibid., 217–218.

7. O'Leary, *Arguing the Apocalypse.*

8. Ibid., 72.

9. Ibid., 90.

10. Ibid., 214.

11. Salem Kirban, *666.* Kirban became something of a celebrity in 1970's prophecy circles, even appearing in a prophecy film as himself titled, *A Distant Thunder.* Other notable 1970's prophecy novels that fit a similar pattern include Carol Balizet, *The Seven Last Years,* and Gary Cohen, *The Horsemen Are Coming.*

12. Frank Peretti, *This Present Darkness* and *Piercing the Darkness.* Evangelical novelist Frank Peretti almost single-handedly catapulted Christian prophecy fiction into the mass market during the 1980's with his first two novels. Featuring action-packed plots and harrowing battles between angels and demons, the quality of Peretti's prose has made him a premier writer in the genre. Interestingly, Peretti began writing with Crossway Books, a small Illinois-based Christian publishing house. Now, Tyndale House—the imprint of the *Left Behind* series—has secured the rights to Peretti's older, more successful material.

See also Larry Burkett, *The Illuminati.* Burkett, a Christian economist, anticipates in many instances the themes found in the *Left Behind* novels. His characters, including computer scientists and assorted techies, also develop ingenious means to resist Antichrist.

13. Susan Harding, "Imagining the Last Days: The Politics of Apocalyptic Language," in *Accounting for Fundamentalisms: The Dynamic Character of Movements,* edited by Martin E. Marty and R. Scott Appleby (Chicago: University of Chicago Press, 1994), 57–78.

14. The Scopes Trial, a watershed event in the history of American evangelicalism/fundamentalism but also important to mainstream American culture, convened in Dayton, Tennessee in 1925. At issue were the teachings of a young biology teacher, John T. Scopes, who defied the state legislature and taught the evolutionary origin of terrestrial life. Defended by famed attorney Clarence Darrow, Scopes lost the trial officially but the events proved embarrassing and devastating to fundamentalists. The prosecutor, the "Great Commoner" and perennial Democratic/Populist presidential candidate William Jennings Bryan, died a week later in Dayton. Scopes won a fellowship to the University of Chicago and became a successful scientist.

15. Writers commenting on the Christian Right often conflate pre-millennialists with post-millennialists—an unfortunate and consequential mistake. Theological differences do indeed matter. Pre-millennialists have certain restraints on

their political involvement which post-millennialists lack. Post-millennialists among American evangelicals are a small but articulate lot. The most important faction among them are the so-called Christian Reconstructionists, a group of highly educated and highly conservative Presbyterians inspired by the ideas of the late Rousas John Rushdoony and presently led by such prolific writers as Greg Bahnsen and Gary North. Christian Reconstructionists seek to reconstruct—as the name suggests—a Protestant America built upon a Biblical model. Pre-millennialists, by contrast, occasionally flirt with such ideas, but are hamstrung for the most part by their belief in the imminent return of Christ.

16. Susan Friend Harding, *The Book of Jerry Falwell: Fundamentalist Language and Politics* (Princeton, N.J.: Princeton University Press, 2000). See also William C. Martin, *With God on Our Side: The Rise of the Religious Right in America* (New York: Broadway, 1996), 156. Martin notes that evangelicals, notably southern Baptists, did not take a rigid stand against abortion immediately after the 1973 *Roe v. Wade* decision that overturned anti-abortion laws. Granted, evangelicals found the practice unsettling, but it did not immediately become the hot-button issue that later characterized evangelical involvement in the political arena. The anti-abortion movement developed first among American Catholics, not conservative Protestants. Not until 1975, with the advocacy of later Surgeon General C. Everett Koop and evangelical thinker Francis Schaeffer did the anti-abortion movement gain momentum among evangelicals.

17. Harding, *The Book of Jerry Falwell*, 244.

18. Martin, *With God on Our Side*, 120–129.

19. Ibid., 117–118.

20. Michael Lienesch, *Redeeming America: Piety and Politics in the New Christian Right* (Chapel Hill: University of North Carolina Press, 1993), 14. Political scientist Michael Lienesch describes the evangelical disenchantment after the retirement of President Reagan, "With the retirement of Reagan and the passing of power to George Bush, their skepticism grew even greater, and alienated activists like Colonel V. Doner, a founder of the lobbying group Christian Voice, concluded that they had been cynically used." See also Martin, *With God on Our Side*, 221–237.

21. See especially, Martin, *With God on Our Side*. Martin directly addresses the early political naivety of evangelicals, but also notes their recent increases in sophistication.

22. Tim LaHaye, *The Race for the 21st Century* (Nashville, Tennessee: Thomas Nelson, 1986), 45.

23. Boyer, *When Time Shall Be No More*, 162.

24. Ibid. See also Chris Wojcik, *The End of the World as We Know It: Faith, Fatalism, and Apocalypse in America* (New York: New York University Press, 1997).

25. Boyer, *When Time Shall Be No More*, 141.

26. Ibid., 146.

27. Ibid., 175.

28. Lindsey, *The Late Great Planet Earth*, 160.

29. Ibid., 66.

30. Boyer, *When Time Shall Be No More*, 152–175.

31. Ronald Reagan quoted in ibid., 162.

32. LaHaye, *The Hidden Censors*, 96–98. Tim LaHaye defends Watt, claiming that two and a half years of media misrepresentation and public ridicule forced him to resign.

33. Boyer, *When Time Shall Be No More*, 141.

34. See also Grace Halsell, *Prophecy and Politics: Militant Evangelists on the Road to Nuclear War* (Westport, Conn.: Lawrence Hill and Co., 1986).

35. Boyer, *When Time Shall Be No More*, 127–128.

36. Grant Wacker, "Planning Ahead: The Enduring Appeal of Prophecy Belief," *The Christian Century*, January 19, 1994, 48–52. Available on-line at http://www.religion-online.org. Last accessed March 28, 2004. See also George M. Marsden, *Fundamentalism and American Culture: The Shaping of Twentieth-Century Evangelicalism: 1870–1925* (New York: Oxford University Press, 1980); *Understanding Fundamentalism and Evangelicalism* (Grand Rapids, Mich.: Eerdman's, 1991); Sandeen, *The Roots of Fundamentalism*; Timothy P. Weber, *Living in the Shadow of the Second Coming: American Premillennialism 1875–1925* (New York: Oxford University Press, 1985). Marsden, Sandeen, and Weber tend to play down political connections, especially to the extent such concerns remove the focus from religious issues. I think any disagreement likely stems from the historical nature of these studies. Conservative evangelicalism (or fundamentalism, if one prefers) became increasingly apolitical as the periods in question progressed.

37. Harding, "Imagining the Last Days," 61, 77.

38. Boyer, *When Time Shall Be No More*, 180. See also Joan Didion, review of *Armageddon: The Cosmic Battle of the Ages* by Tim F. LaHaye and Jerry B. Jenkins, *New York Review of Books*, November 6, 2003. Although most commentators and reviewers tend to miss the complexity of President George W. Bush's relationship to prophecy belief, Didion does not, correctly noting that whether or not Bush is a "true believer," his simplified approach to nuanced political questions has coincided with an alarming sense of absolutism in his administration—whether religiously informed or not.

39. Tim LaHaye, *The Race for the 21st Century*, 98–100. Although LaHaye studiously avoided any mention of President Carter in *The Battle for the Mind*, it is evident that LaHaye had Carter in mind when he published the book in 1980, just months before the election of Ronald Reagan. Carter had, after all, failed to meet LaHaye's expectations of an evangelical president. Moreover, Carter brought a number of "humanists" into his administration, most notably Vice

President Walter Mondale. LaHaye also promoted the agenda of Jerry Falwell's Moral Majority by identifying his own "sleeping majority" as potential supporters of Falwell's organization.

40. LaHaye, *The Race for the 21st Century,* 139–140.

41. Tim LaHaye and Bob DeMoss, *The Mind Siege Project* (Nashville, Tenn.: Word, 2001). LaHaye and cowriter Bob DeMoss depict the nefarious influence of secular humanism on the minds of children in their novel, *The Mind Siege Project.* An idealistic civics teacher, Rosie Meyer, invites eight honor students to participate in a spring break houseboat trip emphasizing diversity and tolerance. The manifest includes two Christians, Heather and Jodi. Jodi becomes a target of the others for her Christian beliefs, while Heather tries to "fit in." As the week passes, Jodi finds herself increasingly isolated. Jodi also chides Heather for not being a stronger witness for Christ. All of this changes when an accident occurs in which Kit, a Wiccan student, falls from a cliff and needs a new kidney, which Jodi—being of the same ultrarare blood type—provides. Jodi's sacrifice allows Kit to survive, an act which astonishes the other students. Even Rosie Meyer, who is otherwise hostile to Christianity, admits that she has "a lot to learn about this Jesus too." *The Mind Siege Project* functions analogously to the *Left Behind* novels in that the authors take a condition of perceived cultural marginality and reverse it, arguing that humanism with its emphasis on diversity and tolerance invariably leads to cultural chaos and intolerance.

42. LaHaye, *The Battle for the Mind,* 14.

43. Ibid., 15.

44. Ibid., 14.

45. Ibid., 17.

46. Ibid., 17–18. The location of LaHaye's "emotional center," ironically enough, corresponds to what New Age practitioners often refer to as the "third eye"—a center of emotional perception and energy located just beneath the center of the forehead.

47. Ibid., 21.

48. Ibid.

49. Ibid., 27–46, 57–83.

50. Ibid., 59.

51. Ibid., 68–69

52. Ibid., 69.

53. Ibid., 72–78.

54. Ibid., 197.

55. Ibid., 46.

56. Ibid., 190.

57. Dante quoted in ibid., 237.

58. LaHaye, *The Hidden Censors,* 64.

59. Michael Kazin, *The Populist Persuasion: An American History,* revised edition (Ithaca, N.Y.: Cornell University Press, 1998).

60. Michael O. Emerson and Christian Smith, *Divided by Faith* (New York: Oxford University Press, 2000).

61. Ibid., 9.

62. Amy Johnson Frykholm, "Reading the Rapture: Christian Fiction and the Social Structures of Religious Belief" (Ph.D. diss., Duke University, 2001).

63. For an engaging exploration of gender in evangelical families, see John P. Bartkowski, *Remaking the Godly Marriage: Gender Negotiation in Evangelical Families* (Camden, N.J.: Rutgers University Press, 2001). Bartkowski discusses how both genders construct their identities, and how this reflects in domestic responsibilities and the balance of power in evangelical families. See also Brenda E. Brasher, *Godly Women: Fundamentalism and Female Power* (Camden, N.J.: Rutgers University Press, 1998). Brasher takes a somewhat different approach from Bartkowski, showing how women at two California fundamentalist churches of divergent cultural and class backgrounds have found ways to resist the patriarchy inherent in their churches and construct a space of empowerment within their congregations.

64. For a more detailed account of LaHaye's view of homosexuality, see Tim LaHaye, *What Everyone Should Know about Homosexuality* (Wheaton, Ill.: Tyndale House, 1978). LaHaye goes into extensive detail, even providing a three-page glossary of terms used in the gay subculture.

65. Frykholm, "Reading the Rapture," 72–77.

66. I must note an obvious difference between nineteenth-century Populism and the populist language of the *Left Behind* novels, however. Unlike *Left Behind* and contemporary evangelical prophecy belief, the uprisings that collectively formed the Populist movement subscribed—for the most part—to an apocalyptic ideology known as post-millennialism, rather than the pre-millennialism advocated by the *Left Behind* novels. Nineteenth-century post-millennialism was much more world-affirming than its contemporary pre-millennial cousin, owing in large measure to its belief that humans could significantly improve the world through social action. They could, in effect, create a world to which Jesus would want to return. As such, Populists utilized the language of evangelical post-millennialism to energize their movements and enhance coherence among disparate elements. Hence, post-millennial Populism served to encourage believers to pursue social and economic reforms without suffering as many restraints as the populist language characteristic of pre-millennial prophecy belief. Although, as I note—especially in chapter 6—the gaps between the two eschatologies may be closing, at least in the *Left Behind* novels.

67. Kazin, *The Populist Persuasion,* 5.

68. Ibid., 12.

69. Lawrence Goodwyn, *The Populist Moment: A Short History of the Agrarian Revolt in America* (New York: Oxford University Press, 1978), 35.

70. Kazin, *The Populist Persuasion*, 13–14.

71. Ibid., 17–25.

72. Ibid., 10–12. Unfortunately, a more complete discussion of the Second Great Awakening lies well outside of the scope of this study. The reader would do well to consult a number of excellent sources on the revivals, including Ahlstrom, *A Religious History of the American People*; Hatch, *The Democratization of American Christianity*; and the excellent regional studies by historians Paul Johnson and Terry Bilhartz, which I will note shortly.

73. Paul E. Johnson, *A Shopkeeper's Millennium: Society and Revivals in Rochester, New York, 1815–1837* (New York: Hill and Wang, 1978), 139–141.

74. Hatch, *The Democratization of American Christianity*, 212.

75. Ibid., 87–88. Hatch notes that the life span of a circuit rider averaged thirty-nine years, although the highest cluster of mortality (35.9 percent) occurred among those between the ages of twenty-three and twenty-nine.

76. Ibid., 75.

77. Ahlstrom, *A Religious History of the American People*, 422–434. For an older but still important chronicle of the camp meeting phenomena, see Charles A. Johnson, *The Frontier Camp Meeting: Religion's Harvest Time* (Dallas: Southern Methodist University Press, 1955).

78. Terry D. Bilhartz, *Urban Religion and the Second Great Awakening: Church and Society in Early National Baltimore* (Teaneck, N.J.: Fairleigh Dickinson University Press, 1986). Paul E. Johnson, *A Shopkeeper's Millennium*, 152–161. Although both Bilhartz and Paul Johnson suggest that church membership increased appreciably during the first half of the nineteenth century, Bilhartz challenges the scope of Johnson's findings not only by his case-study of analogous trends in Baltimore, but also through a closer examination of church membership. Not every member, in other words, was recorded on church membership rosters, especially just prior to the Second Great Awakening. Hence, a more liberal definition of "member," Bilhartz argues, combined with the revival spirit to increase membership—at least as far as the historical record indicates.

79. Goodwyn, *The Populist Moment*, 28–54. The Grange movement consisted of loosely organized farmers who sought higher prices for their goods and cheaper supplies. The Farmer's Alliance, strongest in 1880's Texas, moved further and established cooperatives to force higher prices for their produce. And, when they failed to eliminate the "middle men," they decided to form even more pervasive cooperatives to produce their own supplies. It was more ambitious than the Grange movement, certainly, but became an attractive and aggressive alternative to the Grange.

80. Rhys H. Williams and Susan Alexander, "Religious Rhetoric in American

Populism: Civil Religion as Movement Ideology," *Journal for the Scientific Study of Religion* 33 (March 1994): 8.

81. Goodwyn, *The Populist Moment,* 44–51. Goodwyn discusses the activism of Texan William Lamb, who quickly gained the "pulse of the people" and attempted to organize a more pervasive challenge to American social structures, culminating in the "Cleburne Demands" of 1886. The Cleburne Demands, so-named because of their promulgation in Cleburne, Texas, proved highly controversial even within the Farmer's Alliance, passing by only a seventeen delegate margin (49). The demands centered on the rights and abilities of farmers to extricate themselves from the grappling and expansive tentacles of industrial capitalism, represented especially by financiers, corporations, railroads, and even government land policies. As Goodwyn notes, perhaps the most important aspect of the Cleburne Demands—and the most relevant to the present narrative— was the demand that government officials recognize the legitimacy of farmer's cooperative networks (47). See also Kazin, *The Populist Moment,* 26–46.

82. Kazin, *The Populist Moment,* 15–16, 20–21, 32, 35, 40.

83. Ibid., 34–37.

84. Ibid., 287–290.

85. Ibid., 42–46.

86. David M. Potter, *People of Plenty: Economic Abundance and the American Character* (Chicago: University of Chicago Press, 1954), 121, 157–159.

NOTES TO CHAPTER 3

1. Tim LaHaye, The Prophetic Significance of Sept. 11, 2001, http://www .timlahaye.com/about_ministry/index.php3?p=sept11_tlm&section=Prophetic %20Significance. Last accessed June 26, 2002.

2. Mark C. Taylor, *The Moment of Complexity,* 4–5.

3. Taylor, *About Religion: Economies of Faith in Virtual Culture* (Chicago: University of Chicago Press, 1999), 26.

4. LaHaye and Jenkins, *Left Behind,* 274.

5. See Clarence Larkin, *Dispensational Truth.* Larkin's turn-of-the-century text is best known for its elaborate charts that depict the events of the last days in minute and colorful detail. In a movement characterized by its love of such baroque charts, Larkin's remain the most influential.

6. See www.timlahaye.com. Tim LaHaye also hosts an on-line, fee-based "prophecy club" for those whose financial gifts exceed their gifts of discernment. Although in theory (according to a widely held evangelical belief), God can lead anyone to knowledge of the last days through a careful reading of the Bible, some readers are obviously more gifted than others.

7. Taylor, *The Moment of Complexity,* 5–14.

8. Castells, *The Rise of the Network Society,* 69–72.

9. Ibid., 70.

10. Ibid., 502.

11. Ibid., 71.

12. Ibid.

13. Ibid., 6, 45–46, 163–215. See also Taylor, *Hiding* (Chicago: University of Chicago Press, 1997), 326.

14. Ibid., 72.

15. Ibid., 72–76. See also Taylor, *Hiding*, 326, 329.

16. Ibid., 153.

17. Mark C. Taylor, *The Moment of Complexity*, 4–5.

18. Ibid., 5, 14.

19. Castells, *The Rise of the Network Society*, 6. See also Taylor, *Hiding*, 325–329.

20. Castells, *The Rise of the Network Society*, 6.

21. I extrapolate the foregoing summary from Albert-László Barabási, *Linked: The New Science of Networks* (Cambridge, Mass. Perseus, 2002); Manuel Castells, *The Rise of the Network Society*; and Mark C. Taylor, *The Moment of Complexity*.

22. Taylor, *Hiding*, 327. See also Wouter J. Hanegraaff, *New Age Religion and Western Culture: Esotericism in the Mirror of Secular Thought* (New York: E. J. Brill, 1996), 113–139. Although my argument relies on insights from information, systems, and complexity theories, a detailed examination of such interrelated fields—although no doubt interesting—would take me well beyond my focus on evangelical prophecy literature. Nevertheless, the close connections between information/systems/complexity theories and the emerging face of contemporary religion has not gone unnoticed by recent scholarship. Historian Wouter Hanegraaff notes such interconnections in his study of New Age religion. Hanegraaff's description of the New Age emphasis on "holism"—the belief in an essential unity of God/humans, humans/nature, material/spiritual—bears an uncanny resemblance to Mark C. Taylor's articulation of network culture in his *Moment of Complexity*. Of course, what Taylor from a philosophical perspective and New Agers from a religious viewpoint see as a positive development—a quasi-Hegelian fulfillment of an interconnected yet nontotalizing system for the former and a dawning spiritual age for the latter—evangelicals view with great hostility. That is, for Taylor along with Hanegraaff's New Agers, the collapse of dualism and the concomitant rise of a self-organizing network culture appears to promise limitless possibility, while for evangelicals it marks the rise of Satan's infernal kingdom which eliminates meaningful difference. A couple of key sources undergird both Taylor and Hanegraaff's understandings including Fritjof Capra, *The Turning Point: Science, Society, and the Rising Culture* (New York: Simon and Schuster, 1983); and Ilya Prigogine, *From Being to*

Becoming: Time and Complexity in the Physical Sciences (San Francisco: W.H. Freeman, 1980).

23. Taylor, *The Moment of Complexity*, 14–16.

24. Howard Rheingold, *The Virtual Community: Homesteading on the Electronic Frontier* (New York: Harper, 1993), 7.

25. Castells, *The Rise of the Network Society*, 6–7, 45–46. This section relies heavily on the excellent summary of the Internet and its development provided by Castells.

26. Ibid.

27. Ibid., 49.

28. Ibid.

29. Rheingold, *The Virtual Community*, 6–7. Castells, *The Rise of the Network Society*, 6–7, 46–47.

30. Castells, *The Rise of the Network Society*, 50. See especially Rheingold, *The Virtual Community*, 38–64.

31. Castells, *The Rise of the Network Society*, 46, 50–51.

32. Ibid., 51.

33. Barabási, *Linked*.

34. Ibid., 55–64.

35. Ibid., 3–4.

36. Ibid., 211.

37. Ibid., 209–211. See also Thomas Friedman, *The Lexus and the Olive Tree* (New York: Farrar, Straus & Giroux, 1999). The collapse of the Thai baht and the ensuing Asian currency crisis is also one of Friedman's favorite examples of network culture and its potential downside.

38. Barabási, *Linked*, 109–122. See also Taylor, *Hiding*, 328. Taylor points out that as networks become more highly integrated, they paradoxically become more vulnerable—if attackers direct their assaults at sensitive areas. Taylor calls this the "rule of vulnerability."

39. Barabási, *Linked*, 116–118.

40. Ibid., 80, 102–107. Castells, *The Rise of the Network Society*, 71.

41. Daniel Bell, *The Coming of Post-Industrial Society: A Venture in Social Forecasting* (New York: Basic Books, 1976).

42. Manuel Castells, *The Rise of the Network Society; The Power of Identity: The Information Age—Economy, Society and Culture* (Malden, Mass.: Blackwell, 1997); *End of Millennium* (Malden, Mass.: Blackwell, 1998).

43. Taylor, *The Moment of Complexity*, 202.

44. See also David Lyon, *The Electronic Eye: The Rise of Surveillance Society* (Minneapolis: University of Minnesota Press, 1994).

45. Castells, *The Rise of the Network Society*, 23. See also LaHaye and Jenkins, *Are We Living in the End Times?* x. LaHaye and Jenkins, like prophecy

writer Hal Lindsey before them, ties the flood of information in contemporary culture to prophecies found in Daniel, specifically verse 12:4, which refers to an increase in knowledge during the last days. See also LaHaye, *The Race for the 21st Century,* 14; and *The Beginning of the End,* 97–103.

46. Taylor, *The Moment of Complexity,* 213–214.

47. LaHaye, *The Race for the 21st Century,* 14. LaHaye definitely worries about the contemporary flood of information. He asks, "Where will the inventive brain of man take us? Frankly, I do not know, but everyone acknowledges a high-tech rate of change, which has so increased the amount of information available to us today that experts warn of the dangers of 'an information glut' in this age called the 'Information Age.'" LaHaye's views on the "Information Age," as I will point out in chapter 4, are highly ambivalent.

48. LaHaye, *The Hidden Censors,* 31–33. LaHaye demonstrates his awareness of the fluidity of reality in the Information Age in his discussion of George Orwell's *1984.* LaHaye quotes *1984* at length, explaining to his readers that reality, in effect, is what the media powers want it be, making it paramount that believers seize control of their information (in Taylor's sense of the term in-*formation*).

49. Castells, *The Rise of the Network Society,* 407–459. Castells prefers the terminology of "The Space of Flows," which I have adapted and abbreviated here as informational "flows." See also Jean Baudrillard, *Symbolic Exchange and Death,* translated by Iain Hamilton Grant (London: Sage, 1993), 74, 92. Baudrillard considers the effacement of the "real" within the context of fashion and the increasingly indeterminate and nonreferential character of signs. When difference is reproduced from abstract models rather than life itself, simulacra, or copies of copies that have no original are the result. Baudrillard considers this the triumph of the *hyperreal,* or the new aesthetic of fashion and models of simulation that efface the real. He writes, "There is fashion from the moment that a form is no longer produced according to its own determinations, but *from the model itself*—that is to say, that it is never produced, but always and immediately *reproduced.* The model itself has become the only system of reference."

50. Castells, *The Rise of the Network Society,* 458–459, 495, 506–507.

51. Ibid., 495.

52. Lyon, *The Electronic Eye,* 41.

53. William Gibson, *Neuromancer* (New York: Ace Books, 1984). Gibson's "constructs" are nothing more than "data-images" of once living humans, who have been scanned and transformed into bits of digital information. They perform important tasks in the narrative, but lack critical aspects of humanity (such as the ability to appreciate the affective dimension of embodied existence, although they recall that such a human dimension—now inaccessible to them—exists) and thus seek only the release offered by "death"—the erasure of their construct.

54. Lyon, *The Electronic Eye*, 147–157.

55. Taylor, *The Moment of Complexity*, 213–214. While Taylor has not directly addressed the problematic responses of LaHaye and Jenkins vis-à-vis the network culture in his published writings, he has definitely made his perspectives known in a number of personal communications with the author.

56. Ibid., 194.

57. Castells, *The Rise of the Network Society*, 71.

58. Taylor, *The Moment of Complexity*, 11–12. Taylor, *Hiding*, 327–329. Taylor's nontotalizing system requires what he calls "allelomorphs"—structures that fall between the world of the "real" and the "imaginary." Neither inside nor outside the system, they form the "condition of the possibility" of the volatility and turbulence that prevents the network culture from becoming a stifling, closed system. They open the system up, in other words, to chance, risk, and contingency; which, Taylor adds throughout his work, are really the core characteristics of life in the network culture—hence, one of his favorite illustrations—the hyperreal simulations and risky environs of the Las Vegas strip.

59. Prophecy believers, if one extends Taylor's metaphor, would be wise to roll the dice, so to speak. And, as we will see in chapter 5, LaHaye and Jenkins do introduce such elements of chance, risk, and contingency into their narrative (at least temporarily), despite the seemingly inexorable nature of their apocalyptic framework.

Taylor, *The Moment of Complexity*, 48, 122–123.

60. Castells, *The Rise of the Network Society*, 458–459, 495, 506–507.

61. Ibid., 476.

62. LaHaye, *The Race for the 21st Century*, 13–48. LaHaye cites approvingly (albeit with some reservations) such popular social forecasters as Alvin Toffler (*Future Shock, The Third Wave*) and John Naisbitt (*Megatrends*).

63. Ibid., 46.

64. LaHaye and Jenkins, *Left Behind*, 82.

65. Hermann von Laer, "Der Euro und die Europäische Währungsunion: Eine gefährliche Fehlentscheidung für das gemeinsame Europa," in *Deutschland und Europa, Europa und die Deutschen*, edited by Joachim Kuropka and Wilfried Kürschner (Münster, Germany: Verlag Regensberg, 1998), 141–172. As an economist, von Laer ultimately opposes the introduction of the Euro currency on economic grounds, although he also addresses the connection between currency and cultural identity. Nevertheless, von Laer does not neatly divide the economic consequences from the cultural ones. That is precisely his point. For von Laer—citing Karl Marx—economic *and* cultural issues are both closely bound with the notion of currency.

66. See Michel Foucault, *Discipline and Punish: The Birth of the Prison*, translated by Alan Sheridan (New York: Vintage Books, 1977). The French poststructuralist thinker Michel Foucault extensively analyzes the subtleties of power

in his writings. In *Discipline and Punish,* Foucault discusses the internalization of power, with individuals in effect internalizing the desires and commands of their oppressors, doing precisely what the more powerful agents seek, all the while believing they are acting of their own free will.

67. I owe the phrase "cultural Cuisinart" to the creative, eclectic imagination of one of my teachers, John M. Stroup.

68. LaHaye and Jenkins, *Left Behind,* 295–296.

69. Ibid., 296.

70. Ibid., 297.

71. Antichrist, for example, must deal with a variety of plagues, including foul-mouthed, anthropomorphic locusts, ubiquitous boils, bodies of water converted into blood, and unprecedented heat waves.

72. Quentin J. Schultze, *Televangelism and American Culture* (Grand Rapids, Mich.: Baker, 1991).

73. See Jackson Lears, *No Place of Grace: Antimodernism and the Transformation of American Culture, 1880–1920* (New York: Pantheon, 1981), viii–xviii.

74. Ibid., xiii–xviii.

75. Ibid., 42.

76. Ibid., 4–58, 60–96.

77. Ibid. See also Richard Dawkins, *The Selfish Gene* (New York: Oxford University Press, 1989); and Daniel Dennett, *Consciousness Explained* (Boston: Little, Brown, 1991). Dawkins redirects human volition, or choice, to the microscopic level of individual genes, which take whatever action necessary for their own survival along with that of the traits they code. Dennett, on the other hand, suggests that "memes," or cultural ideas with an almost infectious quality, help explain human behavior on the macro level. A meme, in other words—for example, a catchy pop song—gets replicated from brain to brain with a transmission quality resembling that of a virus. The upshot—at least for the purpose of the point I am making here—is that for the work of both thinkers the active, thinking, conscious, that is, the "Cartesian" human subject, is seriously challenged.

78. Lears, *No Place of Grace,* 32.

79. Ibid., 98–139.

80. William Gibson, *Count Zero* (New York: Ace Books, 1986); *Mona Lisa Overdrive* (New York: Bantam, 1988). For an engaging analysis of Gibson and the cultural significance of the cyberpunk genre, among other topics, see Mark Dery, *Escape Velocity: Cyberculture at the End of the Century* (London: Hodder & Stoughton, 1996).

81. Available on DVD as *The Complete Prisoner Megaset* (New York: New Video, in association with A&E Entertainment and Carlton International Media Limited, 2000). The series originally ran in the United States on the CBS network in 1968 and also briefly in 1969. See also the website *The Prisoner Appre-*

ciation Society: Six of One at http://www.netreach.net/~sixofone/, maintained by
Bruce Clark, for additional insight on *The Prisoner* and its continuing influence
and fan base across the world.

82. Lears, *No Place of Grace,* 118.
83. Michael Kazin, *The Populist Persuasion.*
84. LaHaye and Jenkins, *The Remnant,* 120.
85. Taylor, *The Moment of Complexity,* 224.

NOTES TO CHAPTER 4

1. Quentin J. Schultze, "Keeping the Faith," in *American Evangelicals and
the Mass Media,* edited by Quentin J. Schultze (Grand Rapids, Mich.: Zondervan, 1990), 41.
2. Jack and Rexella van Impe, promotional material for their VHS video,
Marks of the Beast. Online at http://jvim.com. Last accessed February 27, 2003.
3. I do not suggest here that prophecy belief is limited to the American South.
On the contrary, it can be found throughout the United States. This is, in part,
due to the fact that it spreads most readily through informal channels such as
evangelical media outlets, rather than through formal, denominational means.
4. Mary Stewart Relfe, *When Your Money Fails.*
5. Emil Gaverluk and Patrick Fisher, *Fiber Optics: The Eye of the Antichrist,*
cited in Robert C. Fuller, *Naming the Antichrist: The History of an American
Obsession* (New York: Oxford University Press, 1995), 181–182.
6. Quentin J. Schultze, *Televangelism and American Culture,* 15.
7. LaHaye and Jenkins, *Tribulation Force,* 389
8. Ibid., 398.
9. LaHaye and Jenkins, *Desecration,* 100.
10. LaHaye and Jenkins, *Nicolae,* 243.
11. LaHaye and Jenkins, *The Remnant,* 119.
12. LaHaye and Jenkins, *Soul Harvest,* 235.
13. LaHaye and Jenkins, *Assassins,* 50.
14. Ibid., 53.
15. Glenn W. Shuck, "Televangelism," in *Encyclopedia of Protestantism,*
edited by Hans Hillerbrand (New York: Routledge, 2004). Early Federal Communications Commission (FCC) guidelines required networks to donate a small
portion of broadcast time, called "sustaining time," for edifying programs, often
of a religious nature. The National Council of Churches (NCC) informally controlled the disposition of sustaining time, however, leaving evangelically oriented
programming out of the loop. As a result, conservative Protestant broadcasters—who would later be known as televangelists—either bought time or
founded their own networks, the latter occurring with the advent of satellite
technology and cable television.

16. LaHaye and Jenkins, *Armageddon*, 290.

17. LaHaye and Jenkins, *Apollyon*, 61.

18. Schultze, *Televangelism and American Culture*, 52.

19. Ibid., 64.

20. LaHaye and Jenkins, *Assassins*, 401.

21. LaHaye and Jenkins, *The Mark*, 238.

22. Boyer, *When Time Shall Be No More*, 286–288.

23. Ibid., 254.

24. Ibid., 288.

25. Ibid.

26. David Lyon, *The Electronic Eye*, 110, 114.

27. Ibid., 3–21.

28. Ibid., 191, 211.

29. Rheingold, *The Virtual Community*, 289–297. Internet pioneer and analyst Howard Rheingold also notes the contemporary aptness of Foucault's Panopticon reference. Indeed, the proliferation of references to the Panopticon may indicate that it—or some form of it—may represent the underside of the drive toward network culture. Rheingold notes that "if totalitarian manipulators of populations and technologies actually do achieve dominance in the future, I predict that it will begin not by secret police kicking in your doors but by allowing you to sell yourself to your television and letting your supermarket sell information about your transactions, while outlawing measures you could use to protect yourself (293)."

30. Ibid., 62–67.

31. This is a common criticism of Foucault and especially Foucault's earlier work, which depicts in often meticulous detail the development of regimens of discipline that would seem to offer individuals little maneuverability in contemporary Western societies. The later work of Foucault, however, does offer greater possibilities for individuals to engage in what he calls "technologies of the self," or the "care of the self"—essentially ascetic practices of self-transformation. See especially Michel Foucault, "Technologies of the Self" in *Ethics: Subjectivity and Truth,* translated by Robert Hurley et al. and edited by Paul Rabinow (New York: New Press, 1997), 223–252.

32. Lyon, *The Electronic Eye*, 167, 204–208.

33. Ibid., 210.

34. Ibid., 62–78.

35. Ibid., 208–212.

36. Ibid., 65, 212.

37. Ibid., 211.

38. See especially Michel Foucault, *Ethics*, note 31 above; and also *The History of Sexuality, Volume III: The Care of the Self,* translated by Robert Hurley (New York: Random House, 1986).

39. Lyon, *The Electronic Eye*, 212–213.

40. Ibid., 211–217.

41. Ibid., 213.

42. Ibid., 214–217.

43. Ibid., 205.

44. Foucault, *Discipline and Punish*. Again, the means by which Antichrist deploys his power is quite similar to how Foucault suggests power has come to operate in the modern world.

45. Castells, *The Rise of the Network Society*, 505.

46. Ibid.

47. Taylor, *The Moment of Complexity*, 17.

48. Ibid., 202. Augustine quoted in ibid.

49. A number of scholarly observers have recently commented on the phenomenon of the alleged merging of humans and their technologies. See Donna Haraway, *Cyborgs, Simians, and Women: The Reinvention of Nature* (New York: Routledge, 1991). Haraway provides an ironic, although at times disturbingly celebratory look at the phenomenon. See also Scott Bukatman, *Terminal Identity: The Virtual Subject in Postmodern Science Fiction* (Durham, N.C.: Duke University Press, 1993); Mark Dery, *Escape Velocity*; and Kathryn Hayles, *How We Became Posthuman: Virtual Bodies in Cyberspace, Literature, and Informatics* (Chicago: University of Chicago Press, 1999). Bukatman, Dery, and Hayles provide excellent overviews of recent cyberpunk fiction, also considering the ethical consequences of any merger between humans and technology. Finally, although one could select any number of cyberpunk short stories or novels to illustrate this problem, perhaps the best and most concise is "The Girl Who Was Plugged In" by James Tiptree Jr., in *Warm Worlds and Otherwise* (New York: Ballantine, 1975).

50. Timothy P. Weber, *Living in the Shadow of the Second Coming*.

51. See also Fuller, *Naming the Antichrist*, 138–145.

52. "*The Remnant* Chat Transcript." http://www.leftbehind.com/channel-news.asp?pageid=459&channelID=17. Last accessed July 6, 2003.

53. Carl E. Olson, *Will Catholics Be "Left Behind"? A Critique of the Rapture and Today's Prophecy Preachers* (San Francisco: Ignatius Press, 2003), 50–65. American Catholics have obviously taken note of the anti-Catholicism in the *Left Behind* novels, as Olson's text demonstrates. Olson finds—with considerable justification—that anti-Catholicism and evangelical prophecy belief are closely bound up together. Most significantly, Olson worries that "ignorant or nominal Catholics" will fall victim to the seductive nature of the books. Olson even points out that LaHaye describes his own father as having been "delivered" from Roman Catholicism. While Olson provides little more than anecdotal evidence to ground his fears of any widespread impact of evangelical prophecy belief on American Catholicism, his research nevertheless suggests the extent and

potential influence, positive or otherwise, of the *Left Behind* phenomenon throughout American culture—especially among Roman Catholics.

54. Boyer, *When Time Shall Be No More*, 273–274.

55. McGinn, *Antichrist*, 152–157.

56. Ibid., 162–164.

57. Boyer, *When Time Shall Be No More*, 274.

58. McGinn, *Antichrist*, 203.

59. Ibid., 205–206. See also Bernhard Lohse, *Luthers Theologie in ihrer historischen Entwicklung und in ihrem systematischen Zusammenhang* (Göttingen, Germany: Vandenhoeck & Ruprecht, 1995), 345–349. Luther—it must be noted—while not a millennial thinker, most certainly believed in an imminent End and a last judgment of sinners.

60. Fuller, *Naming the Antichrist*, 145–148.

61. Gary M. Cohen, *The Horsemen Are Coming*. Cohen's prophecy novel features an aptly named adversary, Pope Sixtus the Sixth.

62. This is purely a pragmatic cooperation on political, rather than theological issues, however, as LaHaye makes evident in his published writings.

63. LaHaye and Jenkins, *Are We Living in the End Times?* 176–177.

64. Martin, *With God on Our Side*, 219–220, 230–231.

65. *A Distant Thunder*, directed by Donald W. Thompson (Des Moines, Iowa: Mark IV Pictures, 1977). For the UCC symbol, see http://www.ucc.org. Last accessed August 7, 2002. The verse referenced is St. John 17:22.

66. LaHaye and Jenkins, *Are We Living in the End Times?* 176.

67. Ibid., 172.

68. LaHaye and Jenkins, *Apollyon*, 54.

69. Ibid.

70. See also "Esalen's Hot Springs: Esalen in the Popular Evangelical Imagination," in *Esalen in American Religious Culture*, edited by Jeffrey J. Kripal and Glenn W. Shuck (Bloomington: Indiana University Press, 2005). I describe in much greater detail in this article the antagonistic attitudes held by prophecy writers vis-à-vis the so-called New Age Movement.

71. Catherine Albanese, *Nature Religion in America: From the Algonkian Indians to the New Age* (Chicago: University of Chicago Press, 1990).

72. Fuller, *Naming the Antichrist*, 185–190. See also Robert C. Fuller, *Stairways to Heaven: Drugs in American Religious History* (Boulder, Colo.: Westview Press, 2000), 12–16.

73. Starhawk (Miriam Simos), *The Spiral Dance: A Rebirth of the Ancient Religion of the Great Goddess* (San Francisco: Harper, 1999). Starhawk, an author and activist, has influenced not only Wiccan spiritualities but also feminist eco-spiritualities. See also Glenn William Shuck, "The Myth of the Burning Times and the Politics of Resistance in Contemporary American Wicca," *Journal of Religion and Society* 2: 2000. Available on-line at http://moses.creighton

.edu/JRS/2000/2000-4a.html. In this essay, I discuss an interesting sign I observed when visiting a Wiccan group. The sign read, "Our religion is 100% true. We make it up as we go along." The sign may strike one as paradoxical, but to many American Wiccans truth is experiential and thus highly flexible. Truth emerges not from proper belief, in other words, but from effective ritual practice.

74. Fuller, *Naming the Antichrist,* 187. Constance Cumbey, *The Hidden Dangers of the Rainbow,* cited in Fuller.

75. Tim LaHaye, *The Battle for the Mind.*

76. Ibid., 26.

77. Ibid., 130.

78. See also Fuller, *Spiritual, but Not Religious;* Roof, *Spiritual Marketplace;* and Robert Wuthnow, *After Heaven: Spirituality in America since the 1950's* (Berkeley: University of California Press, 1999).

79. Peter L. Berger, *The Sacred Canopy: Elements of a Sociological Theory of Religion* (New York: Anchor Books, 1990), 47.

80. Schultze, *American Evangelicals and the Mass Media,* 29–34.

81. This is not to claim, of course, that God could not use humans and their technologies to accomplish His goals. But to make a potentially complicated point simple, it would seem superfluous for an all-powerful God to use a group of technologically savvy automatons to accomplish His eternal goals. Indeed, even within evangelicalism one finds a rather strong emphasis on human agency that would be contradicted by such a suggestion.

82. Schultze, *American Evangelicals and the Mass Media,* 30–32. Although the origin of Schultze's usage of "technological sublime" is uncertain, it probably derives, ultimately, from historian Leo Marx's *The Machine in the Garden: Technology and the Pastoral Ideal in America* (New York: Oxford University Press, 1964).

83. Schultze, *Televangelism and American Culture,* 54–59.

84. Ibid., 30–34.

85. Ibid., 33.

86. Along with the cyberpunk fiction of William Gibson noted in chapter 3, see also J. G. Ballard, *Crash* (New York: Farrar Straus & Giroux, 1973). Ballard's *Crash,* arguably one of the most important precursors to the cyberpunk genre of science-fiction literature of the 1980's—along with the work of Philip K. Dick (*Do Androids Dream of Electric Sheep, Minority Report*)—highlights the human interaction with the technological dimension in a way that celebrates the closely intertwined elements of eroticism and death. Filled with scenes of mangled bodies and gore, *Crash* provides an ironic cautionary tale against a culture that accepts technology as morally neutral, and demonstrates the morbid appeal of the exciting, alluring, but potentially deadly impact of new technologies taken without ample ethical consideration. The *Left Behind* novels, while not so

graphic, typify the technological obsessions—even erotic fixations with the technological—exemplified in *Crash*, albeit without Ballard's explicit ethical concerns.

87. Melvin Kranzberg and Manuel Castells quoted in Castells, *The Rise of the Network Society*, 76.

88. Mark C. Taylor and Esa Saarinen, *Imagologies: Media Philosophy* (New York: Routledge, 1994).

NOTES TO CHAPTER 5

1. Mark C. Taylor, *The Moment of Complexity*, 202.

2. Ricoeur, *On Paul Ricoeur*, 199.

3. Taylor, *The Moment of Complexity*, 199–205.

4. Marsden, *Fundamentalism and American Culture*, 15–16. Historian George M. Marsden explains that American evangelical thought has historically owed much to a philosophical school known as "Scottish Common Sense Realism," an extension of the early modern epistemological speculations of Francis Bacon. The Baconian view, against the philosophies of Immanuel Kant and John Locke, held that one could obtain immediate knowledge of the world since "the external world was in fact just as it appeared to be." Marsden writes, describing the thought of Common Sense philosopher Thomas Reid, "Everyone in his senses believes such truths as the existence of the real world, cause and effect, and the continuity of the self. The ability to know such things was as natural as the ability to breathe air." Moreover, one could read the external world—the Book of Nature—as commensurate with The Bible. Both complemented the other and revealed important truths about the world. This synthesis between the natural world and the Bible began to break apart late in the nineteenth century, however, as Darwinian evolution among other factors exposed differences between natural and Biblically derived epistemologies. Nevertheless, prophecy writers have clung tenaciously to the Common Sense view—especially in their readings of the Bible—while leaving the Book of Nature to the "Godless humanists." See also Mark A. Noll, *The Scandal of the Evangelical Mind* (Grand Rapids, Mich.: Eerdman's, 1994), 85–86.

5. Lyon, *The Electronic Eye*, 41.

6. Mark C. Taylor, *Hiding*, 125.

7. Ibid., 89. Theologically, LaHaye and Jenkins's turn toward indelible marks—*even for believers*—is more troublesome. As Taylor notes, for example, the Second Council of Nicea in 787 went so far as to proscribe tattooing, declaring such practices in support of idolatry—in essence, producing graven images upon one's body.

8. Fuller, *Naming the Antichrist*, 9.

9. Elaine Scarry, *The Body in Pain: The Making and Unmaking of the World*

(New York: Oxford University Press, 1985), 28–37. See also Michel de Certeau, *Heterologies: Discourses on the Other,* translated by Brian Massumi (Minneapolis: University of Minnesota Press, 1997).

See also Glenn William Shuck, "The Myth of the Burning Times and the Politics of Resistance in Contemporary American Wicca," *Journal of Religion and Society* 2: 2000. Available on-line at http://moses.creighton.edu/JRS/2000/2000-4a.html. I originally worked through Scarry and de Certeau's definitions of torture in my work on American Wicca, although adaptations were certainly needed to fit the evangelical situation.

10. The authors describe "Hail Carpathia!" as complete with backing vocals from a children's choir. Unfortunately, the song does not appear to be commercially available at the moment.

11. Berger, *The Sacred Canopy,* 47.

12. LaHaye and Jenkins, *Tribulation Force,* 275.

13. LaHaye and Jenkins, *The Mark,* 82.

14. Ibid., 85; LaHaye and Jenkins, *The Indwelling,* 284–286.

15. Angela Swafford, "The Era of Implanting People with Identity Chips Is upon Us," *Boston Globe,* May 20, 2003. Swafford's article discusses the literal implantation of personal identity chips in humans, including Swafford herself. Prophecy writers may exaggerate the traits of such chips, but there can be no question that such technologies—and the thorny ethical and civil liberties issues they raise—are indeed "upon us," in more than one sense.

16. Peter Lalonde, *The Mark of the Beast* (Eugene, Oreg.: Harvest House, 1994), 149.

17. Baudrillard, *Symbolic Exchange and Death,* 92. Baudrillard views signs as "floating signifiers" that have no fixed referent, but rather reflect changes in a superficial economy of "fashion" that is uncertain, risky, and speculative. He writes, "There is no more constraint of either coherence or reference than there is permanent inequality in the conversion of gold into floating monies—this indeterminacy implies the characteristic dimension of the cycle and recurrence in fashion (and no doubt soon in economy), whereas determinacy (of signs or of production), implies a linear and continuous order" (92).

18. Mark C. Taylor, *About Religion,* 7–8.

19. Ibid., 21.

20. LaHaye and Jenkins, *The Mark,* 358.

21. LaHaye and Jenkins, *Soul Harvest,* 178–179.

22. Ibid.

23. Ibid., 193.

24. Cf. Wouter J. Hanegraaff, *New Age Religion and Western Culture: Esotericism in the Mirror of Secular Thought* (New York: E. J. Brill, 1996), 139–142. It is interesting that LaHaye and Jenkins describe the Mark of the Believer as holographic, suggesting that holography contributes to the reality of the

Mark of Christ, as opposed to the two-dimensional appearance of the Mark of the Beast. Hanegraaff's discussion of the two figures associated with the development of holography, neuroscientist Karl Pribham and physicist David Bohm, undermines the "reality" of holography. As both understood, a hologram generates verisimilitude but is itself epiphenomenal—generated by the brain of the percipient looking at what is essentially a fuzzy pattern of distortion.

25. Hal Lindsey, *There's a New World Coming: A Prophetic Odyssey* (Santa Ana, Calif.: Vision House, 1973), 119.

26. Carol Balizet, *The Seven Last Years.*

27. LaHaye and Jenkins, *Armageddon*, 140. Consistent with the trajectory of the novels moving from a troubled acceptance of uncertainty to a rigid demand for absolute certainty and security, the authors narrate the miraculous removal of Chang's Mark of the Beast in *Armageddon* (#11). With the disappearance of Chang's wild-card status, the willingness of the authors to make needed compromises with the modern world also seems to vanish.

28. LaHaye and Jenkins, *Are We Living in the End Times?* 197.

29. LaHaye and Jenkins, *Apollyon*, 36.

30. Ibid., 37.

31. Frykholm, "Reading the Rapture," 253–258. Literary theorist Amy Johnson Frykholm also notes the prominence of deception in the *Left Behind* novels, along with the dubious character of the Marks. Frykholm makes a persuasive case that potential deceivers are marginal to evangelical culture, including two women, Amanda White and Hattie Durham. Both have transgressed the boundaries of the traditional evangelical community by refusing to submit to male authority. Moreover, Albie, the Middle-Eastern Tribulation Force pilot, and Chang Wong, the Chinese computer genius, are also suspect. They are traditional outsiders to evangelicalism, and as such come under intense scrutiny. Although the Tribulation Force exists in some sense to preserve patriarchal authority and other evangelical cultural boundaries, as Frykholm asserts, I think an examination of the existential issues involved also proves fruitful. That is, beyond the concerns Frykholm notes, prophecy believers may also feel a significant degree of *spiritual* and *existential* marginalization, perceiving their identity as evangelicals threatened by the emerging network culture. Some of this, as Christian Smith notes in his study *American Evangelicalism,* may be contrived to amplify strategically the differences between evangelicalism and the mainstream culture, but it does take a prominent place in the novels and as such merits closer examination.

32. Taylor, *The Moment of Complexity,* 96–97.

33. LaHaye and Jenkins, *Apollyon*, 311–312.

34. President Roosevelt exempted rare coins (or at least coins having numismatic value well in excess of their bullion worth) from his recall, however. See also Paul van Eeden, "Roosevelt's Number," at www.kitco.com. Last accessed March 17, 2004. Van Eeden's articles make provocative, if perhaps overstated,

assessments of the importance of precious metals in the contemporary global economy.

35. Taylor, *About Religion*, 20.
36. Ibid., 21.
37. Ibid., 11.
38. LaHaye and Jenkins, *Apollyon*, 204–205.
39. Ibid., 239.
40. Ibid., 238.
41. Ibid., 239–240.
42. Ibid., 238.
43. Taylor, *The Moment of Complexity*, 97.
44. Taylor, *Hiding*, 186.
45. O'Leary, *Arguing the Apocalypse*, 214.
46. Ibid., 72–73.

NOTES TO CHAPTER 6

1. LaHaye and Jenkins, *The Remnant*, 248.
2. Nancy Updike, "13,000 Fans of God," *New York Times*, April 21, 2002.
3. Fuller, *Naming the Antichrist*, 200.
4. Hanegraaff, *New Age Religion and Western Culture*, 114.
5. See Shibley, *Resurgent Evangelicalism in the United States*, 83–110. Sociologist Mark A. Shibley compares the tried-and-true stereotypes of evangelicals as rural, low-income, southern, and undereducated with his own findings of a recent phenomenon he dubs "new-style evangelicalism." New-style evangelicals retain most traditional evangelical values, but do so with greater openness toward change, along with a willingness to embrace and "Christianize" aspects of the mainstream popular culture such as rock music. Shibley's study indicates that evangelical churches grow because they combine strong, unambiguous theological positions along with an affirmation of middle-class American values.
6. We must remember, of course, that the novels reflect the ambitions of a career political activist, Tim LaHaye, not necessarily the views of rank-and-file evangelicals. The authors' goal, however—as I have argued throughout this text—is on one level to motivate political action through the deployment of apocalyptic rhetoric.
7. Cf. Clifford Geertz, "From the Native's Point of View: On the Nature of Anthropological Understanding," in *The Insider/Outsider Problem in the Study of Religion*, edited by Russell T. McCutcheon (New York: Cassell, 1999), 55–58.
8. See http://hirr.hartsem.edu/org/faith_megachurches_database.html. Last accessed May 13, 2003. Scholars generally consider a church with more than 2,000 members a "megachurch." *The Hartford Institute for Religion Research* estimates the number of megachurches in the United States at 700. By and large,

megachurches cluster in the South, Southern California, and the Midwest, although exceptions abound. Theologically, they almost always reflect the views of conservative Protestant evangelicalism. *The Hartford Institute for Religion Research* maintains an on-line database detailing the location, affiliation, and membership statistics, among other figures, for megachurches across the United States.

For a straightforward use of the language of commodification by the pastor of an evangelical megachurch, see Haya El Nasser, "Megachurches Clash with Critics Next Door . . . Neighbors Say Enough Is Enough," *USA Today,* http://www.usatoday.com/usatonline/20020923/4470948s.htm. Last accessed May 13, 2003. Nasser writes, quoting a megachurch pastor: "'The reasons why churches are getting bigger are the same reasons why your Costco, your Wal-Mart, your Home Depot and Lowes are expanding and are successful,' says Charlie Bradshaw, executive pastor of North Coast Church, which has 5,500 members in Vista, Calif., a suburb of San Diego. 'They're providing what you're looking for in options and prices, and that's why people are driving by the mom 'n' pop stores.'"

9. Patricia Leigh Brown, "Megachurches as Minitowns," *New York Times,* May 5, 2002. Brown notes, among other things, that megachurches have added many of the attractions of mainstream culture, including shopping malls, gyms, credit unions, cafes, and even a McDonald's restaurant in one case. The article focuses on the self-insulation such megachurches provide, although I would further emphasize the notion that megachurchgoers do not so much escape the world as they unknowingly incorporate and relabel it as "Christian" in their efforts to resist it.

10. Strong academic sources for the "Electronic Church" include Razelle Frankl, *Televangelism: The Marketing of Popular Religion* (Carbondale: Southern Illinois University Press, 1987); Jeffrey K. Hadden, "The Rise and Fall of American Televangelism," *Annals of the American Academy of Political and Social Science* 527 (May 1993): 113–130; Jeffrey K. Hadden and Anson Shupe, *Televangelism: Power and Politics on God's Frontier* (New York: Henry Holt, 1988); Peter G. Horsfield, *Religious Television: The American Experience* (New York: Longman, 1984); J. Gordon Melton, Phillip Charles Lucas, and Jon R. Stone, *Prime-Time Religion: An Encyclopedia of Religious Broadcasting* (Phoenix, Ariz.: Oryx Press, 1997); and Janice Peck, *The Gods of Televangelism: The Crisis of Meaning and the Appeal of Religious Television* (Cresskill, N.J.: Hampton Press, 1993).

11. LaHaye and Jenkins, *Apollyon,* 54.

12. "Lakewood Deal OK'd by Council; Church to Rent Compaq Center for 35 Million over 60 Years," *Houston Chronicle,* December 20, 2001.

13. Michel Serres, *The Parasite,* translated by Lawrence R. Schehr (Baltimore: Johns Hopkins University Press, 1982).

14. Michel de Certeau, *The Practice of Everyday Life,* translated by Steven Rendall (Berkeley: University of California Press, 1984), 37.

15. LaHaye and Jenkins, *Tribulation Force,* 405.

16. Ibid., 424.

17. Serres, *The Parasite,* 9.

18. Ibid., 3.

19. LaHaye and Jenkins, *The Indwelling,* 26.

20. J. Hillis Miller quoted in Taylor, *The Moment of Complexity,* 97–98.

21. See http://www2.tribforcehq.com/fiction/display_story.asp?StoryID=568. Last accessed July 6, 2003. The *Left Behind* novels have inspired a large complement of "fan fiction" narratives written by fans based upon the plots and protagonists of the *Left Behind* series. Fan authors have an unusual fascination with Chang, especially his avoidance of decapitation. They are clearly bothered by his ambivalent status. In one story, written by "His Lamb," Chang rips the Mark out of his forehead with a knife, before holding off the GC with his gun. He then places himself in a guillotine and commits suicide—albeit, one assumes, a Church-sanctioned form of suicide.

22. Taylor, *The Moment of Complexity,* 115.

23. LaHaye and Jenkins, *Apollyon,* 185.

24. Ibid., 186.

25. LaHaye and Jenkins, *The Indwelling,* 180–182.

26. Serres, *The Parasite,* 53.

27. LaHaye and Jenkins, *Apollyon,* 127. The discovery of personal journals, especially the attribution of elaborate schemes indirectly through such journals, recalls the narrative strategy of the nineteenth-century Christian existentialist Søren Kierkegaard. Authorship, it seems in the *Left Behind* novels—moral or otherwise—often comes from unexpected or unintended sources.

28. Ibid., 196.

29. Ibid., 198.

30. Frykholm, "Reading the Rapture," 110.

31. See especially R. Laurence Moore, *Selling God,* 244–255.

32. Goodwyn, *The Populist Moment,* 28–54.

33. See Michael Kazin, *The Populist Persuasion;* and Lawrence Goodwyn, *The Populist Moment.*

34. Christian Smith, *Christian America?*

35. Cf. Mark Juergensmeyer, *Terror in the Mind of God: The Global Rise of Religious Violence* (Berkeley: University of California Press, 2000). Juergensmeyer's description of the organizational structures of religious terrorism networks uncannily parallels the fictional movement envisioned by LaHaye and Jenkins. Groups such as the Irish Republican Army possess their own political wing, Sinn Fein, while Islamic groups such as Hamas have community centers, political activists, and, of course, militants. Juergensmeyer notes that all such

groups view their acts of terrorism as justifiable acts of self-defense and do not see themselves as terrorists. By the same token, LaHaye and Jenkins take pains in the *Left Behind* series to defend the Tribulation Force from charges of terrorism as they suggest that the protagonists simply act to defend their own status as evangelicals. As interesting as this connection might appear, however, it is critical to remember that the *Left Behind* series is a fictional device, and it is highly unlikely that LaHaye and Jenkins's apocalyptic vision will translate to the kind of violence carried out by the groups Juergensmeyer studies. And even the violence found in the novels appears quite tame by contemporary standards.

36. LaHaye and Jenkins, *The Remnant*, 120. One can find a similar phenomenon in the development of megachurches. If one conceives of megachurches as small cities, or at least small towns, the cities include numerous "neighborhoods" and "blocks" led by prayer captains, who form a chain to the executive pastor. Local pastors often shift the emphasis from the size of their congregations onto the metaphor of a nostalgic small town of shared values.

37. Ibid., 252.

38. Serres, *The Parasite*, 52.

39. LaHaye and Jenkins, *The Remnant*, 401. I am also making a thinly veiled allusion to Christian novelist Frank Peretti's best-selling novel, *Piercing the Darkness*.

40. Ibid., 191.

41. Ibid., 180.

42. Ibid., 316.

43. Ibid., 287–297.

44. Ibid., 330–338.

45. Ibid., 357.

46. Ibid., 362–364.

47. LaHaye and Jenkins, *Armageddon*, 133–140.

48. LaHaye and Jenkins, *The Remnant*, 80–83.

49. Put simply, orthodox Calvinism—a product of reformer John Calvin's sixteenth-century theological reflections—posited that since God was all-powerful, humans had no power over their ultimate fate. It followed that God had presumably chosen whom to save, and whom to damn, since humans had no choice in the matter. As historian Mark Noll suggests, Orthodox Calvinist thought gradually eroded in the United States, as waves of reformers and itinerant evangelists made salvation more compatible with the ethos of an emerging democratic culture, offering instead that individuals could choose—with God's assistance, of course—their ultimate status. See Noll, *The Scandal of the Evangelical Mind*, 62.

50. Ibid., 222.

51. LaHaye and Jenkins, *The Remnant*, 238–242.

52. Ibid., 248.

53. Ibid., 260.

54. O'Leary, *Arguing the Apocalypse*, 214.

55. LaHaye and Jenkins, *Armageddon*, 17–18.

56. *The Omega Code*, written and produced by Paul and Matthew Crouch (Santa Clara, Calif.: TBN Films, 1999).

57. O'Leary, *Arguing the Apocalypse*, 214.

58. Serres, *The Parasite*, 52–55.

59. Mark C. Taylor, *The Moment of Complexity*, 115.

60. See Mark Noll, *The Scandal of the Evangelical Mind*; and George M. Marsden, *Fundamentalism and American Culture*. Noll and Marsden, two of the foremost historians of American evangelicalism, provide ample insight into the intellectual underpinnings of evangelical belief; and Noll, specifically, examines the evangelical dependence on Enlightenment developments and evangelicalism's resultant focus on questions of selfhood and free will.

NOTES TO THE EPILOGUE

1. Carpenter, *Revive Us Again*, 242.

2. O'Leary, *Arguing the Apocalypse*, 71.

3. Gary North and Gary DeMar, *Christian Reconstruction: What It Is, What It Isn't* (Tyler, Tex.: Institute for Christian Economics, 1991). North and DeMar, two of the leading figures in contemporary Christian Reconstructionist thought, provide a concise and articulate summary of Christian Reconstructionist viewpoints and goals, with an extensive bibliography of Christian Reconstructionist literature.

4. Castells, *The Rise of the Network Society*, 76.

5. Carpenter, *Revive Us Again*, 141–160. See also Christian Smith, *American Evangelicalism*, 9–13. I am indebted to both authors for their descriptions of these important events.

6. Carpenter, *Revive Us Again*, 153.

7. Smith, *American Evangelicalism*, 11, 13–15.

8. Carpenter, *Revive Us Again*, 165–167, 172.

9. Smith, *American Evangelicalism*, 150.

10. Smith, *Christian America?* 7–9.

11. See Michel de Certeau, *The Practice of Everyday Life*, 165–176. Certeau describes the act of reading as a much more active process than many observers assume. The text, in other words, may take on a life of its own in the hands of its readers. He writes that "the reader takes neither the position of the author nor an author's position. He invents in texts something different from what they 'intended.' He detaches them from their (lost or accessory) origin. He combines their fragments and creates something unknown in the space organized by their capacity for allowing an indefinite plurality of meanings" (169).

Granted, if one looks at the many fan-fiction sites on the Internet dedicated to the *Left Behind* series, one sees that readers do not stray too far from the meanings suggested by LaHaye and Jenkins. Nevertheless, a variability—and with it an unpredictability—exists, making it certain that although the novels have significant rhetorical impact on their readers, the readers are not strictly limited by the dictates of the authors. A creative process is at work, one that will take years to unfold. That is, while I suggest possible readings for the novels, only with time will we know how readers interpret and apply the texts to their lives as evangelicals, despite a number of suggestive possibilities. For an applied study of what Certeau calls "poaching"—albeit dealing more with audiovisuals (but still reading "texts")—see Henry Jenkins, *Textual Poachers: Television Fans and Participatory Culture* (New York: Routledge, 1992).

Select Bibliography

PRIMARY SOURCES

Balizet, Carol. *The Seven Last Years*. Lincoln, Va.: Chosen Books, 1978.

Betzer, Dan. *Beast: The Novel of the Future World Dictator*. Lafayette, La.: Prescott Press, 1985.

Bloomfield, Arthur. *How to Recognize the Antichrist*. Minneapolis: Bethany Fellowship, 1975.

Bragg, Robert. *Babylon Is Fallen*. New York: Vantage Press, 1977.

Burkett, Larry. *The Illuminati*. Nashville, Tenn.: Thomas Nelson, 1991.

Cohen, Gary. *The Horsemen Are Coming*. Chicago: Moody Press, 1974.

Jeffrey, Grant R. *Surveillance Society: The Rise of Antichrist*. Toronto, Ont.: Frontier Research Publications, 2000.

Johnson, Carl. *Prophecy Made Plain for Times Like These*. Chicago: Moody Press, 1972.

Kirban, Salem. *666*. Chattanooga, Tenn.: AMG Publishers, 1998.

LaHaye, Tim. *What Everyone Should Know about Homosexuality*. Wheaton, Ill.: Tyndale House, 1978.

———. *Battle for the Mind: You Are Engaged in a Battle for the Mind*. Old Tappan, N.J.: Revell, 1980.

———. *The Battle for the Family*. Old Tappan, N.J.: Revell, 1982.

———. *The Hidden Censors*. Old Tappan, N.J.: Revell, 1984.

———. *The Race for the 21st Century*. Nashville, Tenn.: Thomas Nelson, 1986.

———. *The Beginning of the End*. Wheaton, Ill.: Tyndale House, 1991.

———. *Revelation Unveiled*. Grand Rapids, Mich.: Zondervan, 1999.

LaHaye, Tim, and Bob DeMoss. *The Mind Siege Project*. Nashville, Tenn.: Word, 2001.

LaHaye, Tim, and Jerry B. Jenkins. *Left Behind: A Novel of the Earth's Last Days*. Wheaton, Ill.: Tyndale, 1995.

———. *Tribulation Force: The Continuing Drama of Those Left Behind*. Wheaton, Ill.: Tyndale, 1996.

———. *Nicolae: The Rise of Antichrist*. Wheaton, Ill.: Tyndale, 1997.

———. *Soul Harvest: The World Takes Sides*. Wheaton, Ill.: Tyndale, 1998.

———. *Apollyon: The Destroyer Is Unleashed*. Wheaton, Ill.: Tyndale, 1999.

———. *Are We Living in the End Times? Current Events Foretold in Scripture . . . and What They Mean*. Wheaton, Ill.: Tyndale, 1999.

———. *Assassins: Assignment: Jerusalem, Target: Antichrist*. Wheaton, Ill.: Tyndale, 1999.

———. *The Indwelling: The Beast Takes Possession*. Wheaton, Ill.: Tyndale, 2000.

———. *The Mark: The Beast Rules the World*. Wheaton, Ill.: Tyndale, 2000.

———. *Desecration: Antichrist Takes the Throne*. Wheaton, Ill.: Tyndale, 2001.

———. *The Remnant: Countdown to Armageddon*. Wheaton, Ill.: Tyndale. 2002.

———. *Armageddon: The Cosmic Battle of the Ages*. Wheaton, Ill.: Tyndale, 2003.

Lalonde, Peter. *The Mark of the Beast*. Eugene, Oreg.: Harvest House, 1994.

Larson, Bob. *Abaddon*. Nashville, Tenn.: Thomas Nelson, 1993.

Lindsey, Hal, with C. C. Carlson. *The Late Great Planet Earth*. Grand Rapids, Mich.: Zondervan, 1970.

Lindsey, Hal. *There's a New World Coming: A Prophetic Odyssey*. Santa Ana, Calif.: Vision House, 1973.

———. *The 1980's: Countdown to Armageddon*. New York: Bantam, 1983.

Meier, Paul. *The Third Millennium: A Novel*. Nashville, Tenn.: Thomas Nelson, 1993.

Pentecost, J. Dwight. *Will Man Survive?* Chicago: Moody Press, 1971.

Peretti, Frank. *This Present Darkness*. Westchester, Ill.: Crossway, 1986.

———. *Piercing the Darkness*. Westchester, Ill.: Crossway, 1989.

———. *Prophet*. Westchester, Ill.: Crossway, 1992.

———. *The Oath*. Dallas, Tex.: Word, 1995.

———. *The Visitation*. Nashville, Tenn.: Word, 1999.

Relfe, Mary Stewart. *When Your Money Fails: The 666 System Is Here*. Birmingham, Ala.: Ministries, Inc., 1981.

Scofield, Cyrus I., ed. *The Scofield Reference Bible: King James Version*. 1945 edition. New York: Oxford University Press, 1945.

Smith, Chuck. *The Final Curtain*. Costa Mesa, Calif.: Word for Today, 1984.

Thompson, Donald W., director. *A Thief in the Night*. Reissue. Des Moines, Iowa: Mark IV Pictures, 1995.

———. *A Distant Thunder*. Reissue. Des Moines, Iowa: Mark IV Pictures, 1995.

———. *Image of the Beast*. Reissue. Des Moines, Iowa: Mark IV Pictures, 1995.

———. *The Prodigal Planet*. Reissue. Des Moines, Iowa: Mark IV Pictures, 1995.

van Impe, Jack. *11:59 and Counting!* Royal Oak, Mich.: Jack van Impe Ministries, 1983.

Wade, Ken. *The Orion Conspiracy.* Nampa, Idaho: Pacific Press, 1993.

Webber, David, and Noah Hutchings. *Computers and the Beast of Revelation.* Shreveport, La.: Huntington Press, 1986.

Whisenant, Edgar. *Eighty-Eight Reasons Why the Rapture Will Be in 1988.* Nashville, Tenn.: World Bible Society, 1988.

White, John Wesley. *The Coming World Dictator.* Minneapolis: Bethany Fellowship, 1981.

Wilson, Nathan D. *Right Behind: A Parody of Last Days Goofiness.* Moscow, Idaho: Canon Press, 2001.

Wood, Leon. *The Bible and Future Events.* Grand Rapids, Mich.: Zondervan, 1973.

SECONDARY SOURCES

Ahlstrom, Sidney E. *A Religious History of the American People.* New Haven, Conn.: Yale University Press, 1972.

Albanese, Catherine. *Nature Religion in America: From the Algonkian Indians to the New Age.* Chicago: University of Chicago Press, 1990.

Ammerman, Nancy. *Bible Believers: Fundamentalists in the Modern World.* Camden, N.J.: Rutgers University Press, 1987.

Ballard, J. G. *Crash* (New York: Farrar, Straus & Giroux, 1973.

Balmer, Randall. *Mine Eyes Have Seen the Glory: A Journey into the Evangelical Subculture.* New York: Oxford University Press, 1992.

Barabási, Albert-László. *Linked: The New Science of Networks.* Cambridge, Mass.: Perseus, 2002.

Barber, Benjamin. *Jihad vs. McWorld: How Globalism and Tribalism Are Reshaping the World.* New York: Ballantine, 1996.

Barkun, Michael. *Disaster and the Millennium.* New Haven, Conn.: Yale University Press, 1974.

———. *Radical Religion in America: The Origins of the Christian Identity Movement.* Chapel Hill: University of North Carolina Press, 1997.

Bartkowski, John P. *Remaking the Godly Marriage: Gender Negotiation in Evangelical Families.* Camden, N.J.: Rutgers University Press, 1991.

Baudrillard, Jean. *Symbolic Exchange and Death.* Translated by Iain Hamilton Grant. Thousand Oaks, Calif.: Sage Publications, 1993.

Berger, Peter L. *The Sacred Canopy: Elements of a Sociological Theory of Religion.* New York: Anchor Books, 1990.

"The Bible and the Apocalypse." *Time,* June 1, 2002. On-line version: http://www.time.com/time/covers/1101020701/theology2.html. Last accessed: June 25, 2002.

Bilhartz, Terry D. *Urban Religion and the Second Great Awakening: Church and*

Society in Early National Baltimore. Teaneck, N.J.: Fairleigh Dickinson University Press, 1986.

Boyer, Paul S. *When Time Shall Be No More: Prophecy Belief in Modern American Culture.* Cambridge, Mass.: Harvard University Press, 1992.

Brasher, Brenda E. *Godly Women: Fundamentalism and Female Power.* Camden, N.J.: Rutgers University Press, 1998.

Carpenter, Joel A. *Revive Us Again: The Reawakening of American Fundamentalism.* New York: Oxford University Press, 1997.

Castells, Manuel. *The Power of Identity.* Malden, Mass.: Blackwell, 1997.

———. *End of Millennium.* Malden, Mass.: Blackwell, 1999.

———. *The Rise of the Network Society.* Malden, Mass.: Blackwell, 2000.

de Certeau, Michel. *The Practice of Everyday Life, Volume I.* Translated by Stephen Rendall. Berkeley: University of California Press, 1984.

———. *Heterologies: Discourses on the Other.* Translated by Brian Massumi. Minneapolis: University of Minnesota Press, 1997.

The Complete Prisoner Megaset. New York: New Video, in association with A&E Entertainment and Carlton International Media Limited, 2000.

Dawkins, Richard. *The Selfish Gene.* New York: Oxford University Press, 1989.

Dayton, Donald W., and Robert K. Johnston, eds. *The Variety of American Evangelicalism.* Knoxville: University of Tennessee Press, 1991.

Dennett, Daniel. *Consciousness Explained.* Boston: Little, Brown, 1991.

Dery, Mark. *Escape Velocity: Cyberculture at the End of the Century.* London: Hodder & Stoughton, 1996.

Emerson, Michael O., and Christian Smith. *Divided by Faith: Evangelical Religion and the Problem of Race in America.* New York: Oxford University Press, 2000.

Eskridge, Larry, and Mark A. Noll, eds. *More Money, More Ministry.* Grand Rapids, Mich.: Eerdman's, 2000.

Fiedler, Leslie. "Close the Border—Cross the Gap." *Playboy.* December 1969.

Foucault, Michel. *Discipline and Punish: The Birth of the Prison.* Translated by Alan Sheridan. New York: Vintage Books, 1977.

———. *The History of Sexuality, Volume III: The Care of the Self.* Translated by Robert Hurley. New York: Random House, 1986.

———. *Ethics: Subjectivity and Truth.* Translated by Robert Hurley et al. Edited by Paul Rabinow. New York: New Press, 1997.

Frankl, Razelle. *Televangelism: the Marketing of Popular Religion.* Carbondale: Southern Illinois University Press, 1987.

Friedman, Thomas. *The Lexus and the Olive Tree.* New York: Anchor Books, 2000.

Frykholm, Amy Johnson. "Reading the Rapture: Christian Fiction and the Social Structures of Religious Belief." Ph.D. diss., Duke University, 2001.

Fuller, Robert C. *Naming the Antichrist: The History of an American Obsession.* New York: Oxford University Press, 1995.

————. *Stairways to Heaven: Drugs in American Religious History.* Boulder, Colo.: Westview Press, 2000.

————. Spiritual, but Not Religious: Understanding Unchurched America. New York: Oxford University Press, 2002.

Gibbs, Nancy. The Bible and the Apocalypse: The Biggest Book of the Summer Is about the End of the World. It's Also a Sign of Our Troubled Times." *Time,* July 1, 2002. On-line version: http://www.time.com/time/covers/0,8816,265345,00.html. Last accessed: June 23, 2002.

Gibson, William. *Neuromancer.* New York: Ballantine, 1984.

————. *Count Zero.* New York: Ace Books, 1986.

————. *Mona Lisa Overdrive.* New York: Bantam, 1988.

Goetz, David. "Suburban Spirituality: The Land of SUVs and Soccer Leagues Tends to Weather the Soul in Peculiar Ways . . ." *Christianity Today,* June 23, 2003. On-line version: http://www.christianitytoday.com/ct/2003/007/1.30 .html.

Goodwyn, Lawrence. *The Populist Moment.* New York: Oxford University Press, 1978.

Gross, Michael Joseph. "The Trials of the Tribulation." *Atlantic Monthly,* January 2000. http://www.theatlantic.com/issues/2000/01/001gross.htm.

Grundmann, Herbert. *Studien über Joachim von Floris.* Leipzig, Germany: G. B. Teubner, 1927.

Hanegraaff, Wouter J. *New Age Religion and Western Culture: Esotericism in the Mirror of Secular Thought.* New York: E. J. Brill, 1996.

Harding, Susan Friend. *The Book of Jerry Falwell: Fundamentalist Language and Politics.* Princeton, N.J.: Princeton University Press, 2000.

Harvey, David. *The Condition of Postmodernity.* London: Basil Blackwell, 1992.

Hunter, James Davison. *Evangelicalism: The Coming Generation.* New York: Oxford University Press, 1987.

————. "Fundamentalism in Its Global Contours." In *The Fundamentalist Phenomenon: A View From Within: A Response From Without.* Edited by Norman J. Cohen. Grand Rapids, Mich.: Eerdman's, 1990.

Johnson, Paul E. *A Shopkeeper's Millennium: Society and Revivals in Rochester, New York, 1815–1837.* New York: Hill and Wang, 1978.

Juergensmeyer, Mark. *Terror in the Mind of God: The Global Rise of Religious Violence.* Berkeley: University of California Press, 2000.

Kaplan, Jeffrey. *Millenarian Movements from the Far Right to the Children of Noah.* Syracuse, N.Y.: Syracuse University Press, 1997.

Kazin, Michael. *The Populist Persuasion: An American History.* Ithaca, N.Y.: Cornell University Press, 1998.

Kermode, Frank. *The Genesis of Secrecy: On the Interpretation of Narrative.* Cambridge, Mass.: Harvard University Press, 1979.

Kirkpatrick, David D. "Evangelical Sales Are Converting Publishers." *New York Times,* June 8, 2002.

von Laer, Hermann. "Der Euro und die Europäische Währungsunion: Eine gefährliche Fehlentscheidung für das gemeinsame Europa." In *Deutschland und Europa, Europa und die Deutschen.* Edited by Joachim Kuropka and Wilfried Kürschner. Münster, Germany: Verlag Regensberg, 1998.

Lears, Jackson. *No Place of Grace: Antimodernism and the Transformation of American Culture, 1880–1920.* New York: Pantheon, 1981.

Lienesch, Michael. *Redeeming America: Piety and Politics in the New Christian Right.* Chapel Hill: University of North Carolina Press, 1993.

Lohse, Bernhard. *Luthers Theologie in ihrer historischen Entwicklung und in ihrem systematischen Zusammenhang.* Göttingen, Germany: Vandenhoeck & Ruprecht, 1995.

Lyon, David. *The Electronic Eye: The Rise of Surveillance Society.* Minneapolis: University of Minnesota Press, 1994.

Marsden, George M. *Fundamentalism and American Culture: The Shaping of Twentieth-Century Evangelicalism, 1870–1925.* New York: Oxford University Press, 1980.

———. *Evangelicalism and Modern America.* Grand Rapids, Mich.: Eerdman's, 1984.

———. *Understanding Fundamentalism and Evangelicalism.* Grand Rapids, Mich.: Eerdman's, 1991.

Martin, William. *With God on Our Side: The Rise of the Religious Right in America.* New York: Broadway, 1996.

Marty, Martin E., and R. Scott Appleby. *Fundamentalisms and the State.* Chicago: University of Chicago Press, 1991.

———. *Fundamentalisms Observed.* Chicago: University of Chicago Press, 1991.

———. *Fundamentalisms and Society.* Chicago: University of Chicago Press, 1992.

———. *Accounting for Fundamentalisms.* Chicago: University of Chicago Press, 1994.

———. *Fundamentalisms Comprehended.* Chicago: University of Chicago Press, 1995.

Marx, Leo. *The Machine in the Garden: Technology and the Pastoral Ideal in America.* New York: Oxford University Press, 1964.

McCutcheon, Russell T., ed. *The Insider/Outsider Problem in the Study of Religion.* New York: Cassell, 1999.

McGinn, Bernard. *Visions of the End: Apocalyptic Tradition in the Middle Ages.* New York: Columbia University Press, 1979.

———. *Antichrist: 2000 Years of the Human Fascination with Evil.* New York: Harper, 1994.

———. *Apocalypticism in the Western Tradition.* Brookfield, Vt.: Variorum, 1994.

Mehegan, David. "Appeal Spreads for Series that Spreads The Word." *Boston Globe,* February 27, 2002.

Miller, Timothy, ed. *America's Alternative Religions.* Albany: State University of New York Press, 1995.

Moore, R. Laurence. *Selling God: American Religion in the Marketplace of Culture.* New York: Oxford University Press, 1984.

Noll, Mark A. *The Scandal of the Evangelical Mind.* Grand Rapids, Mich.: Eerdman's, 1994.

O'Leary, Stephen D. *Arguing the Apocalypse: A Theory of Millennial Rhetoric.* New York: Oxford University Press, 1994.

Olson, Carl E. *Will Catholics Be "Left Behind"? A Critique of the Rapture and Today's Prophecy Preachers.* San Francisco, Calif.: Ignatius Press, 2003.

Potter, David M. *People of Plenty: Economic Abundance and the American Character.* Chicago: University of Chicago Press, 1954.

Rabey, Steve. "No Longer Left Behind." *Christianity Today,* April 22, 2002. Online version: http://www.christianitytoday.com/ct/2002/005/1.26.html.

Reeves, Marjorie, and Warwick Gould. *Joachim of Fiore and the Myth of the Eternal Evangel in the Nineteenth Century.* New York: Oxford University Press, 1987.

Rheingold, Howard. *The Virtual Community: Homesteading on the Electronic Frontier.* New York: Harper, 1993.

Ricoeur, Paul. *On Paul Ricoeur: Narrative and Interpretation.* Translated and edited by David Wood. New York: Routledge, 1991.

Ritzer, George. *The McDonaldization Thesis: Explorations and Extensions.* Thousand Oaks, Calif.: Sage Publications, 1997.

Roof, Wade Clark. *Spiritual Marketplace: Baby Boomers and the Remaking of American Religion.* Princeton, N.J.: Princeton University Press, 1999.

Sandeen, Ernest R. *The Roots of Fundamentalism: British and American Millenarianism, 1900–1930.* Chicago: University of Chicago Press, 1970.

Scarry, Elaine. *The Body in Pain: The Making and Unmaking of the World.* New York: Oxford University Press, 1985.

Schultze, Quentin J. *Televangelism and American Culture.* Grand Rapids, Mich.: Baker, 1991.

———, ed. *American Evangelicals and the Mass Media: Perspectives on the Relationship between American Evangelicals and the Mass Media.* Grand Rapids, Mich.: Zondervan, 1990.

Serres, Michel. *The Parasite.* Translated by Lawrence R. Schehr. Baltimore: Johns Hopkins University Press, 1982.

Shibley, Mark A. *Resurgent Evangelicalism in the United States: Mapping Cultural Change since 1970.* Columbia: University of South Carolina Press, 1996.

Shuck, Glenn W. "Televangelism." *Encyclopedia of Protestantism.* Edited by Hans Hillerbrand. New York: Routledge, 2003.

Smith, Christian. *American Evangelicalism: Embattled and Thriving.* Chicago: University of Chicago Press, 1998.

———. *Christian America? What Evangelicals Really Want.* Berkeley: University of California Press, 2000.

Stout, Harry S. *The New England Soul: Preaching and Religious Culture in Colonial New England.* New York: Oxford University Press, 1986.

Strozier, Charles. *Apocalypse: On the Psychology of Fundamentalism in America.* Boston: Beacon Books, 1994.

Stunt, Timothy C. F. *From Awakening to Succession: Radical Evangelicals in Switzerland and Britain (1815–1835).* Edinburgh: T&T Clark, 2000.

Taylor, Frances Grandy. "'Left Behind' Sales Surged in September." *Hartford Courant,* November 10, 2001.

Taylor, Mark C. *Err/ing: A Postmodern A/Theology.* Chicago: University of Chicago Press, 1984.

———. *Altarity.* Chicago: University of Chicago Press, 1987.

———. *Hiding.* Chicago: University of Chicago Press, 1997.

———. *About Religion: Economies of Faith in Virtual Culture.* Chicago: University of Chicago Press, 1999.

———. *The Picture in Question: Mark Tansey & The Ends of Representation.* Chicago: University of Chicago Press, 1999.

———. *The Moment of Complexity: Emerging Network Culture.* Chicago: University of Chicago Press, 2002.

———, ed. *Critical Terms for Religious Studies.* Chicago: University of Chicago, 1998.

Taylor, Mark C., and Esa Saarinen. *Imagologies: Media Philosophy.* New York: Routledge, 1994.

Updike, Nancy. "13,000 Fans of God." *New York Times,* April 21, 2002.

Wacker, Grant. "Planning Ahead: The Enduring Appeal of Prophecy Belief." *Christian Century,* January l9, l994.

Wainwright, Arthur W. *The Mysterious Apocalypse.* Nashville, Tenn.: Abingdon Press, 1993.

Weber, Eugen. *Apocalypses: Prophecies, Cults, and Millennial Beliefs through the Ages.* Cambridge, Mass.: Harvard University Press, 1999.

Weber, Timothy. *Living in the Shadow of the Second Coming: American Premillennialism (1875–1925).* New York: Oxford University Press, 1979.

Webster's New Collegiate Dictionary. Cambridge, Mass.: G. C. Merriam, 1959.

Williams, Rhys H., and Susan Alexander, "Religious Rhetoric in American Populism: Civil Religion as Movement Ideology." *Journal for the Scientific Study of Religion* 33 (March 1994): 8.

Wojcik, Chris. *The End of the World as We Know It: Faith, Fatalism, and Apocalypse in America*. New York: New York University Press, 1997.

Wuthnow, Robert. *After Heaven: Spirituality in America since the 1950s*. Berkeley: University of California Press, 1998.

Wyschogrod, Edith. *Saints and Postmodernism: Revisioning Moral Philosophy*. Chicago: University of Chicago Press, 1990.

———. *The Ethics of Remembering: History, Heterology, and the Nameless Others*. Chicago: University of Chicago Press, 1998.

Index

About the Author

Glenn W. Shuck is Visiting Assistant Professor of Religion at Williams College. He recently obtained his Ph.D. from Rice University, with specializations in the religions of North America and the history of Christianity. He is also the co-editor, with Jeffrey J. Kripal, of the forthcoming *Esalen in American Religion Culture* (Indiana University Press). His research interests center on questions of religious and cultural identity.